Việt Nam

Ohio University Research in International Studies

This series of publications on Africa, Latin America, Southeast Asia, and Global and Comparative Studies is designed to present significant research, translation, and opinion to area specialists and to a wide community of persons interested in world affairs. The series is distributed worldwide. For more information, consult the Ohio University Press website, ohioswallow.com.

Books in the Ohio University Research in International Studies series are published by Ohio University Press in association with the Center for International Studies. The views expressed in individual volumes are those of the authors and should not be considered to represent the policies or beliefs of the Center for International Studies, Ohio University Press, or Ohio University.

Executive Editor: Gillian Berchowitz
Southeast Asia Series Editors: Elizabeth F. Collins and William H. Frederick

Việt Nam

Tradition and Change

Hữu Ngọc

Edited by Lady Borton and Elizabeth F. Collins

OHIO UNIVERSITY RESEARCH IN INTERNATIONAL STUDIES
SOUTHEAST ASIA SERIES NO. 128
OHIO UNIVERSITY PRESS
ATHENS

NHÀ XUẤT BẢN THẾ GIỚI — WORLD PUBLISHERS
HÀ NỘI

Published by Ohio University Press, Athens, Ohio 45701
ohioswallow.com
All rights reserved

To obtain permission to quote, reprint, or otherwise reproduce or distribute material from Ohio University Press publications, please contact our rights and permissions department at (740) 593–1154 or (740) 593–4536 (fax).

Printed in the United States of America
Ohio University Press books are printed on acid-free paper ⊚ ™

26 25 24 23 22 21 20 19 18 17 16   5 4 3 2 1

Library of Congress Cataloging-in-Publication Data

Names: Hữu Ngọc, author. | Borton, Lady, editor. | Collins, Elizabeth Fuller, editor.
Title: Viet Nam : tradition and change / Huu Ngoc ; edited by Lady Borton and Elizabeth F. Collins.
Other titles: Research in international studies. Southeast Asia series ; no. 128.
Description: Athens, Ohio : Ohio University Press, [2016] | Series: Ohio University Research in International Studies Southeast Asia series ; no. 128 | Includes bibliographical references and index.
Identifiers: LCCN 2016016840| ISBN 9780896803015 (hc : alk. paper) | ISBN 9780896803022 (pb : alk. paper) | ISBN 9780896804937 (pdf)
Subjects: LCSH: Vietnam—Civilization. | Vietnam—Social life and customs.
Classification: LCC DS556.42 .H877 2016 | DDC 959.7—dc23
LC record available at https://lccn.loc.gov/2016016840

Table of Contents

Foreword

Short, clear introductions to the cultures of Southeast Asian nations are difficult to find. For years, I cobbled together collections of short articles and selections of literature for my university-level introduction to Southeast Asia and presented the historical framework in lecture. My goal was to entice students to investigate the material on their own or in a more advanced class.

On a trip to Việt Nam, an area outside my own research field in the Bahasa world of Indonesia and Malaysia, I had a chance to meet Hữu Ngọc and was given a copy of *Wandering through Vietnamese Culture*, a collection of his essays, which is over 1,200 pages. It served as a wonderful guide, containing answers to so many of the questions that had presented themselves. When Ohio University Press was considering publication of an excerpted version of *Wandering through Vietnamese Culture*, I was asked in my role as editor for the O.U. Press's Southeast Asia Series to accept the Press's invitation to make the initial selection of essays.

Hữu Ngọc originally wrote his essays as newspaper columns for international readers who, living in Việt Nam, had some acquaintance with the country. Yet all of us working on this project, including and especially Hữu Ngọc, wanted also to think of those for whom Việt Nam is completely new. Starting from an early draft Table of Contents, with Hữu Ngọc as expert and author, we worked together to crystallize his oeuvre into a first-taste introduction to Vietnamese history and culture, emphasizing the structure, factors, and individuals he feels are particularly important.

Việt Nam: Tradition and Change shimmers with Hữu Ngọc's thoughtful reflections and insight. The collection is designed for students in introductory classes and for other readers interested in Việt Nam. I hope they will also fall in love with the rich cultural heritage of the people and nation that is Việt Nam.

Hữu Ngọc's central thesis—"All tradition is change through acculturation"—twines through each of the book's ten sections and through many of these short essays. In the first section, "The Vietnamese Identity," Hữu Ngọc portrays what it means to be Vietnamese. He describes the values that shape Vietnamese character, such as the untranslatable word "*nghĩa*," and explores the meaning of the customs that embody Vietnamese ideals: ancestor veneration, worship of mother goddesses, the naming of a child, the arrangement of a traditional Vietnamese house, and the deep emotional attachment Vietnamese have to the communal houses of their home villages. In encounters with "others"—the Chinese, French, Japanese, and American overlords who have tried to rule Việt Nam—the Vietnamese absorbed new values, translating them into their own Vietnamese vernacular. Hữu Ngọc shows that the Vietnamese are martial, but not militaristic; they are willing to fight to defend their nation but never forget the anguish that war brings. We see how the Vietnamese have blended their ancient Austronesian cultural heritage and language together with Buddhist traditions brought from India and China, with the value that Confucian ethics from China place on order, harmony, and scholarly learning, and then with the Western influence of humanism and individual liberty. Nevertheless, for Hữu Ngọc, Buddhism remains the "heart" of the Vietnamese village, while Confucian ethics and learning and rites are still its "head." The ancient, quintessentially Vietnamese rites of ancestor veneration that bind a family, clan, and village together and the awe at the legendary powers of the spirits of nature as well as the spirits of national and local heroes are the roots that anchor Việt Nam today.

The second section, "The Four Facets of Vietnamese Culture," illuminates how the ancient Việt (Kinh) ethnic group had its roots in Southeast Asia and defines the Việts' earliest cultural descriptors (e.g., a wet-rice-growing culture and bronze drums) that Việt Nam shares with other Southeast Asian countries. However, Hữu Ngọc specifies the cultural aspects (e.g., matriarchy, mother goddesses, myths, and legends) that are quintessentially Vietnamese. He clarifies the four major facets of Vietnamese culture—the original Southeast Asian roots and the subsequent Indian-Chinese, French, and regional-global branches—and shows how the Southeast Asian base of Vietnamese culture persists today within a dynamism created by tradition and change through acculturation. Central to the features specific to Việt Nam and important in the Việts' preservation of their cultural essence during foreign occupations is the Vietnamese language. Vietnamese has been the mother tongue of the Việt for millennia and, today, is the mother tongue for 85 percent of the country's population, which includes fifty-four ethnic groups. Many nations, particularly former colonies in Africa and Asia, do not have this unifying feature of a common language, which is both ancient and modern.

Hữu Ngọc takes us deeper into Vietnamese Confucianism and Buddhism in the sections, "Việt Nam's Confucian Heritage" and "Buddhism in Việt Nam." Hữu Ngọc helps us understand the ethics Confucianism espoused and the cultural overlay it brought. He contrasts the Machiavellian *Realpolitik* of twentieth century international relations with the Confucian ethical spirit that condemns corruption, but he also criticizes Confucianism for its conservatism, for its contempt of commerce (an attitude, which produced poverty) and for its misogyny (which altered the deep roots of Vietnamese matriarchy and institutionalized rigid and destructive gender inequality).

Like Confucianism, Buddhism is a theme spreading throughout this book. We meet the "Bearded Indian," who played an early role in Vietnamese Zen Buddhism. We also learn about retired King Trần Nhân Tông, who established Việt Nam's Bamboo Forest Zen branch at Yên Tử Mountain, which we as readers visit. The section on Buddhism features an essay devoted to the female Bodhisattva, Avalokitesvara (Quan Âm or Quan Thế Âm), the Buddhist Goddess of Mercy, who appears quite often in other sections, helping us to feel her pervasive cultural presence. We can sense how Vietnamese Buddhism honors the fragile and impermanent beauty of nature and inspires aesthetic sensibilities. Taken together, these Buddhist traditions constitute a rich spiritual heritage without dogmatism or rigidity.

The essays in the section entitled "Exemplary Vietnamese" tell the stories of the national heroes (known and not well known) who embody Vietnamese values and love of country. These include the Trưng sisters, Việt Nam's first historical personages, who defeated the Chinese in 40 CE, and Lady Triệu, who took up arms against the Chinese two centuries later, "her flag raised, breasts tossing, her elephant charging." We have the great generals, Lý Thường Kiệt and Trần Hưng Đạo, who defended Việt Nam from Chinese and Mongol invasions in the 1000s and 1200s respectively, as well as Lê Lợi, who also defeated the Chinese and then became King Lê Thái Tổ in the 1400s, and we have the Tây Sơn rebel leader who defeated the Chinese and became King Quang Trung in the late 1700s. In his essay about Hoàng Diệu, whose warning to the emperor in 1882 about French intentions to attack Hà Nội went unheeded, Hữu Ngọc reminds readers that the cost of failure in a Confucian society was disgrace or an honorable suicide. He explores the dilemmas faced by Vietnamese searching for the best way to serve their nation under colonial rule. Particularly poignant are his essay on the Catholic Trương Vĩnh Ký (Pétrus Ký) and on Nguyễn Văn Vĩnh, who are seen by some as traitors to their country.

We hear stories of the teachers, writers, artists, and activists who fostered a love of Vietnamese literature and history and who kept alive the dream of an independent nation despite colonial repression. Hữu Ngọc's essay on Hồ Chí Minh explores how the founder of modern Việt Nam himself embodied tensions that animate Vietnamese culture and history—tradition and revolution; idealism and realism; reason versus heart; and Eastern versus Western values. Hữu Ngọc shows us Hồ Chí Minh through the eyes of Western contemporaries, those who admired him and those who fought against him, describing how Hồ Chí Minh learned from the West while never losing the love of his country and its people that was at the center of all he did.

The essays in "Vietnamese Literature: An Expression of the Nation's Spirit" are the heart of this book. Hữu Ngọc begins with *The Tale of Kiều,* which he describes as "the Vietnamese soul," for "as long as *Kiều* lives on, our Vietnamese language shall live on. And as long as our language lives on, our nation will not die." The love story at the heart of this narrative poem, the national epic written in Vietnamese ideographic script (*Nôm*), gives expression to the conflict between Confucian duty and the rebellious call of freedom. This tension appears over and over again in the writings of the Vietnamese poets we meet—the anti-Confucian feminist Hồ Xuân Hương, the bitter scholar-administrator poet Nguyễn Công Trứ, the rebel poet Cao Bá Quát (who was such an exception), and poets Nguyễn Đình Chiểu and Nguyễn Khuyến (who wrote about patriotism and not just about love).

In 1926, Phạm Tất Đắc, a high school student and author of the incendiary poem "Invocation for the Nation's Soul," set Việt Nam on fire with his call for revolution by joining Confucian piety to rising nationalism. Hữu Ngọc also describes the 1930s New Poetry Movement that gave voice to the young writers who sought to escape from traditional Vietnamese and Chinese literary conventions and who altered Vietnamese literature into a dynamism shifting between the romantic and the realistic. He quotes poet Xuân Diệu to help us understand the tectonic shift to the appearance of the personal pronoun "I" in common usage and in literature. The poems, short stories, and novels from the New Poetry Movement explored the individual's struggle in a society that had stifled individualism with outmoded customs and conventions. We feel the "I" most profoundly in the excerpts of poems by the "leper poet," Hàn Mặc Tử, a devout Catholic succumbing to Hansen's Disease yet both proclaiming his faith in "Ave Marie" and portraying deep angst in *Poems of Madness*.

Hữu Ngọc celebrates "Culture and the Arts" with essays on contributions unique to Việt Nam, including the Đông Hồ folk woodcut prints, *tuồng* (Vietnamese classical opera), *chèo* (popular opera), *ca trù* performances in villages of the Red River Delta in northern Việt Nam, and the *cải lương* (renovated theater) of the Mekong Delta in southern Việt Nam. He brings alive the water puppets (unique to the Red River Delta of northern Việt Nam) by taking us to a local performance in one of the villages where the puppets originated some two thousand years ago. This essay gives us a taste of rural, farming life devoid of urban influences. We see this both through the visit to the village and in the characters and skits the farmer-puppeteers create. The essays on the romantic music of the 1930s and early 1940s and the paintings by Nam Sơn (co-founder of the Indochina Fine Arts College in 1925) and the "four pillars" of successive generations of Vietnamese painters embody the push-pull, repulsion-attraction of the Vietnamese response to French influences.

The section on "The Vietnamese Landscape and the Vietnamese Spirit" helps us understand the inextricably intertwining of these two determinants. Hữu Ngọc describes how the Vietnamese landscape has forged the character of Việt Nam's people, how the harsher climate and floods in northern Việt Nam led to tight-knit communal villages, while a wilder frontier spirit prevailed in the southern part of the country. His essays introduce the reader to places beloved for their historical significance, beauty, and local customs as well as to the illustrious individuals and ordinary inhabitants associated with those sites. He takes us to Ancient Hà Nội and inside the Royal Palace in the 1700s, more than a century before French colonialism, through a long excerpt written by a Vietnamese doctor, Lê Hữu Trác, who arrives to treat the crown prince.

Hữu Ngọc also takes us to the Hà Nội of his childhood through his own reflections and a rich excerpt by Hoàng Đạo Thúy about traditional "Grand Tết" (Lunar New Year) in the early 1900s, "when the newly established colonial administration had only blurred the festival's traditions." This section ends with Côn Đảo Island and its infamous prisons off the coast of Sài Gòn and a tribute to Confucian scholar Phan Châu (Chu) Trinh, whose sense of honor did not bind him to tradition but, rather, made him one of Việt Nam's most famous patriotic opponents to French rule. Phan Châu Trinh combined Confucian ethics with democratic ideals in an attempt to create a harmonious, independent country achieved through non-violence. Phan Châu Trinh's poem, "Smashing Rocks at Côn Lôn," which he wrote on the prison wall, weaves together landscape, Confucian ethics, patriotism, and Vietnamese endurance.

In the book's final two sections, "Vietnamese Women and Change" and "*Đổi Mới* (Renovation or Renewal) and Globalization," Hữu Ngọc turns his attention to more modern times. Once, teeth lacquering was thought to enhance one's beauty. In the 1930s, the *áo dài* was created, with French influence; it is now considered traditional Vietnamese dress. In these essays, Hữu Ngọc's subtle commentary suggests that customs and traditions must be thoughtfully assessed for the ways they shape people's lives. Some should be preserved, some reformed, others discarded. Hữu Ngọc reflects on the difficulties confronted by women in the era of *Đổi Mới*, which began in late 1986. He exposes the ways in which Confucian traditions once limited women's lives and the new challenges women face now. The essays on *Đổi Mới* consider the problems Việt Nam addresses as it builds an economy linked to global markets, a step that inevitably opens the society once again to outside influences.

Hữu Ngọc argues that national culture "must hold a central position and play the coordinating and regulating role" in economic development and that economic statistics are not an adequate measure of the quality of life of a people. The unfettered expansion of world markets poses a threat to the environment, and there is great danger that the wealth produced will be appropriated by a minority of elites, leaving the mass of people dependent and poor. To shape a different kind of identity, Việt Nam must restore a balance between national traditions fostering patriotism, a strong sense of community, and discipline on one hand and universal values (such as human rights) and the need for economic development on the other.

We find here essays on the impact of a market economy on marriage, divorce, attitudes toward tradition in the "cicada" generation born after 1990, class differences, the traditional village, the value placed on education, and corruption in government. Hữu Ngọc suggests that the traditional family, which is at the heart of national culture, should be modernized, divesting itself of disdain for women. His reflections are nuanced, returning always to the theme, "All tradition is change through acculturation," yet encouraging readers to make their own evaluation of the balance between national values and the values of the market.

Having read these essays, a foreigner sees Việt Nam through new eyes. Written during *Đổi Mới*, the essays reflect modern times but reach into the rich past of Hữu Ngọc's memory and scholarship. These essays are also a reminder to young Vietnamese and to all of us of the vibrant cultural heritage that distinguishes Việt Nam. The essays can be read in any order. They invite readers to dip in here or there, according to impulse and interest. Taken together and read from beginning to end, they transform one's understanding of Việt Nam, its culture, and its people.

Elizabeth F. Collins
Professor
Ohio University
Athens, Ohio

Introduction

If I were to choose one person to accompany visitors on their first trip to Việt Nam, my choice would be Hữu Ngọc. If I were to choose one book for those about to visit Việt Nam or those unable to visit, my choice would be Hữu Ngọc's *Việt Nam: Tradition and Change*. At age ninety-eight by Western counting (ninety-nine according to Vietnamese), Hữu Ngọc is among Việt Nam's most famous general scholars. Born with limited eyesight, he reads by holding a text three inches from his near-sighted eye. Yet with his unusual linguistic ability, prodigious memory, and his longevity, he is among Việt Nam's keenest observers of traditional Vietnamese culture and recent history. For twenty years, Hữu Ngọc wrote a Sunday column in French for *Le Courrier du Vietnam* (The Việt Nam Mail). An English version appeared as "Traditional Miscellany" in *Việt Nam News*, Hà Nội's English-language newspaper. He collected 1,255 pages from these essays into *Wandering through Vietnamese Culture*, the only English-language book to win Việt Nam's Gold Book Prize.

Việt Nam: Tradition and Change is a selection from the many treasures in *Wandering through Vietnamese Culture*.

Hữu Ngọc was born on Hàng Gai (Hemp Market) Street in Hà Nội's Old Quarter in 1918, when Việt Nam did not yet have its own name on world maps. At that time, the French name for Việt Nam was Annam, which was also the French name for one of Việt Nam's three regions—Tonkin (Bắc Kỳ, the Northern Region); Annam (Trung Kỳ, the Central Region); and Cochin China (Nam Kỳ, the Southern Region). The Vietnamese people in all three regions endured colonialism's rigid and often lethal grasp. The literacy rate among Vietnamese was from 5 to 10 percent. The schools recognized by the French provided education in *Quốc Ngữ* (Vietnamese Romanized script) and French to train a small group of Vietnamese students to be administrators at French offices. The curriculum in the country's few high schools centered on French literature, French history, mathematics, and the sciences, with Vietnamese taught as a foreign language.

During Hữu Ngọc's student years, Hà Nội had only two state-run high schools—Bưởi School for Vietnamese and Lycée Albert Sarraut for French children as well as for Vietnamese children from the privileged class. Hữu Ngọc was one of two students from Bưởi along with several from Sarraut to place highest in the special examinations. The prize was a ride in the first airplane to circle above Hà Nội.

"This was 1936," Hữu Ngọc says. "Airplanes were rare in Việt Nam. How extraordinary, how amazing to be up in the sky! Such a wide-open view!"

Việt Nam was still under French rule when Hữu Ngọc completed a year of law school in Hà Nội and taught French in Vinh and Huế, two cities in the Central Region. Việt Nam's Declaration of Independence placed the Democratic Republic of Việt Nam (DRVN) on the world map on September 2, 1945. Hữu Ngọc joined the Revolution that same year.

However, nationwide independence was short-lived. The French re-invaded Việt Nam's Southern Region on September 23, 1945, three weeks after the Declaration of Independence, arriving on British ships carrying American materiel. Then, in late 1946, the French re-invaded Việt Nam's Northern Region and its Central Region, again with American materiel. By this time, Việt Nam was divided into two shifting zones—French-occupied and liberated.

Hữu Ngọc was in the liberated zone. There, he took an examination with forty candidates to choose four who would become English teachers. He placed first. He laughs about this now: "The examiner for the verbal section asked about Wordsworth's 'The Daffodils,' my favorite poem. I could be unusually fluent, and so I placed first. Wordsworth changed my life!"

He taught English in Yên Mô District, Ninh Bình Province and in the liberated zone of Nam Định Province, where he also served as chair of the Cultural Committee for the Nam Định Province Resistance. While in Nam Định, he created, wrote, and edited a French agitprop (agitation and propaganda) newspaper intended for troops in the French Far-East Expeditionary Corps. Only one known copy of the newspaper remains. Its red banner proclaims *L'Etincelle* (The Spark). That issue has an article about General Võ Nguyên Giáp, complete with a photograph.

Hữu Ngọc would tie his contraband newspapers to his bicycle's luggage rack. He remembers passing through a Catholic village. He was biking down a narrow alley when he spotted several French-affiliated African troops, who had arrived for a mopping-up operation. They were on foot and heading toward him.

"Halt!" the soldiers shouted.

"I had to remain calm," Hữu Ngọc says. "I ducked down an alley. I heard the click of gun triggers engaging. I was sure the soldiers would shoot me in the back. But I was lucky. I had just enough time to turn into another lane and disappear."

In 1950, the DRVN government called up adult men in the liberated areas to join the army. By then, the French had re-occupied the liberated areas in the Red River Delta. Hữu Ngọc walked hundreds of kilometers out to the Việt Bắc Northern Liberated Zone in the mountains. As an army officer, he supervised the Section for Re-Education of European and African Prisoners of War (POWs). At that time, the DRVN kept the POWs at houses of local Tày and Nùng ethnic-minority people in "prisons without bars." Hữu Ngọc remembers sitting with three POWs around a hearth in a house-on-stilts. "One POW was French," he says, "one was an English former officer who'd served in the Royal Air Force, and one was German. We were chatting about anything and everything. I was speaking three foreign languages in the same conversation! I learned a great deal about foreign cultures from the POWs."

Several thousand Germans had joined the French Foreign Legion, a French mercenary force, after World War II for assignments to Việt Nam. Some deserted to the Việt Minh side. "I worked closely with Chiến Sĩ (Militant, a.k.a. Erwin Borchers), an anti-Nazi German intellectual," Hữu Ngọc says. "Chiến Sĩ had joined the French Foreign Legion and then deserted to the Việt Minh *before* our 1945 Revolution. He handled our agitprop among German POWs. We were close friends. That's how I learned German."

The Foreign Legion and the French Far-East Expeditionary Corps in Việt Nam had nearly twenty different nationalities. Many POWs had come from the French colonies in Northern and Central Africa. Hữu Ngọc and his colleagues organized lectures and printed training materials on nationalism to persuade POWs (particularly those from other French colonies) that they had been assisting the French in an unjust war.

Then the Vietnamese periodically released their "best students" back to the French side to organize within French ranks. The French soon caught onto the scheme and sent the newly released POWs back home. Once they were back home, many of these liberated African POWs began to organize for their own national revolutions. Perhaps it is no accident that some Algerians identify the beginning of their revolution as May 8, 1954, the day after the Vietnamese victory over the French at the famous Battle of Điện Biên Phủ.

Hữu Ngọc received a People's Army Feat-of-Arms Award for his agitprop work. His assignments during the French War had taken him between POW camps-without-bars to staff headquarters and to other sites in liberated Việt Bắc. Like many other army officers, he hiked along mountain paths. One day, at an intersection between two trails, he met one of his former Nam Định students, a lovely young woman, who by then was an army nurse and who, before long, would become a pediatrician. The two courted in the mountains and married in a simple wedding with tea, cigarettes, and their friends' congratulations. They shared three days off in the special honeymoon hut Hữu Ngọc's colleagues had built. Then he and his wife returned to their assignments, seeing each other whenever possible. Their first child was born in the mountains. After Hà Nội was liberated in October 1954, Hữu Ngọc and his family moved back to the capital. These days, he and his wife live with one of their sons and his family. Without fail, their children, grandchildren, and great grandchildren gather each Sunday for lunch, rotating from one household to another. Over the years, foreigners from many countries have joined Hữu Ngọc's family for Sunday lunch, formerly sitting in a circle on a reed floor mat but now sitting around a large, polished table, yet always conversing in many languages.

During the American War (the term Vietnamese use for what Americans call "the Vietnam War"), Hữu Ngọc was deputy director of Việt Nam's Foreign Languages Publishing House. He and Nguyễn Khắc Viện, the publishing house director, edited and translated Vietnamese poetry and prose for their thousand-page *Literature Vietnamienne* (Vietnamese Literature, 1979). Publication of this work was a major cultural event. *Le Monde* (The World), the leading newspaper in France, noted: "Every day, a hundred American B-52s pummeled North Việt Nam. Nevertheless, the Vietnamese did the work to publish this major anthology of their literature in French."

The Foreign Languages Publishing House (also known as Red River Press) printed books in Arabic, Chinese, English, French, German, Portuguese, Russian, Spanish, and other languages, including Esperanto (a constructed international language).

"The Esperanto period was so interesting!" Hữu Ngọc says. "Not many people knew Esperanto, but those who did were fanatical. They would translate from Esperanto into their own languages. Esperanto multiplied our efforts at the publishing house because Esperanto translators worked in both the communist and the capitalist blocs."

Hữu Ngọc was director of the publishing house from 1980 until his retirement in 1989. When Việt Nam began to open, he changed the name to Thế Giới (World) Publishers because all countries in the communist/socialist bloc had a Foreign Languages Press. Hữu

Ngọc wanted to signal that Việt Nam was not only unique but also open to the whole world, including the West.

During the American War, the publishing house had paid particular attention to English. Those books and *Vietnamese Studies*—a quarterly founded by Nguyễn Khắc Viện in 1964 and still published today—reached American activists and scholars.

Between the end of the American War in April 1975 and September 1989, Việt Nam faced war on two fronts: 1) the Khmer Rouge incursions into southern Việt Nam with the subsequent war in Cambodia and 2) the Chinese invasion into six Vietnamese border provinces. The then US government politically backed the genocidal Khmer Rouge and the Chinese invasion. Thus, although many say the American War ended in 1975, in truth, re-unified Việt Nam first enjoyed peace only in 1990.

The United States responded to the war in Cambodia by enforcing an even stricter embargo, which entangled all Western countries except Sweden. The embargo kept out not only Western goods and spare parts for any machine produced or patented in the West but also books, including medical journals. Việt Nam's leadership had already instituted a rigorous, intensely collectivized socio-economic system, which stymied individual incentives in agriculture, trade, business, education, and scholarship. Although Việt Nam received military aid from the former Soviet Union, with the exception of Sweden, the country essentially had no outside assistance for food, medicines, and post-war reconstruction. Everything was rationed. Everyone was gaunt. Typhoons, floods, and droughts compounded the stress. Nevertheless, by the mid-late 1980s, Hữu Ngọc was already looking ahead to normalized relations between Việt Nam and the United States. He had published works about French, Japanese, Lao, and Swedish culture. Now, he wanted to write about American culture.

Hữu Ngọc often cites this caution: "You can go to Paris for three weeks and write a book, but if you live there thirty years, you dare not write a word."

With his own caveat in mind and long before the Internet, Hữu Ngọc read everything he could about American culture. He asked any Americans he met to send books with the next visitor and to write articles. He went on to create a thousand-page volume in Vietnamese with essays from friends, summaries from his own research, and a very extensive bibliography. *Hồ Sơ Văn Hóa Mỹ* (A File on American Culture) remains in print today after twenty years. Hữu Ngọc's oeuvre also includes many books about Vietnamese culture. Perhaps most important among them is his *Dictionary of Traditional Vietnamese Culture,* which has been available in Vietnamese since 1994 but was published in English only in 2012. This must-have book holds gems on every page.

When Hữu Ngọc was still in his late eighties, he walked to work, carrying his bag of books and covering the five kilometers in a little more than an hour. He used his far-sighted eye to negotiate Hà Nội's famously horrendous traffic while reciting poetry in Chinese, English, French, German, and Vietnamese, with William Wordsworth still among his favorite poets. And so, it is no accident that Hữu Ngọc's *Wandering through Vietnamese Culture* opens with his favorite lines from Wordsworth's "The Daffodils."

Several years ago, Hữu Ngọc's family moved too far from World Publishers for him to walk to work. Now, for exercise, he walks forty-five minutes every day, covering three kilometers inside his house, often reciting the ten Buddhist precepts. He begins with the first precept, then recites the first and second precepts, then the first and second and third. When he finishes all ten precepts, he starts over again. Then Hữu Ngọc continues his day, writing his essays in heavy black ink, a felt-tip marker as his pen.

Hữu Ngọc has a rather wry approach to his prolific writing. "Do you know why I write?" he will say, pointing to the shelves of books he has written and edited. "When I need to check something, I know where to look!"

Three days a week, Hữu Ngọc rides on the back of his son's motorbike to his office at World Publishers. He is a mentor to many. His door is open. Whoever pops in is welcomed, introduced, and linked to anyone already in the room. His open door emphasizes the great role of "the random" in life. Hữu Ngọc says his own life has been a continuous series of random events. As a youth in

Hà Nội, he dreamed of marrying a girl from the mountains and nesting in a house by a stream. However, the random from an interview question and lines from his favorite Wordsworth poem led him to teaching. In 1945, he joined the Việt Minh because of random events of history. His limited eyesight and assignment to work with POWs and the random in life led him to a career as a researcher in culture. Yet, despite his belief in "the random," Hữu Ngọc recognizes opportunity without being an opportunist. Those who take advantage of his open door know that he has an unusual ability to discern and develop a new idea or a novel approach.

After retiring as chairman of the Vietnam-Sweden Cultural Fund and of the Vietnam-Denmark Cultural Fund, in 2012 Hữu Ngọc established the Cultural Charity Fund to provide children in remote areas with world literature. The translated books range from works by American John Steinbeck to Russian Boris Pasternak to the newest Harry Potter books. He has also given rural children the chance to study English first hand by organizing courses taught by English-speaking volunteers.

Hữu Ngọc continues to give his ever-changing lecture, "Three Thousand Years of Vietnamese History in One Hour." He will hand *Wandering through Vietnamese Culture* to a listener in the first row. "Take a look," he says. "Pass it around." One by one, members of his audience marvel at the book's weight and peruse its 1,255 pages, pausing here and there to measure the book's depth.

For this volume, Professor Elizabeth Collins from Ohio University has worked with Hữu Ngọc to select essays from *Wandering through Vietnamese Culture*. This was a huge task, one I had seen as important for years but had found overwhelming. Hữu Ngọc worked over successive drafts of the Contents, restructuring some sections, making minor changes in other sections, and adding a few pieces, which do not appear in *Wandering through Vietnamese Culture*.

A weekly newspaper column is like a ticking metronome rushing the writer on and leaving little time to ponder chords, trills, and grace notes. However, collecting columns into a book of essays gives the writer a chance to revisit his work—to consolidate some pieces, expand and tighten others, and to play with the melodies and harmonies of language. At ninety-eight, Hữu Ngọc is still writing weekly essays and assembling books. He is busy moving forward. For that reason, he asked me to assume responsibility for shifting his selected newspaper columns into the essays that appear in this volume.

That task provided me an opportunity for many random discussions of this text in Hữu Ngọc's office. In consultation with the author, I have updated paragraphs, made corrections, and inserted some sentences and phrases for clarity and context. I have left in repetitive details because readers may approach the essays out of order. I have also added a note on the Vietnamese language, a historical timeline, and an index.

Additions made to Hữu Ngọc's text include the titles of the works he quoted, with the Vietnamese titles in parentheses and the English translation in italics or quotation marks in the body of the text. This intentional reversal of usual practice is for easier reading; it does *not* indicate that the quoted excerpt is from a work that has been translated into English. Indeed, very few of these works have been translated in full.

Vietnamese Literature, the English version of the French anthology, was the source for many of the excerpts from poetry and prose that Hữu Ngọc quoted in his newspaper columns. The Vietnamese works in *Vietnamese Literature* had been translated sometimes from Chinese (*Hán*) or Vietnamese (*Nôm*) ideographic script into Romanized Vietnamese script (*Quốc Ngữ*), then into French, and, only then, into English. As a result, understandably, many English translations in *Vietnamese Literature* and in Hữu Ngọc's original newspaper columns were rather distant from the original texts.

For this reason, I have re-translated all the quotations from Vietnamese works, returning to the original Romanized Vietnamese versions and, when relevant, to the transliterated *Hán* and *Nôm* versions of the ancient poems and prose. By adding the Romanized Vietnamese titles, I hope to encourage interested readers to explore the original texts, many of which are available on the Web at <www.thivien.net> in *Quốc Ngữ* and, for the ancient works, also in *Hán* or *Nôm* at that same website. Some of our translations in this volume appear in our other books and articles and will appear in the new edition of *Vietnamese Literature.*

Hữu Ngọc chose not to read the final manuscript for this book because he wants to conserve his time to work on new projects. His son, Hữu Tiến, read the manuscript and alerted me to several errors. Phạm Trần Long, deputy director of World Publishers and the book's editor in Việt Nam, is always a careful, helpful reader. Trần Đoàn Lâm, the director of World Publishers, is well versed in Chinese *Hán* script and Vietnamese *Nôm* ideographic script. In addition, he is fluent in Russian and English and can read French. Mr. Lâm has checked our translations with the original texts (*Hán, Nôm, Quốc Ngữ,* and French). As director of World Publishers, he is also the book's final Vietnamese reader. Trần Đoàn Lâm brings to any text an extraordinary ability to think broadly yet concentrate on the smallest detail.

This book does not attempt to be a systematic study of Vietnamese culture or of Việt Nam's traditions and changes. Rather, it is a compilation of some of the essays from *Wandering through Vietnamese Culture* that reflect that theme. As a result, there may be important events, people, and issues not covered in this collection.

Now, with many of us working together and with assistance from many other colleagues in Việt Nam at World Publishers and in the United States at Ohio University Press, we have *Việt Nam: Tradition and Change,* an accessible and absorbing tour of Việt Nam's history and culture with scholar-writer Hữu Ngọc as our guide.

Lady Borton
Hà Nội, Việt Nam

The Vietnamese Identity

Nghĩa

Of all the beautiful verses in *The Tale of Kiều* (Truyện Kiều), the immortal work in 3,254 lines by our national poet, Nguyễn Du (1766–1820), this couplet in six-word, eight-word meter about Kiều, when she is beset by lost love, seems to me the most beautiful:

> Sorrowful, the remnant of old love,
> The thread of a lotus root still lingering.

> *Tiếc thay chút nghĩa cũ càng*
> *Dẫu lìa ngó ý còn vương tơ lòng.*

I believe only Vietnamese can really appreciate this couplet's beauty and, in particular, can understand "*nghĩa*," which in this context means "love." But that's not all. "*Nghĩa*," a Sino-Vietnamese word, is a traditional Vietnamese ethical concept, which can be understood as moral obligation, justice, duty, debt of gratitude, and mutual attachment based on duty. *Nghĩa* has to do with both the heart and the mind, which are closely linked in important phrases, such as "*nghĩ bụng*" (think with the belly) and "*nghĩ trong lòng*" (think with the bowels). Traditionally, belly and bowels are the locus of feelings.

"*Nghĩa*" is the phonetic transcription of the Chinese character for "justice," a key word in Confucianism. Actually, Confucius (551–479 BCE) placed greater stress on humanism (*nhân*) than on justice. Mencius (372–289 BCE), for his part, insisted on "*nghĩa*" as meaning "the right thing to do, even to the detriment of one's own interest." Moral obligation can take different forms depending on concrete social relationships (suzerain – vassal; parents – children; teacher – student; friends, etc.). The best definition for "*nghĩa*" may be found in the lines I just quoted. The definition has three components:

- duration: A proverb says, "*Nghĩa* can arise from one ferry trip" (*Chuyến đò nên nghĩa*). This means that one trip across a river is enough for passengers to feel bound together by *nghĩa*.
- mind: The mind is symbolized by the lotus stem. When snapped, the stem's tenuous filaments keep the two halves linked.
- heart: The tenuous filaments represent the heart.

In brief, far from being a dictate of conscience, *nghĩa* mixes reason and feeling—the mutual, moral, and sentimental obligation born from human contacts, however brief. *Nghĩa* governs relationships with other people as well as within the family, village, and country.

Love in Việt Nam generally leads to marriage and family. Conjugal love based on affection and loyalty is expressed by "*yêu thương*," a compound word, which is very difficult to translate. "*Yêu*" means "love;" "*thương*" means "to have compassion, understanding, or pity." "*Yêu*" implies passion, desire, affection, and fondness. "*Thương*" implies care, even tolerance. However, conjugal love can be best translated by "*tình nghĩa*," with "*tình*" expressing "love," and "*nghĩa*" capturing "mutual, moral, and sentimental obligation born out of love."

Nghĩa will keep a married couple together at a later life stage, when passion no longer reigns supreme and when affection has become a habit. But even then, because of *nghĩa*, a conjugal relationship will not be governed solely by reason. Husband and wife endure with each other because *nghĩa* binds them. *Nghĩa* explains why so many couples remain physically faithful despite long absences, especially during war.

The Vietnamese Character

A few years back, I spoke with Sociology Professor Göran Therbom about the Swedish mentality. We agreed that circumspection is indispensable in questions of national character, the psychology of peoples, cultural identity, and traditional values, lest one enter the trap of racism.

Since Việt Nam's August 1945 Revolution, we have held dozens of seminars and have published an abundance of literature devoted to the character and cultural identity of the Vietnamese people. The research, which tended to stress positive aspects, established the following points about the traditional Vietnamese character:

- strong adherence to the community: formation of the nation (unifying the family, village, and state) at an early stage to fight foreign invasions and natural disasters (e.g., building dikes against floods); formation of the village as the basic social, political, and economic unit

- an essential element: love for one's country

- an ancient culture: importance of the Việt language and love of learning

- ardor for work: intelligence, innovativeness, skillfulness, thrift, and the influence of wet-rice cultivation

- primordial role of the family: language use of personal pronouns according to the presumed age of the interlocutors and their position in the wider cultural family

- relationships: filial piety, respect for aged persons, and solidarity (family, village, and nation)

- adaptability: ability to survive, suppleness of comportment, sense of realism, preference for concreteness, eclecticism, and empiricism

- lifestyle: sobriety and simplicity, greater sensitivity to the simple, skillful, lovely, and graceful than to the imposing and monumental

- spectrum of feelings: tendency to be more sentimental than rational

- philosophical tendencies: little inclination toward philosophical speculations or metaphysical flights

- religious feelings: religiosity rather than fanaticism, with a large presence of autochthonous beliefs (animism)
- profound influences: Confucianism and Buddhism
- priority: preference for the good rather than the beautiful, hence the predominant role of morals and virtues

Our researchers analyzing Vietnamese character and cultural identity tend to highlight positive points. Very few discuss negative aspects. This attitude was justified during the long wars for national liberation, since we needed to emphasize positive national traditions to galvanize our Resistance. However, we need truly scientific research in today's increasing competition on a world scale to reveal our people's weaknesses and strengths in order to help shape capable and highly motivated citizens. According to our researchers, the main negative traits of traditional Vietnamese character and cultural identity may be listed as follows:

- social development and socio-economic structures: inability to evolve normally because of war and other interruptions
- in opposition to the strong sense of community: exaggerated concern for face-saving, difficulty for individuals to gain self-affirmation; localism and regionalism
- in opposition to fidelity toward traditions: conservatism and reluctance to embrace reforms and renovation of the economy, technology, and society
- patriarchal traditions inherited from traditional society: sectarianism, anarchism, and the cult of personality; too much emphasis on artisans and small-scale agriculture; lack of discipline, foresight, planning, and accounting; weak concern for profitability
- lack of logical and analytical sense: emphasis on empiricism and reliance on chance

Not all the traits enumerated can be taken as gospel truth. Nevertheless, they provide material for serious research and discussion.

The Vietnamese "I" and "We"

To understand the Vietnamese community, we should explore the strong socio-affective ties binding the "I" to the "we," that is, binding the individual to the community, large or small. We can trace these ties back to the formation of the nation. Việt Nam, lying in the heart of Southeast Asia, developed its own life and culture as early as the Bronze Age (first millennium BCE) and before exposure to Indian and Chinese influences. The Vietnamese nation was formed through the sporadic multiplication of villages (*làng, xã*), which were political, social, and economic units with solidarity forged through successive struggles against natural elements and foreign aggression. The Vietnamese language, which symbolizes the Vietnamese community, has no general word for "I." The first person singular cannot be expressed uniformly but must vary to suit different relationships the speaker has with others, including equals, parents, children, older or younger persons, and persons from different social conditions.

The pronoun "*ta*" may signify "I" or "we" depending on the context. The interrogative pronoun "*ai*" may mean "I," "you" (singular or plural), "he" or "she," "they," as well as "him" and "her" and "them," with a hint of tenderness, melancholy, or mild reproach. Consider this couplet in six-word, eight-word meter from an eleven-line oral folk poem (*ca dao*):

> *Ai đi muôn dặm non sông*
> *Để ai chất chứa sầu đong vơi đầy*

When translated literally, these lines are virtually meaningless:

> Who crossed myriad mountains and rivers,
> Leaving who fraught with melancholy, which defies measure.

With an understanding of the variations possible in "*ai,*" the lines become:

You are away, across many mountains,
Leaving me fraught with melancholy, which defies measure.

The Vietnamese: A Warlike People?

A favorite anti-Vietnamese press theme during the 1960s, 1970s, and 1980s was: "The Vietnamese are the Prussians of Asia." As ideological issues fade with time, perhaps future historians will agree among themselves that, at its base, all that fighting was for national liberation. If we consider the often bloody conflicts that tore apart Southeast Asian states in gestation during the second millennium, we can see that most wars fought by Việt Nam were in resistance to foreign aggression.

If it is true that literature mirrors a people's psyche, then we might point out that the literature of Việt Nam's majority ethnic group (the Kinh or Việt) does not have epics or other works exalting war for its own sake or singing the grandeur of massacres. On the contrary, the work second in popularity only to *The Tale of Kiều* (Truyện Kiều, the masterpiece by Nguyễn Du [1766–1820]) is a long anti-war poem, "Lament of a Wife Whose Husband Has Gone to War" (Chinh Phụ Ngâm). For two centuries, this lament enjoyed the love and esteem of both common people and learned scholars. This poem in 103 quatrains with eight-word meter exudes a poignant despair, which leads to instinctive hatred of war. As a woman subjected to Confucian education, the wife never directs the least reproach toward war's initiators—the kings, lords, and other feudalists. Instead, she simply describes her loneliness and suffering. Her only solace is hope for her husband's return. Memories of the separation from her beloved cast a constant shadow on her waking hours:

The brook rippling beneath the bridge is pure,
The roadside grass is still a tender green.
Seeing him off leaves her anguished,
Once he's astride his horse, aboard his boat.

The rushing water can never cleanse her grief,
The fragrant grass can never ease her memories.

Let us note that the Vietnamese text of this lament is a translation by the poetess Đoàn Thị Điểm (1705–1748) from the original version, which male poet Đặng Trần Côn (1710–1745) wrote in classical Chinese characters (*Hán*). Đoàn Thị Điểm condensed the original 477 lines into 412 lines in Vietnamese ideographic script (*Nôm*). During the Resistance War Against France, Hồ Chí Minh taught this long poem to his staff while on long jungle treks.

Are There Differences in the Mentality of Northern and Southern Vietnamese?

After first visiting southern Việt Nam and before traveling to the country's northern region, a foreign friend asked me, "Have differences affected your national identity because of the regional interests and disparities in northern and southern mentalities that were deepened by twenty years of war and separation characterized by two different political and cultural systems?"

In answering such a question, it would first be useful to define "north" and "south" in Việt Nam, because these words have very different meanings depending on the time in our nation's history.

The Nguyễn and Trịnh lords, under the pretext of serving the Lê Dynasty (1533–1788), split the country into two by waging a war, which lasted two centuries (from 1570 to 1786, among many dates used). The demarcation line was the Gianh River in Quảng Bình Province, north of Huế. Foreigners—in particular Portuguese and Dutch traders—called the northern part of Việt Nam "Tonkin" and the southern part, "Cochin China." Quang Trung (a.k.a. Nguyễn Huệ, life: 1753–1792; reign: 1788–1792) re-unified the country.

But then the French conquered Việt Nam in the mid-1800s. During colonial reign (1884–1945), France divided Việt Nam into three parts—the Northern Region, which the French called Tonkin

(Bắc Kỳ); the Central Region, called Annam (Trung Kỳ); and the Southern Region, called Cochin China (Nam Kỳ). The French ruled Tonkin and Annam as protectorates and administered Cochin China as a colony. On September 2, 1945, Hồ Chí Minh proclaimed the independent Democratic Republic of Việt Nam (DRVN) and re-unified the country. After nine years of war, the Geneva Conference ended the First Indochina War Against France and divided Việt Nam into North Việt Nam and South Việt Nam at the 17th parallel. This division lasted two more decades (1954–1975) during the Second Indochina War Against the United States.

Thus, the border between the North and the South changed three times, with the Center sometimes in play. In each case, the words "North" and "South" are capitalized, since they refer to distinct regimes. After 1975, there has been only one regime, one country, with formal re-unification on July 2, 1976. This is a little complicated, but lower case for "north," "center," and "south" and variations of those words should be used after April 30, 1975 and for periods before French colonialism except from 1570 to 1786 (the War of the Trịnh-Nguyễn Lords during the Lê Dynasty).

At present, when speaking of "the people of the south" in re-unified Việt Nam, we think of the inhabitants of the Mekong Delta. Although their mentality is different from the mentality of Vietnamese in other areas, it is by no means secessionist. The French colonialists failed to realize this when they attempted to create the autonomous Republic of Cochin China in 1946. The US military made the same mistake during the American War when trying to sever the Hồ Chí Minh Trail, which connected North Việt Nam and South Việt Nam.

One cannot deny the different mentalities of our northern and southern people. In Europe, Nordics are generally less easy to approach and less talkative than Mediterranean peoples. The same might be said traditionally of northerners and southerners on the US East Coast. In a way, the same also applies to Việt Nam. But in Việt Nam, explanations should be sought by carefully considering history. The ethnic Việt were wet-rice farmers, who created an original cultural identity in the Red River Delta during the first millennium BCE. After freeing themselves in 938 CE from a thousand years of Chinese domination, the Việt began advancing southward, reaching the Mekong Delta during the 1600s.

The Mekong Delta's first Việt settlers—famished peasants, peasant-soldiers, adventurers, and banished criminals—cleared virgin land. They did not experience the hard work and chronic deprivation of northern farmers plagued by scarce land and frequent natural calamities, such as typhoons and floods. The villages built by the Việt who moved southward were not, as in the north, isolated communities surrounded by bamboo hedges and burdened by age-old Confucian customs, rites, and taboos. New religions, such as Cao Đài and Hòa Hảo, which were unknown in northern Việt Nam, attracted millions of followers. No distinction was made between guest and host villagers.

The Việt lived in harmony with the region's other ethnic groups, such as the Chăm, Khmer, Mạ, Xtiêng, and Chinese. There were enough resources for all. The Chinese, many of whom were political refugees, engaged in a thriving trade. Direct French colonial rule and, later, the capitalist economy under American sway reinforced the psychology of the "people of the former South," some traits of which call to mind the American frontier spirit.

On Naming a Child

My first daughter-in-law, Lan, glows with happiness. She has just given birth to a baby girl; her nine-year-old is a boy. One boy, one girl—both "glutinous and ordinary rice," as the saying goes—is the dream of Vietnamese couples after the family-planning limit of two children. My other two daughters-in-law have two daughters each. Having a male descendant is still the wish of all couples, although the custom decreeing that only a male descendant can perpetuate ancestral worship is waning.

While all our family was busy looking after Lan and the baby, it fell to me as paternal grandfather to choose a name for my new granddaughter. This rather pleasing spiritual exercise brought a challenge in poetic logic. Since my daughter-in-law's name is Lan (Orchid), what system should I use to choose her daughter's name? I could select an ideogram from a classical verse, a moral maxim, or an old adage containing the word "*lan*" to accompany my choice as an adjective. Or I could choose the name of a plant or flower, since "orchid" is both. Or I could opt for the name of one of the more than 10,000 orchid varieties!

In the end, a name—"Cúc Hoa" (Chrysanthemum Flower)—flashed through my mind from a treasury of childhood memories. Cúc Hoa is the heroine in a folk tale written in verse with ideographic Vietnamese ideograms (*Nôm*) during the 1700s. The story is set in China during the early first millennium. I remember being moved to tears when, at age eight or nine, I saw a *chèo* (popular opera), *Phạm Công and Cúc Hoa* (Phạm Công Cúc Hoa), based on this tale. In a particularly moving scene, two children find solace in the arms of their mother, Cúc Hoa, who returns from the Other World to protect them.

Here, in a few lines, is the story:

Phạm Công was very young when he lost his impoverished woodcutter father and had to beg in the market to support his mother. A kind-hearted scholar looked after his education. A fellow student named Cúc Hoa fell in love with Phạm Công and, with her parents' agreement, married him. However, the couple faced hard times. Cúc Hoa was expecting a baby, yet they owned nothing. Phạm Công presented himself for the royal examinations. He earned the first laureate degree and the offer of marriage to the Ngụy king's daughter. When Phạm Công declined the marriage offer, the Ngụy king banished him to the Hán Kingdom.

There, Phạm Công was again honored with the first laureate title and a marriage offer to the Hán princess. When Phạm Công refused this marriage, the Hán king ordered the young scholar's hands severed, his eyes gouged, and his teeth pulled. The Emperor of Heaven punished the tyrant king and restored the victimized scholar's health. On his way home, Phạm Công passed through the Triệu Kingdom. This king also honored him with the first laureate title and a royal bride, but Phạm Công managed to escape and was reunited with Cúc Hoa. The couple had a daughter in addition to their elder child, a son. Alas, Cúc Hoa fell ill and died as foreign troops invaded. Phạm Công, who was an army commander, set off to fight the enemy, carrying his wife's coffin on his back. When the campaign ended in victory, Phạm Công took a second wife, Tào Thị, hoping she would tend to the two children. Three years later, Phạm Công became governor of Việt Nam's Cao Bằng Province. In his absence, Tào Thị took a lover and turned Phạm Công's two children out of the house. Cúc Hoa, by then in the Land of Shades, was broken-hearted. She returned to the World of Mortals to comfort her children. Before going back to the Land of Shades, she wrote letters deploring her children's fate and sewed the letters into her children's clothes. On his return, Phạm Công learned the truth and repudiated Tào Thị, who subsequently died from a lightning strike. He went to the Other World to search for Cúc Hoa. The couple's sorrow so moved the King of Darkness that he allowed Phạm Công to take Cúc Hoa back to the World of Mortals. At last, the couple knew happiness.

My choosing "Cúc Hoa" also has another reason. A line in *The Tale of Kiều* (Truyện Kiều), the masterpiece by Nguyễn Du (1766–1820), matches "chrysanthemum" ("*cúc*") with "orchid" ("*lan*"):

Spring's <u>orchid</u>, autumn's <u>chrysanthemum</u>, they are
equally alluring.

Xuân <u>lan</u> thu <u>cúc</u> mặn mà cả hai.

The Traditional Village: For and Against

Over the centuries, the Việt (ethnic Vietnamese or Kinh) nation took shape through the spread of villages, which were the political-socio-economic groupings that united the Việt people in continuous struggle with nature and against foreign invaders.

Another term for a Vietnamese "village" is "commune," which is not a communist term but, instead, comes from the French word, "*commune*," for the lowest-level governmental administrative unit. The Vietnamese village with its staunch sense of community binds residents together within the three-step structure of family, village, and state. Villages allowed the Việt to survive on wet-rice cultivation by building and maintaining large communal irrigation and drainage systems. On a wider scale, Việt Nam's thick network of villages supported the Việt resistance to invasions by powerful foes, such as the Mongol armies in the 1200s.

In many countries, military defense has relied on urban citadels. The fall of a fortress was a military disaster. However, in Việt Nam, *each* village was a bastion. The Ba Đình Resistance Against France in 1886 is a perfect example. "*Ba đình*" (meaning "three communal houses") refers to the three villages in Thanh Hóa Province that joined together, connecting themselves with deep, defensive trenches. They held at bay thirty-four hundred French colonial troops supported by four gunboats during the thirty-five-day siege conducted by Captain (later, Marshal) Joseph Jacques Césaire Joffre (1852–1931).

Other factors in addition to self-defense and community irrigation systems strengthen the communal character of Vietnamese villages. Traditionally, villages were autonomous units within the state. The central authority, which was represented by district mandarins, assessed each commune for head taxes, land taxes, and unpaid labor. However, village councils of male elders assisted by elected agents met those obligations. A popular saying summarizes the village's unusual stature: "Royal decrees yield to village customs."

The village population had several groupings, including the hamlet, *giáp*, family clan, and guild. The *giáp*, a vestige of the primitive agricultural commune, was an egalitarian and democratic male association, which grouped the men into classes by age regardless of their titles, functions, or fortunes. A man's passage from a lower to a higher class in the *giáp* gave him greater prestige. In certain cases, elders would bring sensitive matters before the *giáp* for a preliminary consensus to avoid a stormy discussion in the broader village.

The periodic distribution of communal village fields among registered male villagers every three, four, or six years was another democratic village institution and a vestige of the primitive agricultural community. Vietnamese practiced this recurring privatization of public land from the 1100s to the early 1800s and, in some areas, even into the 1900s. Communal fields still existed in some villages on the eve of the Land Reform Campaign conducted in the 1950s. The traditional communal lands brought the state more revenue than private lands because of higher tax rates; those taxes also supplied funds to pay village administrators and assist widows, the elderly, orphans, and others without adequate support.

The traditional village was also the repository of our nation's spiritual and artistic traditions. Many mandarins and scholars retired to their home villages after public service; their literary creations were both learned and popular. Today, village temples remain the sites for spring and autumn ritual celebrations, which draw communities together through popular merriment. These temples display some of the best examples of ancient Việt architecture. They also house a majority of the remaining Việt sculptures because Vietnamese hid their national art (which was in fact popular art) in the countryside during the long periods of Chinese and French domination.

Despite its positive aspects, the traditional Vietnamese village is far from a Rousseau-esque model. During the early 1900s, "village" was synonymous with oppression and extortion, intellectual backwardness, and moral stagnation. The democracy apparent in the examples above became a delusion. Communal lands were reduced and no longer played a significant role. Elders imposed their tyranny. The communal hierarchy buttressed by Confucianism divided villagers into socio-economic classes: scholars, soldiers, artisans, traders, and peasants. The lowest class—the peasants—bore the burden of taxes and forced hard labor.

In fairness to the French, it should be said that the colonial administration attempted several reforms, but those were formalities.

During French colonialism, the traditional village was still pre-capitalist, essentially agricultural, and self-sufficient. One result was a severely limited national economy with little foreign trade. Despite Việt Nam's long coastline, the Việt were not seafarers like the Malays. The absence of Vietnamese foreign trade hampered the country's economic advancement.

Before the August 1945 Revolution, young Western-trained Vietnamese intellectuals converted some patriotic Confucian scholars to the Western idea of progress. These patriots criticized the archaic character and structure of the traditional Việt village. During the Resistance War Against France (1945–1954), the vast majority of residents in French-occupied villages functioned undercover on the patriots' side by secretly supplying food and intelligence. Many Vietnamese left French-occupied villages to help transport rice by shoulder poles and pack bicycles hundreds of kilometers to the Battle of Điện Biên Phủ. This Herculean effort made possible the Vietnamese defeat of the French army in 1954. Võ Nguyên Giáp, the victorious Vietnamese general, noted that when the French tallied the balance of armed forces before the battle, they neglected to appraise accurately the role of Vietnamese peasant porters.

Later, Ngô Đình Diệm, whom the Americans had brought in from the United States in 1954 to be premier of South Việt Nam, tried in vain to dismantle traditional Vietnamese villages. His troops drove southern Vietnamese peasants from their homes into policed, barbed-wire-encircled camps called strategic hamlets. During the American War, US aircraft tried without success to destroy the traditional Việt socio-economic-cultural village bonds by bombing two-thirds of the rural communities across the country, in both North Việt Nam and South Việt Nam.

The August 1945 Revolution, the Land Reform Campaign of the 1950s, the creation of agricultural co-operatives in the 1960s, and the two resistance wars for national liberation and re-unification (1945–1975) subjected traditional villages to profound upheavals. Now, it is up to us to keep the positive values within this heritage.

A Village Landscape

I shall never forget this reading lesson, which I learned by heart (but of course in Vietnamese!) at primary school, when I was eight:

My Village

My village is near the province. All around my village is a bamboo hedge so thick that those outside cannot see our houses. At the head and foot of my village is a brick gate. Most houses are thatch. Each household has a courtyard, a garden, and usually a pond. A bamboo hedge surrounds each house, while the garden has vegetables, sweet potatoes, and fruit trees. Only one main road runs through the village, but we have many meandering lanes. Recently, the small lanes were laid with bricks, making those paths much cleaner. Before, whenever it rained, the lanes were slushy with mud and unpleasant for walking.

The village bamboo hedge, in some cases reinforced by an earthen embankment and a moat, turned the traditional rural community into an islet in a sea of green rice fields. The hedge not only protected villagers against bandits and typhoons but also supplied materials to repair or build temples, bridges, markets, and other public works. A village usually had four gates (north, south, east, and west) but sometimes fewer. Guards closed these gates at nightfall. Banyan or ceiba (kapok) trees in front of the main gate cast refreshing shade for farmers returning from the fields or travelers drinking a cup of tea at a stall nestled among the trees. A few villages in Việt Nam's northern delta, the cradle of our nation, kept these traditional traits when facing Western influence and urbanization.

Topography determines four villages types in northern Việt Nam:

- villages behind a river dike, which also serves as a road, since the dike is higher than the flooded rice fields

- villages built on raised ground in swampy lowlands, where fields are often under water
- villages scattered on upland slopes, where the population is sparse and the land is not fertile
- coastal villages among sand dunes, which residents have turned into arable fields

Villages in the Mekong Delta of southern Việt Nam seem like descendants of northern villages in the Red River Delta but with their own character. The ethnic Vietnamese who settled southern Việt Nam were famished peasants, demobilized soldiers transferred to agricultural colonies, adventurers, and political refugees from China. They settled on alluvial land, building new villages along the delta's myriad rivulets.

Communities in southern Việt Nam developed along intertwining waterways, which replaced the village lanes common in the north. These villages did not have hedges and were not separated from each other. Compared with northern villages, they were young communities with a more heterogeneous population, including Chinese, Chăm, and Khmer minorities. The age-old Confucian strictures common in northern Việt Nam did not bind people in these newly formed communities. Fertile land and a mild climate spared these new southerners from the toil and suffering that had been their lot in the Red River Delta.

The Traditional Vietnamese House

The Vietnamese word "*nhà*" (house) has an emotional, sociological, and ideological resonance, which is greater and more profound than "house" in Western languages. Whereas individualism is imbedded in Western cultures, Vietnamese culture relies primarily on community spirit and particularly on family spirit. For generations, more than 90 percent of the Việt lived in rural areas, where they practiced wet-rice farming and rarely stepped outside the bamboo hedges encircling their villages. Their rice paddies held their ancestors' graves and the joys and sorrows of their own lives. Houses had a sacred, mystical character, since they sheltered the altar for the family's ancestors and secondary altars for the mother goddesses and the Genie of the Home and the Genie of the Sun. Thus, the building of any house entailed rites and sacrifices, since people and supernatural beings—the living and the dead—would share the same abode.

The traditional Vietnamese house evolved in northern Việt Nam's Red River Delta, the nation's cradle, beginning with the Bronze Age in the first century before Christ. In early times, the rural Việt built their mud, wattle-and-daub houses (*nhà tranh vách đất*) with walls made from a mixture of clay, rice husks, and straw. They made their roofs from thatch. The Việt modified the basic model as they extended their territory southward after a thousand years of Chinese domination. The variations reflect Việt acculturation with other ethnic groups, including the Chăm in the country's center and the Khmer and overseas Chinese in the south.

The typical Việt house has three rooms (*ba gian*) and two attached lean-tos (*hai chái*), with the foundation (*nền*) higher than the courtyard, which is used for drying rice and corn. The *gian* are not closed-off rooms but, instead, are compartments separated by bamboo or hardwood columns. The central room (*gian giữa*, the largest) contains the ancestral altar. The head of the family hosts visitors on a bed in front of the altar, and he also sometimes sleeps there. The two adjacent *gian* have beds for the male and female members of the family. There are two attached lean-tos (one to the left and one to the right). One is the sleeping area for the head of the family and his wife, and the other is a storage area for rice, clothes, and tools. In order to deter thieves, traditional houses have no doors on the side or back. In the old days, the floors of even rich houses were made from packed earth to symbolize the harmony between Heaven and Earth and the universal principles of *yin* (female) and *yang* (male). In later wooden houses, the roof was supported by large columns, heavy beams, and joists with mortise-and-tenon joints to hold the weighty roof tiles. Lattice walls, which were independent of the roof, obscured the interior and blocked the tropical sun. The effect was solid yet graceful.

Rural houses are usually one story and face south within an enclosed compound (*khuôn viên*) formed by a hedge of spiked bamboo, cactus, or some other trimmed shrub. The front gate usually faces the middle room of the house. The family may have flower beds alongside the courtyard and may also plant trees and vegetables behind the house, where they may have a well, pig sty, cow or buffalo shed, and latrine. Most rural house compounds also have dug ponds stocked with fish. Behind the house, families will often build a small temple dedicated to the Genie of the Earth, or they will have a pedestal in front of the house with an urn for burning incense to the genie. The kitchen is in a separate building.

Construction of a residence for both the living (*nhà ở*) and the deceased (*mồ mả*) becomes a semi-mystical task. The owner must prepare for the happy or unhappy future of his family members. The deceased ancestors must do the same for their descendants by fostering riches, honor, longevity, and many offspring. Although the building materials for a house are simple, construction requires complicated rites. Decisions about a favorable site (with configuration of terrain and orientation), the dimensions for the house, and the proper time (the specific day and hour) to begin construction require the magical competence of a geomancer (*thầy địa lý*), who performs certain rites. For example, when it's time to raise the ridgepole (*thượng lương*), the geomancer attaches to the pole some red fabric (representing the Genie of Fire) and a cycad leaf (*thiên tuế*, a fernlike tropical evergreen representing ten thousand years and, therefore, permanence). During the 1800s and 1900s, the traditional lattice walls began to disappear in favor of brick. A geomancer tending to a brick house will define two walls to establish the spread of the beams.

The homeowner offers a feast for all these ceremonial occasions.

Vietnamese usually orient their houses toward the south, since the south is the principle (*yang*, male) direction and provides access to fresh ocean breezes. A popular saying recommends:

When marrying, you take a woman;
When building a house, you face it to the south.

Using his compass, the geomancer determines the house site and orientation. However, it is the astrologer (*thầy phù thủy*) who protects a new house from possible adversity. He creates a paper model of the future house, on which he places five reeds representing five destructive devils (*ngũ quỷ*). He burns the model and mannequin reeds during the ceremonial rites.

In Vietnamese, "*nhà*" (house) takes on many meanings, including religious identification (*nhà chung* = a Catholic priest; *nhà chùa* = a Buddhist monk or nun); a political era (*nhà Lý* = the Lý Dynasty); professions (*nhà báo* = a journalist); and political definitions (*nhà nước* = government). "*Nhà*" also designates esteemed professions, including writers (*nhà văn*), poets (*nhà thơ*), and mandarins (*nhà quan*). "*Nhà*" can imply a level of intimacy not found in the Western word "house." For example, "*nhà*" can be the pronoun "you" when speaking to one's spouse or with someone for whom the intimate French pronoun "*tu*" might be used. Further, "*cả nhà*" (literally, "the entire house" and therefore "the entire household") can mean "family."

Poet Nguyễn Du (1766–1820) used "*nhà*" more than a hundred times in Việt Nam's national epic, *The Tale of Kiều* (Truyện Kiều), which he wrote in 3,254 lines of six-word, eight-word meter. A profusion of Vietnamese sayings and proverbs relies on "*nhà*" to crystalize Vietnamese culture in a few words. Among the most famous sayings are:

- "Life's two main tasks: build a home for the living and a home for the dead."

- "Men build the houses, women guard the doorways."

- "Children without a father are like a house without a roof."

- "Householders near the market leave debts to their children."

- "While guests eat for three, household members splurge and feast for seven."

- "For advice about a trip, ask the elders; for the truth within the home, ask the children."

- "Once you leave home, you are lost."
- "For a wanderer at night, any place is his home, and any place he lies down is his bed."
- "A master leaves his home, his chickens freely roam."
- "Only when a house burns, do the rats appear" warns that only amidst trying circumstances does a person's real personality show.
- "Corrupt households are corrupt from the roof down" uses "*nhà*" to refer to a family, society, a business, or a government.
- "When the house lights go out, rich and poor are alike" warns of the equalizing effect of life's challenges.

The Communal House

Lines from an oral folk poem describe a traditional Vietnamese village's communal house. Here, "*nón*" is the emblematic Vietnamese conical hat.

> Crossing the bridge, tilting her *nón*,
> The bridge, many spans: How she misses him.
> Passing the communal house, tilting her *nón*,
> Its roof, many tiles: How she loves him.

Nearly half a century ago, Chu Hồng Quý, a ten-year-old boy hunkering in a bomb shelter, composed the following lines in six-word, eight-word meter to begin his poem, "The Ceiba Trees at Our Communal House" (Cây Gạo Đình Chung). The ceiba (kapok), sometimes called a "cotton tree," has a straight trunk and red flowers.

> My village has a communal house,
> Its well water dances with the moon's glow;

Nearby, ceiba trees watch the sky,
A winding, sandy road runs past the gate.

Ceiba flowers cover everything in March,
Half the flowers for fish, half for birds;
The communal house seems sleepy-eyed,
Its roof curving upward, looking at the sky.

A noted painter, Phạm Tăng (1924–), also writes poems. He speaks wistfully with six-word, eight-word lines in "Song for My Ancestral Home" (Bài Ca Quê Hương), which is the opening poem in his collection *Phạm Tăng: Poems* (Phạm Tăng: Thơ, 1994):

Gone: the village banyan's roots, the river's flow.
Is our well's water still clear?
Do lotus blooms cover the communal-house pond?

These quotations show the vivid presence of the *đình* (communal house) for ordinary Vietnamese as a temple, a town hall, a house of culture, and the focus of village life. The *đình* dominates a traditional community's spiritual life, together with the Buddhist pagoda (*chùa*), Confucian shrine (*văn chỉ*), and the many small shrines (*đền*) dedicated to spirits in Vietnamese animistic worship, which has been tinged with Taoism. English speakers sometimes use "temple" when referring to a Buddhist place of worship. However, in Việt Nam, to avoid confusion with the temples for the worship of ancestors and tutelary spirits, we use "pagoda" when referring to a building for the worship of Buddha.

Villagers meet at their communal house to worship their village tutelary god, *thần thành hoàng*, literally, "god" (*thần*) of the "rampart" (*thành*) and the "moat" (*hoàng*) surrounding the citadel. This god could be a historical personage (such as a national or local hero), the benefactor who taught the villagers a trade or helped them claim virgin land, a mythical figure (such as a celestial being like the God of Mount Tản Viên), a deified animal, or an unidentified person (in some instances even a thief or a beggar, who died a cruel death at a sacred hour). Residents conduct their major rituals honoring the tutelary spirit in spring (at Tết, the Lunar New Year), autumn, and on the anniversaries of the god's birth and death. These solemn ceremonies and joyous festivities may last several days. Village leaders organize games and entertainment on the *đình* grounds, including *tuồng* and *chèo* operas, traditional wrestling matches, buffalo and cock fights, and human chess games with young men and women, who are moved about as the players' chess pieces.

In contrast to the Buddhist pagoda, which is a closed building in a secluded place for funeral rites and for events affecting future life, the communal house is an open structure conveniently situated for social activities and meetings. There, adult male villagers meet to address administrative matters (distribution of taxes and communal lands, recruitment of soldiers, allotment of labor) and to settle minor judicial proceedings (conflicts between neighbors and punishment for transgressors of village customs). In former times, the communal house guarded the Confucian order, which determined village social structure during the Lê Dynasty (1428–1788). The *đình* probably first appeared in the 1500s and peaked in the 1600s and 1700s but declined during the 1800s because of feudal disintegration and French intervention.

The traditional communal house began in northern Việt Nam and spread southward with Vietnamese territorial expansion. However, some scholars suggest ethnic-minority longhouses in the Central Highlands may have been the model for Vietnamese communal houses, while other scholars cite boat-like images engraved on the Đông Sơn bronze drums from the first millennium BCE. In any case, Vietnamese communal houses constitute a priceless cultural patrimony with traditional architecture and collections of ancient wooden sculptures. The most famous examples of communal houses are: Tây Đằng (late 1400s, early 1500s, Hà Tây Province, now part of Hà Nội); Lỗ Hạnh (1576, Bắc Giang Province); Thổ Hà (1500s to 1600s, Bắc Giang Province); and Đình Bảng (1736, Bắc Ninh Province).

The Head and the Heart of the
Traditional Village

To understand the soul of the traditional village, you must visit the countryside. There, lies the village, the social cell and the administrative, economic, and spiritual unit that is the repository of Việt Nam's oldest cultural values. Each village has a communal house (*đình*) dedicated to its tutelary god; temples (*đền, miếu, phủ*) for the worship of spirits or saints (deified heroes and tutelary gods); one or two pagodas (*chùa*) to worship Buddha; and sometimes a temple (*văn miếu*) or a shrine (*văn chỉ*) for the worship of Confucius.

Despite a very strong religious syncretism, one can classify these buildings into two groups according to the endogenous (internally caused) or exogenous (externally caused) origin of the worshiped divinities. The first group—the *đền, miếu,* and *phủ*—are used to worship spirits and ghosts of autochthonous (indigenous) origin, that is, the veritable Vietnamese religion according to French researcher Léopold Cadière (1869–1955). Some popular animist beliefs of the Việt from the Red River Delta date to the beginning of recorded history. These include worship of natural forces (thunder, lightning, rain, rocks, plants, and animals), ancestors, the mother goddesses (*mẫu*), and heroes. The second group of religious buildings serves beliefs imported from India and China. Buddhism and Confucianism were grafted onto autochthonous stock (the worship of spirits), which was already firmly rooted and which remains alive today.

In the traditional village, the four elements—the autochthonous animist stock, Buddhism, Taoism, and Confucianism—harmonize and amalgamate. In particular, Buddhism and Confucianism complement each other in meeting two needs. Confucianism responds to the social element and reason, while Buddhism addresses the individual and sentiments. In brief, Confucianism and Buddhism represent the head and the heart.

Confucianism as the "head" reflects Chinese influence. Strictly speaking, Confucianism is not a religion but, rather, a philosophy of social ethics. Confucianism summarizes the precepts for all social relations to achieve universal harmony (*hòa*) by virtue of humanity (*nhân*) governed through rites. In a strongly hierarchical and patriarchal Confucian society, everyone—from kings and mandarins to scholars, peasants, artisans, and workers, to men and women, husbands and wives, parents and children—must accept his or her specific role in society and accomplish his or her duty. How does Confucianism manifest itself at the village level and on the cultural plane?

The Confucian rites at local temples (*văn từ, văn chỉ*) recall the pre-eminence of the Doctrine of the Master (Confucius, 551–479 BCE) and his followers. The *đình* (which serves as the office for the temple, mayoralty, and local tribunal) represents the rational Confucian order in all its strictness, including ritual ceremonies to the tutelary god accredited by royal decrees, a rigid order of precedence, distribution of land taxes and labor duties, and the enforcement of customary laws, which are sometimes very severe, for instance, against unmarried mothers.

In the village, Buddhism as the "heart" addresses feelings and provides solace amidst Confucianism's rigorous norms. The pagoda is a peaceful haven, which calms suffering and assuages sorrow and social injustices. Villagers often evoke Buddha Amitabha (A Di Đà), who is ready to help all who are suffering, and they also call upon Bodhisattva Avalokitesvara (Quan Âm), who, as Amitabha's auxiliary, can implement the most disinherited person's terrestrial wishes. The word "*Bụt*" for Buddha is synonymous with "pity" or "compassion." However, the Buddhist concepts of existence and non-existence remain the domain of educated Buddhist scholars, particularly in the Zen (Thiền) school. For ordinary villagers, karma and metempsychosis (transmigration at death) are reduced to simple beliefs: One must do good deeds to be reborn in human form in the Afterlife and to attain Nirvana, which is conceived as a paradise endowed with terrestrial pleasures. Wicked people are led to Hell by devils, who submit them to atrocious torture.

Buddhism and Confucianism—heart and head—have influenced the Vietnamese psyche for centuries, creating a necessary equilibrium.

The Four Facets of
Vietnamese Culture

The Four Facets of Vietnamese Culture

To understand Việt Nam, you must first understand the country's name. Since the Vietnamese language is monosyllabic, Vietnamese write and pronounce "Việt Nam" as two words, even though foreigners sometimes write our country's name as well as "Hà Nội," "Sài Gòn," and other names as one word. "*Việt*" refers to the Việt (or Kinh), the largest of our fifty-four ethnic groups with 85 percent of the population. Thus, Việt Nam is the land of the Việt, just as, etymologically speaking, France is the country of the Francs and England is the land of the Angles. Since "*Nam*" means "South," "*Việt Nam*" means "the country of the Việt of the South."

Yet if we modern-day Vietnamese are descendants of the Việt of the South, where are the Việt of the North?

They became Chinese.

And so, I define modern-day Vietnamese as members of the Việt ethnic community who did not want to become Chinese, who do not want to become Chinese, and who will never want to become Chinese, even though Chinese culture has imbued Vietnamese culture. Ill-informed foreigners sometimes regard Vietnamese culture as an appendage to Chinese culture, with a tinge of Hindu culture. Chinese and Vietnamese cultures were and are two different cultures. China has Chinese culture, while Việt Nam has Vietnamese culture.

The cradle of Chinese culture is the Hoang Ho (Yellow River) Basin, which is north of the Yangtze (Blue) River. In contrast, modern-day southern China south of the Yangtze belonged to former Southeast Asia. Việt Nam is still farther south. Việt Nam's first identity emerged three thousand years ago (around 1000 BCE) not in China but in the Red River Delta, or present-day northern Việt Nam, as a typical wet-rice-growing Southeast Asian culture. Many attributes from that ancient Southeast Asian civilization remain in

29

present-day Vietnamese culture, for example, rice-growing traditions, myths, popular beliefs, language usage, and the Vietnamese lifestyle.

We can represent the two cultures—Vietnamese and Chinese—with two archeological artifacts. A bronze drum typifies Việt Nam, whereas a bronze incense burner typifies ancient China north of the Yangtze.

The Việt grew wet rice, which requires a long rainy season. Whenever the Việt lacked rain, it is said that they beat their bronze drums to summon the dragon—a positive presence in Eastern cultures—to bring rain. The Việt bronze drums with their finely wrought engravings date back three thousand years, when the engravers faced wild beasts, inclement weather, and hunger. Archeologists have found similar bronze drums in all Southeast Asian wet-rice-growing countries—Cambodia, Indonesia, Laos, Malaysia, Myanmar, the Philippines, Thailand, and Việt Nam. In contrast, the Chinese north of the Yangtze lacked the hot, wet, tropical climate needed to grow wet rice. Instead, they grew dryland crops, which require less water.

Over the centuries, the Vietnamese people have preserved the substratum of their own Southeast Asian culture while enriching it with the foreign contributions—mainly Chinese (Vietnamese Middle Ages) and French (modern times)—that Vietnamese have grafted onto their own culture.

Việt Nam's geographical position and configuration determined its vocation and destiny. Situated in the heart of Southeast Asia, Việt Nam is also part of East Asia. The Pacific Ocean brought the first Western contacts. Those three geographical factors—Southeast Asia, East Asia, and the Pacific—engendered the four cultural facets making up traditional Vietnamese culture and Việt Nam's unique identity. Throughout centuries, Vietnamese have preserved their Southeast Asian substratum—the first facet—as the essential characteristic of Vietnamese culture and then added enriching foreign elements.

The second facet of Vietnamese culture is its East Asian side. Beginning before the Common Era, Chinese empires dominated

Việt Nam for more than a thousand years. The Vietnamese waged persistent struggles to preserve their identity and avoid Siniciza- tion. In 938 CE, the Việt won national independence, which they maintained for nine hundred years, until the 1800s. During the two thousand years before French colonization, Chinese influence translated into a double movement of repulsion from and attrac- tion toward Chinese culture, which was richer and more varied than the Việts' Southeast Asian culture. Together with Japan and Korea, Việt Nam integrated into the cultural system of eastern Asia under strong Chinese influence. This included direct influ- ence (e.g., ideographs, Chinese Buddhism), but we should not forget other indirect Asian influences (e.g., Indian Buddhism and Hinduism).

The third facet of Vietnamese culture is Western influence, which first arrived by way of the Pacific Ocean and the East Sea (sometimes called the South China Sea) in the 1600s and 1700s through trade and religious evangelization. Colonization followed in the 1880s. The dynamic of acculturation to foreign rule trans- lated into repulsion from and attraction toward the French rul- ers' culture. The contributions of Western culture changed the old Vietnamese culture with regard to science, technology, the arts, religion, and even everyday life, such as the consumption of bread, coffee, cabbage, and carrots. Thus, at the historic moment of the 1945 Revolution, Việt Nam's traditional culture consisted of three facets: Southeast Asian, East Asian, and Western.

The fourth facet of Vietnamese culture—internationalization and integration into the world community—began with the Au- gust 1945 Revolution and the re-conquest of national indepen- dence. Since then, the country has survived great upheavals, which have been both national (social revolution, thirty years of war, and policy renovation) and international (regional and global integra- tion). The turning point in Việt Nam's recent history was adoption of world integration a decade after the end of the war in 1975 in the framework of globalization. This change was inspired by *Đổi Mới* (Renovation or Renewal, late 1986), which had two main points: adoption of the market economy (thence creation of a private sector and promotion of competition) and an open-door policy (when possible, relationships with all countries irrespective of ideology). Over the last decades, *Đổi Mới* has testified to its effectiveness in Việt Nam's economic development but has demonstrated its weakness in cultural development. Accelerated economic development has enhanced Western cultural influence, including increased individualism, which may erode our Vietnamese cultural identity based on community spirit. Thus, there arises a conflict between economic and cultural development. To solve this dilemma, we have adopted the following national motto: A country with a prosperous people strong enough to defend ourselves and with a democratic and humanistic culture.

Back to the Source in Southeast Asia

In 1973, the Việt Nam Social Sciences Committee established the Southeast Asian Institute. One cannot overstate this institute's growing and multi-faceted importance, since the Asia-Pacific Region will surely play a prominent role during the twenty-first century. However, for us Vietnamese—and no doubt for all peoples in Southeast Asia—the interest in the region goes far beyond politico-economic questions of the day to include rediscovering our cultural identity, which has been obscured by several historical factors, particularly the glowing aura of Chinese and Indian cultures and the impact of Western colonization.

The word "Indochina" (referring to Việt Nam, Laos, and Cambodia) was probably coined in the late 1800s to designate the peninsular part of Southeast Asia (itself comprised of Brunei, Cambodia, Indonesia, Laos, Malaysia, Myanmar, Philippines, Singapore, Thailand, and Việt Nam). "Indochina" highlights acculturation from the two major Asian cultural centers (India and China). However, it obscures the fact that Southeast Asia peoples had built their own specific cultures on common ground well before they came under Indian and Chinese influence.

Over time, many independent states, which had been Indianized or Sinicized, came into being, breaking the region's geographical and socio-cultural unity. Through the vicissitudes of history, some of these states forgot the brilliant epochs of their past, for example, the Angkor civilization. Under the colonial regimes, which lasted from the second half of the 1800s to the end of World War II in 1945, French, Dutch, and British scholars—prominent Indianists and Sinologists often with an Eurocentric prism tinged with Indianism or Sino-centrism—devoted more time and effort to the study of Indian and Chinese influence in Southeast Asian countries than to the exploration of the substratum of indigenous cultures. Japanese historian Yoshiharu Tsuboi's *The Vietnamese Empire Facing France and China: 1847–1885* (L'Empire Vietnamien: Face à la France et à la Chine, 1847–1885, Paris, 1987) rightly chose Việt Nam itself as the study's starting point and avoided a base on views oriented toward France and China.

After World War II, the idea of Southeast Asia as a geo-cultural-political entity took shape following formation of the great powers' spheres of influence, the process of decolonization, and the awareness of newly independent states with a common past yet each in search of national identity. The lifting of ideological barriers between the countries of ASEAN (Association of South-east Asian Nations, which grew out of the Southeast Asian Treaty Organization—SEATO) and the countries of what once was French Indochina has created an irresistible rapprochement and unification among Southeast Asians. Việt Nam has followed the same impulse on the cultural plane. Having faced two major foreign influences—the Chinese in our Middle Ages and Western (mostly French) in modern times—Việt Nam is returning to sources in Southeast Asia as its primary identity.

In Việt Nam, Rice is the Source of Life

It was proper that the United Nations declared 2004 the International Year of Rice, for rice is a staple for more than half the world's population and the principle source of income for more than one billion people, most of whom are farmers. During 2004, the Food and Agriculture Organization (FAO) hoped to encourage greater access to rice, increased production, a reduction in hunger and poverty, and greater environmental protection in rice-producing countries. Việt Nam took great interest in the promotional year because 80 percent of our population lives in rural areas and essentially survives on rice farming. Then, too, many of us still remember the double yoke of Japanese and French occupation at the end of World War II, when famine took two million lives. The Đổi Mới (Renovation or Renewal) policy, which began in late 1986, ended our perennial food shortage. In recent years, Việt Nam has consistently ranked as the world's second largest exporter of rice.

Rice was a weed until man began to cultivate it six thousand years ago. As of 2012, 85 percent of rice was grown in Asia and fed 40 percent of the world's population. In Việt Nam, rice dates to the Mesolithic Culture of Hòa Bình and Bắc Sơn Provinces. By the dawn of the Vietnamese identity in the Red River Valley in the first millennium of the Bronze Age, rice-growing had become culturally ingrained in Việt Nam as well as in neighboring Southeast Asian countries.

Rice is the source of life in Việt Nam. It's fitting that the English word "rice" has many different words in Vietnamese. To name a few, "lúa" is the rice plant; "thóc" is raw, unhusked rice; "gạo" is raw, polished rice; and "cơm" is ordinary, steamed rice. In the old days, a woman unable to breast feed would feed her child rice porridge ("cháo"), and when the child was old enough, the mother would chew "cơm" to feed the baby. When a person dies, he or she is said to have taken "xôi" (glutinous or "sticky" rice), probably because sticky rice is usually among the votive offerings for the deceased.

Việt Nam practices dry-rice agriculture in mountainous areas and wet-rice agriculture in irrigated fields on the plains. Following the August 1945 Revolution, farmers assisted each other through mutual-aid groups. When the War of Resistance Against France ended in 1954, the Land Reform Campaign returned land to the tillers in liberated North Việt Nam. The country benefited from the 1960s Green Revolution, which brought greater productivity through high-yield seeds, mineral fertilizers, pest control, improvement in irrigation, and various short-stemmed varieties developed by the International Rice Research Institute (IRRI) in the Philippines. These varieties concentrated the energy generated from photosynthesis onto the rice plant's ear instead of in its stem.

In the 1960s, household rice plots were regrouped into village co-operatives. During the War of Resistance Against the United States, these agricultural co-operatives filled the void left by the young men who had become soldiers by providing rice, food, and other labor to the soldiers' families and other villagers. All villagers shared the work collectively, with women taking a great role in food production. After the war, unfortunately, many co-operatives became ineffective because of bureaucratic mismanagement and ineffective distribution of produce. Gradually, the co-operative became moribund; in the early 1980s, many farmers refused to harvest co-operative fields.

The new policy of *Đổi Mới* instituted in late 1986 curbed a prolonged economic crisis and revived agriculture by giving farmers control of the full scope of rice production. The success was spectacular. Previously, everyone had been hungry. Then, in 1989, Việt Nam *exported* two million tons of rice and quickly reached third place as the largest world rice exporter, after Thailand and the United States and then moved to second place after Thailand.

Myths Die Hard in Việt Nam

Emerging from a subway in New York's Time Square, American author Joseph Campbell was immersed in the crowd waiting at a crosswalk and thought he saw more than one ancient myth coming to life right before his eyes. According to this eminent mythologist, in our presumably de-mythicized world, myths are still essential to understanding history as well as a society's modern aspirations:

"It [mythology] is where all the inventions of the common people's imagination meet up with archeology and history."

Let us begin with the Vietnamese myth of origin from the period of the Hùng Kings before 2000 BCE, during the Bronze Age: The Vietnamese people were born from the union of a dragon and a fairy. Throughout the course of history, many Confucians and more than one modern patriot (for example, Hồ Chí Minh in writing our Declaration of Independence) have invoked this mythic origin to mobilize the masses in national struggle against Chinese feudalism and French colonization.

Triệu Quang Phục (a.k.a. Triệu Việt Vương, life: ?–571 CE; reign: 548–571), hero of resistance to Chinese domination, is one. He established his guerrilla base in the swamps of the Lake of One Night (Đầm Nhất Dạ Trạch), which is associated with Chử Đồng Tử, a mythic god from the time of the Hùng kings. Chử Đồng Tử descended from Heaven on a dragon to give Triệu Quang Phục, the country's new savior, the fabled animal claw that assured invincibility and legitimacy. Such, at least, was the claim of Triệu Quang Phục, who knew the myth's power.

Other myths have survived for millennia, entering popular practices. For example, the betel quid expresses love and consecrates marriage; Tết cakes (*bánh giầy* and *bánh chưng*) represent the round sky and the square earth; ceremonies honor the Mountain Spirit, whose struggle against the Water Spirit protects the Vietnamese against the Red River's floods; Boy Genie Gióng, who conquered the Ân invaders from the North (China) and flew away on his iron horse into the sky, symbolizes the Việts' patriotism.

Hà Nội's founding intertwines with Việt Nam's history, illustrating the ties between myths, archeology, and history. We have many examples, including the Dragon King as forefather of the Vietnamese people, the Mountain Spirit as conqueror of the annual Red River floods, the child (Gióng) with Herculean strength beating back the An hordes from the North (China), the Soaring Dragon in all its glory presiding over the birth of the capital, and the Dark Guardian of the North. All these myths of great national significance remain alive in our capital's streets, resurfacing in the city's landscape and in our everyday activities.

Hà Nội has artifacts dating from the Neolithic Period and the Bronze Age, including the period when the first two Việt states, together with the core Việt cultural identity, were born (c. 1000 BCE). After over a thousand years of Chinese domination (c. 200 BCE – 938 CE), the Việts defeated the Chinese and regained their independence. In the beginning of the eleventh century, the Việts established their capital at Thăng Long (City of the Soaring Dragon), which has since become Hà Nội.

The deepest aspirations and dilemmas of the Vietnamese people can be understood through our culture's myths. Joseph Campbell, is correct to say, "Myths allow the spiritual potential of human life to be realized."

The Lord of the Sacred Drum Finally Regains His Artefact

Vietnamese are proud of the famous Đông Sơn bronze drums that are vestiges of the culture of the same name, which defined the Việt from the millennium preceding the Christian era. I can never stop wondering how—3,000 years ago—our ancestors could craft such marvels, such objects with sensuous shapes and decorated with precise geometric lines and perfect human and animal figures reflecting a clear cosmology.

My admiration prompted me one fine spring day to make a pilgrimage to Đan Nê Hamlet in Yên Thọ Commune (Yên Định District, Thanh Hóa Province), which is two hundred kilometers south of Hà Nội. Đan Nê has a temple dedicated to the spirit, Đồng Cổ, ("*đồng*" = "bronze," and "*cổ*" = "drum"). Legend has it that King Hùng, founder of the Việt nation, was on Mount Đan Nê during a military campaign and dreamed about a spirit, who promised him miraculous assistance. During the following day's battle, thunderous rhythms resounded all around, filling the king's army with irresistible strength. After the victory, the grateful king awarded his mysterious supporter the title, "Đồng Cổ Đại Vương"—"Great Lord of the Bronze Drum," and made him guardian spirit of that locality.

Another Đồng Cổ Temple is in Bưởi, a community on the southwestern side of Hà Nội's West Lake. According to legend, Prince Phật Mã from the eleventh-century Lý Dynasty prayed for assistance while billeting his troops at Bưởi during their southern advance to drive back a Chăm Pa invasion. The local spirit brought Prince Phật Mã victory and helped him foil a court plot. After his coronation as King Lý Thái Tông (life: 1000–1054; reign: 1028–1054), Phật Mã built a temple outside the royal citadel to honor his benefactor and ordered court officials to make annual pilgrimages to the temple and pledge loyalty to him as their monarch.

Village elders in Đan Nê confirm the existence in their village of an ancient bronze drum and say that the drum could have been donated by a cousin of Emperor Quang Trung (life: 1753–1792; reign: 1788–1792). French Governor-General Pierre Pasquier (governor-general: October 4, 1926 – May 16, 1927 and December 26, 1928 – January 15, 1934) visited the temple and contributed twenty-five piasters for its maintenance. The event was engraved in French on a marker. Unfortunately, the valuable drum disappeared around 1932. One person has reported seeing in a Paris museum a bronze drum with a placard citing Đan Nê as its origin.

To replace their irreparable loss, the villagers made do with a huge wood-and-buffalo-hide drum. Sensing their frustration, the Vietnam-Sweden Cultural Fund made a generous donation for a replica of an authentic Đông Sơn drum displayed at Việt Nam's History Museum. Nguyễn Trọng Hạnh, a gifted artisan from a long line of bronze casters, crafted the substitution.

Perhaps Đồng Cổ, the Great Lord of the Bronze Drum, is pleased to have a replica of his drum return to his home village.

The Worship of Mother Goddesses

Việt Nam's truly indigenous religious foundation is the worship of spirits, including mother goddesses (*thờ mẫu*). This belief based on animist religious practices dates back to prehistoric times.

Mother goddesses deserve our attention as an example of religious syncretism involving the popular Vietnamese religious credo that survives despite numerous borrowings from other faiths. Among the religious borrowings, we can include the Buddhists' merciful Bodhisattva Avalokitesvara (Quan Âm) as supreme sovereign as well as Taoist saints and spirits, particularly the Jade Emperor of the Sky (Ngọc Hoàng). We can also point to loans from Confucianism, with its teachings about good and evil and some of its sacrificial rites.

The worship of mother goddesses falls within traditional worship of female spirits in Việt Nam. Women have always dominated *thánh mẫu,* the original belief devoted to the mother goddesses. However, a later branch sanctified General Trần Hưng Đạo (1228–1300), the heroic victor over the Mongols.

Generally speaking, three factors contributed to the worship of mother goddesses: animism, respect for women, and rice cultivation. Later, Taoism, Buddhism, and Confucianism (which despised women) influenced the worship of mother goddesses. However, Vietnamese society is, at its base, a matriarchal system honoring women. The innate Vietnamese worship of mother goddesses is traditionally more important than imported beliefs because women's work sowing, transplanting, and harvesting rice played a key role in Việt Nam's wet-rice civilization. For this reason, ancient Vietnamese deified land, water, and sky—important factors in wet-rice cultivation—by referring to them as Mother Earth, Mother Water, and Mother Sky. Animist believers also raised women to goddesses because of women's role in procreation.

Over the millennia, sporadic and local forms of worship became generalized and revealed a common denominator. A national belief was born—the worship of mother goddesses—which is also known as the worship of the Three Palaces (Tam Phủ) or the worship of the Four Palaces (Tứ Phủ). Divinities—all benevolent—among the mother goddesses in hierarchal order include:

- Mother Goddesses of the Three or Four Palaces (Tam Tòa Thánh Mẫu-Tam Phủ or Tứ Phủ)

- Mother Goddess of the Sky (Mẫu Thượng Thiên), whose sacred color is red. Her avatar, Liễu Hạnh, who is of human origin, is very popular.

- Mother Goddess of the Mountains and Forests, of the Dead and the Faithful (Mẫu Thượng Ngàn), whose sacred color is green

- Mother Goddess of Water (Mẫu Thoải), whose sacred color is white

- Mother Goddess of Earth (Mẫu Địa), whose sacred color is also white

- Five Royal Mandarins (Ngũ Vị Vương Quan), sons of the Spirit Dragon of the Eight Seas (Bát Hải Đại Vương). Their number may reach ten.

- Four Lady Saints (Châu Bà or Thánh Bà), avatars of the Four Mother Goddesses. Their number may reach twelve.

- Ten Princes (Thập Ông Hoàng), sons of the Spirit of the Dragon of the Eight Seas (Bát Hải Đại Vương). They live in the Water Palace.

- Twelve Royal Maids (Thập Nhị Vương Cô), servants of the mother goddesses and the ladies

- Twelve Page Boys (Thập Nhị Cậu), avatars of children who died before age nine, retainers of the Princes

- Five Tiger Mandarins (Quan Ngũ Hổ)

- Sir Lốt, the Snake Spirit (Ông Lốt)

The worship of mother goddesses includes male divinities with their sacred color, indigo. They are integrated into the worship of the Three or Four Palaces under the Palace of the Trần Dynasty (Phủ Trần Triều). This belief is devoted to General Trần Hưng Đạo, his son (Trần Quốc Tảng, 1252–1313), his two daughters, and his first lieutenant (Phạm Ngũ Lão, 1255–1320).

Divinities and spirits of secondary or marginal importance in the pantheon, which are rarely incarnated, include:

- Buddhist divinities, particularly the Bodhisattva Avalo-kitesvara (Quan Âm) and the Buddha Amitabha (A Di Đà)

- Taoist divinities, such as the Jade Emperor of the Sky (Ngọc Hoàng), who governs the Realm of the Immortal

- many spirits, which cannot be classified, for instance, Guan Yu (Kuan Yu, Quan Vũ, or Quan Công, 162–219, a great Chinese warrior during the Three Kingdoms) as well as the souls of the ancestors

An essential characteristic of these beliefs is the divinities' mediums.

One might ask: How does someone become a medium? Each mortal is presumed to have an individual destiny governed by one or several spirits from the Three or Four Palaces. People with a heavy destiny (*căn số nặng*) are often sick and prone to misfortune because they are persecuted (*hành*) by an invisible master, who wants to use these individuals as servant soldiers (*lính hầu*). Those wishing to submit to this recruitment must undergo an initiation ceremony, *tôn nhang*, in which they carry on their heads a tray with a vase of joss sticks. If the spirit does not immediately agree to a recruit's petitions, the applicant must hold a ceremony for entry into service of the concerned spirit or spirits (*lễ trình đồng*). This very costly ceremony lasts from two to three days. The recruit must present himself or herself to the spirits (*trình đồng*) and be accepted by them as a medium (*đồng*) through the shadow rite (*hầu bóng*), during which the spirits become incarnated in a professional medium.

The shadow rite is the key ceremony in the worship of mother goddesses. A female medium (*bà đồng*) seats herself in front of the altar, her head and upper body draped in a large red veil, which sets her apart from the World of Mortals. During a session, which usually lasts from two to seven hours, the divinities descend (*giáng đồng*) on the soul of the medium to incarnate themselves. Not all divinities descend, and each medium has his or her preferred divinities. For each successive incarnation (*giá đồng*), the medium possessed by the divinity must wear the proper costume, use the correct attributes (color, objects), and behave according to the particular divinity's temperament (sweet or violent, young or old).

As the rite unfolds, the medium's head begins to nod more and more quickly, which sets her upper body in motion. She enters a trance, dancing and speaking while the incarnation takes place. As a spirit, she distributes favors to the faithful in fulfilment of their wishes. A liturgical singer (*cung văn*) plays a very important role as animator for each session. A novice who has completed the shadow rite may become a professional medium.

Ancestor Worship

Yesterday was the death anniversary of my mother, who died several decades ago. I placed on our ancestral altar a tray of flowers, a cup of plain water, and a few dishes of food. Then, with my hands clasped in prayer, I bowed three times to her photograph. All the while, my four-year-old grandson looked on, intrigued.

"Is your mother home with us today, Grandpa?" he asked.

"Yes," I answered.

In general, my generation, which experienced the Revolution and the two wars of resistance (1945–1975), does not believe in the Other World. Still, we are attached to old memories. For this reason, despite limited living conditions, each family will reserve the best place in the house for the family's ancestral altar. This altar may be only a shelf fixed to the wall at a sufficiently high level to be apparent but not obstructive. On it are photographs of the deceased, a joss-stick holder, two candlesticks, and, sometimes, an incense-burner. Wealthier families can afford a room especially for the altar, while rural people worship the deceased in the central section of their house.

Many Vietnamese believe that the departed are not separated from the living, that their souls hover about the ancestral altar, and that their spirits will return to stay with the living on festive occasions, especially at Tết (the Lunar New Year) and on death anniversaries. Traditionally, Vietnamese honor only death anniversaries, not birthdays, the latter being a recent Western importation and a luxury for the rich. The deceased are believed to share the joys and pains of the living. Thus, the living make offerings to the departed whenever memorable family events occur, for example, the birth of a child, a child's first day at school, a successful exam, construction of a new house, engagements, weddings, deaths, voyages, and even bankruptcies. The living invoke the deceased to help, and they offer to the departed votive paper objects, including paper hats, suits of paper clothes, cardboard beds, and even paper maché horses, motorcycles, and cars.

Since *Đổi Mới* (Renovation or Renewal, which began in late 1986), we have witnessed a return to spirituality, particularly the revival of ancestor worship. This practice, which is rooted in the Vietnamese collective subconscious, was abandoned to oblivion during the wars' hardships and a vague notion of atheist materialism. More stable living conditions and relative well-being brought about by current economic renovation and, coupled with the desire to heal the bitter seasons' wounds, have encouraged our people's return to traditional ancestral spirituality. Vietnamese have restored their family altars. They visit and tend family graves and expand their gatherings for ancestral worship. Family members come together, particularly on death anniversaries, to join in ritual worship and to share a meal.

Could ancestor worship be an anchor preserving national identity at the family level during modern-day family disintegration and a decline in traditional moral values?

The Study Center on Child Psychology founded by Nguyễn Khắc Viện says, "Yes." The Center undertook a research project on ancestor worship in an urban environment. The survey involved thirty-five Hà Nội families, who answered questions, including the following: Will ancestor worship disappear with urbanization and industrialization? Is ancestor worship causally linked to the extended family? Can ancestor worship play a stabilizing role? Does ancestor worship influence child psychology?

Ancestor worship is not actually a religion but a body of animistic beliefs accepted by almost the entire society, including followers of every religion (in many instances, even by Catholics and other Christians). Through rites, each individual is tied not only to the family's living members but also to the ancestors. Members of the same lineage can still be found in fairly large numbers in major urban areas. The ties linking them are symbolic, contributing to the education and emotional health of children and adults. A child acquainted with the rites of ancestor worship receives distinct socio-cultural values. A woman widowed late in life might feel less lonely if, during the first hundred days after her husband's burial, she places a tray of food on the family altar at lunch time and dinner time and then lights a few joss sticks. The presence of the ancestral altar in each Vietnamese house and the periodic acts of worship support the spirits of the deceased to remain present in the lives of the living and to encourage the living to preserve and honor the family.

Village Alliances

In traditional Việt Nam, the village was like an islet encircled by a bamboo hedge and seeming to float amidst rice paddies. Indeed, the village was an autonomous administrative, economic, and cultural unit. An old saying held, "Royal decrees yield to village customs." Each village has its own tutelary spirit, communal rules, and customs. However, this isolation was tempered by a quite widespread practice, *giao hiếu* or *giao hảo,* an agreement between two or more neighboring villages and sometimes between several distant villages. These allied villages never brought legal proceedings against each other; rather, they provided mutual aid during floods, typhoons, fires, and epidemics, and they fought in coordination against pirates. The people of one village often sent a delegation and gifts to the festivals of an allied village. Every five or ten years, they would organize a joint festival.

Văn Xá and Văn Lâm Villages are twenty kilometers apart in two different districts of former Hà Nam Ninh Province in the Red

River Delta. Despite this distance, spiritual links unite the two, for their tutelary spirits are said to be husband and wife. Legend has it that during the Lý Dynasty (1009–1225), a fisherman named Cao Văn Phúc lived in Văn Xá Village. A woman, Từ Thị Lang, lived in Văn Lâm Village, where she caught field crabs and snails. Fate led them to meet at the market and become a happy couple. Poor as they were, their hearts were benevolent.

One day, while hoeing their field, the couple found two eggs, which could not be broken or boiled. The eggs hatched into two snakes, one marked "elder" on the belly and the other marked "younger." Since husband and wife had no children, they surrounded the snakes with love. Cao Văn Phúc's medicinal recipes stopped a horrible epidemic in Văn Xá. After his death, grateful villagers honored him with a temple. Before long, the two snakes went to live near the temple. Văn Lâm villagers built a temple to Từ Thị Lang. That same year, a flood breached the dike protecting the two villages. The snakes slithered out to the dike, inflated their bodies, and formed a giant dam, which checked the rising waters.

The worship of the divine spouses led to the alliance between Văn Xá and Văn Lâm, with customs handed down for generations. Villagers commemorate the two spirits' death anniversaries together. Although twenty kilometers separate the two villages, they now share the same name, Văn Xá. To show mutual respect, the residents greet one another, calling out "Uncle!" or "Aunt!" whenever they meet.

These two villages engage in mutual aid, including reinforcement of local dikes, relief during flooding, assistance in fish rearing and river fishing, and participation in festivals. They hold their large joint festival every ten years; both villages make voluntary donations, with residents contributing as they can. Funds from selling fish raised in ponds at the two communal houses help cover the joint festival and other common expenses. The village honoring the female spouse has a deep well with, according to legend, its water connecting to the Red River. Từ Thị Lang is said to send a message to the village of her husband's spirit in the pomelos that villagers drop into the well. (Pomelos are rather like large, sweet grapefruits with thick, green rinds.)

Vietnamese Cultural Identity

Obviously, eighty years of French colonization influenced Việt Nam's cultural identity. During colonization, some people from the upper social strata prided themselves on speaking French fluently and despised their mother tongue, which they considered fit only for peasants. A Molière-type Vietnamese comedy, *The Annamite French Man* (Ông Tây An Nam, by Nam Xương, 1931), aimed its cutting comments at the key character—a Vietnamese national returning from France. This lead character acts as if he has forgotten how to speak Vietnamese and must hire an interpreter! In fact, at that time, pro-French snobbishness gnawed into traditional Vietnamese culture. After the 1945 Revolution returned independence to Việt Nam, we stressed our cultural identity to enhance the confidence of our people, who once again faced foreign aggression. During colonialism, French was the language of instruction in tertiary education. After the Revolution, we used the Vietnamese language in all educational levels, including higher education, because language is crucial to cultural identity.

For several decades, globalization has forced Việt Nam to redefine its cultural identity after defending it for thirty years (1945–1975) during two wars of national liberation. Now, Việt Nam must preserve and enrich its national culture while opening to world culture. Cultural identity is not permanent, for "All tradition is change." I like this title of a Swedish treatise on Sweden's traditional arts and crafts. A closed culture will wither and die. Cultural identity evolves with time and space. A new tradition may be refashioned in the national mold from a foreign source. The same tradition may take different forms according to time periods.

Let me cite some examples.

Most foreigners agree that modem Vietnamese lacquer painting has a markedly Vietnamese stamp setting it apart from Chinese and Japanese lacquer. Indeed, modern Vietnamese lacquer is a marriage between our traditional handicraft and Western pictorial technique. Another example from art is paintings by Phạm Tăng (1924–), a Vietnamese famous in Europe, especially in Italy. He breathed the Vietnamese soul into an abstract Western style. A further example is the famous Vietnamese long tunic (*áo dài*), which emphasizes the fine silhouette of Vietnamese women. This garment appeared in the 1930s through Westernization of the traditional Vietnamese four-piece, multi-colored women's tunic. More than one Western dictionary mentions "*nem*" (spring rolls) and "*phở*" (soup made with flat rice noodles) as typically Vietnamese dishes. These foods appeared in Việt Nam during the early 1900s. However, they are only indigenous adaptations of foreign dishes of little renown.

A Hyphen between Two Worlds: Indian and Chinese Influences

Việt Nam's location in the center of Southeast Asia makes our country like a hyphen between two worlds, India and China. Southeast Asia has a common heritage marked by these features: matriarchal traditions, predominance of agriculture, and cultivation of rice, betel, areca, and mulberries. Villages were characterized by houses-on-stilts, spinning, bronze drums, bronze gongs, tattoos, loincloths, and kite flying. Spiritual life revolved around special funeral rites and the worship of spirits and fecundity.

Within this common background, Southeast Asians modeled their cultures according to their own geo-political conditions. Since ancient times, Vietnamese have faced two huge challenges: first, the struggle against natural calamities, particularly the Red River's floods; and second, the unbalanced struggle against foreign aggressors. These ordeals gave the Vietnamese certain characteristics:

strong communities fighting for survival, a hard-working nature, sobriety, care for real issues rather than metaphysical abstractions, dexterity, facility with imitations, resistance to physical and moral suffering, and a great ability to adapt. Animism as a pantheist framework characterized the country's spiritual life. The worship of spirits and genies flourishes today, although sometimes diluted by imported religions. Such is the substratum of Vietnamese culture—a Southeast Asian substratum on which Indian and Chinese cultures were grafted during the Christian era.

The first contact with India came early in the Christian era through the Indian traders who ventured into Southeast Asia, seeking gold and spices. While waiting for the northeast monsoon, these traders propagated their culture, in particular their Hindu and Buddhist faiths. The Hindu states of Funan, Chenla, and Chăm Pa emerged. Later, the Khmer and Chăm peoples integrated with the Vietnamese as ethnic minorities.

Vinitaruci (Tỳ Ni Đa Lưu Chi, ?–594 CE), an Indian monk, came to Việt Nam from China and established Việt Nam's first school of Zen (Thiền) Buddhism around 580 CE at Luy Lâu in Hà Bắc Province. This cradle of Vietnamese Buddhism is located at Dâu Pagoda in Thuận Thành District, Bắc Ninh Province, which is about twenty kilometers east of Hà Nội. Later, political upheavals interrupted direct Indo-Vietnamese acculturation. Chinese monks traveling overland replaced Indian preachers and traders. Contact with India resumed only in the 1900s, during our two countries' shared struggle against colonization.

Indian influence is still apparent in southern Việt Nam. There, about a million ethnic minority people (Chăm, Ra Glai, Ê Đê, Gia Rai, and Chu Ru) speak the Chăm language. From 10 to 20 percent of the words in Chăm, which belongs to the Malayo-Polynesian language group, come from Pali, a dead language found in many extant Buddhist manuscripts. Words also coming from Sanskrit, Khmer, and Chăm scripts sprang from the ancient Brahmin writings of India. Many geographical terms in southern Việt Nam, where these two ethnic minorities live today, have Indian origins but were Sinicized (in pronunciation or meaning) before they were

Vietnamized in pronunciation. Thus, "Phan Rang" (the name of a coastal city and bay in Ninh Thuận Province) is a phonetic rendition of "Panduranga," a name for the Chăm state. The Vietnamese language includes words brought by the early Indian missionaries and traders, with most of those words migrating from Sanskrit or Pali into Chinese (*Hán*) and then into Vietnamese. One example is "Buddha," which appears in Vietnamese as "*Bụt*" (a direct phonetic transcription from Sanskrit) and "*Phật*" (through a Sino-Vietnamese word).

Indian influences are visible in Chăm temples and Khmer pagodas, where Brahmin and Buddhist designs stand side by side. Indian cultural influences were deeper and more direct on the culture of the Khmer and Chăm ethnic minorities than on the Kinh (Việt) majority. The effect on the Việt came largely through osmosis from exchanges between Chăm, Khmer, and Vietnamese compatriots. Whereas Indian dance and literature—especially the *Ramayana*—certainly affected Vietnamese culture, India's influence on Việt Nam through Buddhism was profound and durable.

The Chinese introduced Confucianism to Việt Nam after their conquest in the second century BCE, but Confucianism tightened its social grip only after the 1500s. As opposed to Buddhism, Confucianism supports a philosophy of social ethics and the improvement of life on earth but leaves untouched the question of individual salvation. The doctrine of Confucius (551–479 BCE) is based on rules for social relations (e.g., king – subject, father – child, husband – wife, master – disciple, and brother – sister). Relations are hierarchized for social harmony as an element of universal harmony. The Confucian edifice rests on strong, moralizing rules, with "the virtue of humanity" as its foundation.

Pre-Chinese Vietnamese culture caused these strict rules to lose their rigor in Việt Nam compared with China. Nevertheless, Confucianism brought to Việt Nam a political philosophy, *trung*, based on allegiance to the monarch, thereby supporting Vietnamese cohesion and the country's unity. As paradoxical as it may seem, Vietnamese Confucian scholars animated by the ideals they had borrowed from China struggled relentlessly against the

Chinese for Việt Nam's independence. "The Proclamation of Victory over the Ngô [Ming Chinese]" (Bình Ngô Đại Cáo) written by Nguyễn Trãi (1380–1442) and promulgated by King Lê Lợi (life: 1385–1433; reign: 1428–1433) illustrates this paradox.

Traditional Confucian order flourished in ethical, social, political, and cultural domains. Vietnamese adoption of the Chinese model for education (the role of the master, ideograms, triennial examinations) and administration (a mandarin bureaucracy) fostered Confucian ethics. The Vietnamese emphasized moral virtues and literacy but scorned material wealth, economics, and technology. Empiricism replaced science, while patriarchy edged out matriarchy, and men dominated women. An unwritten code of conduct reigned in the village and in the family.

However, many pre-Chinese Southeast Asian cultural values survived in Việt Nam because the Chinese colonial administration never fully penetrated the villages. There, Vietnamese maintained and developed their own popular culture alongside scholarly Confucian culture; thus, the prime Vietnamese cultural identity continued to blossom. Today, Confucianism continues in Việt Nam as a philosophy of social duty, order, and hierarchic discipline. In a word, Confucianism represents "reason." On the other hand, Buddhism searches for individual happiness, relaxation, and compassion. In one word, Buddhism represents "feelings." These two apparent opposites are complementary and contribute to equilibrium in villages, where pagodas for worshipping Buddha co-exist with communal houses and other temples for Confucian rituals.

Analyzing the influence of Buddhism on Vietnamese culture is complex, because Indian traders and monks first introduced Buddhism. Later, Chinese Buddhism reigned. Nevertheless, Buddhism in Việt Nam, even in its most Sinicized form, remains fundamentally a product of Indian spiritualism, as, for example, in the Zen (Dhyana, Thiền) sect. As a religion, Vietnamese Buddhism does not advance the existence of divinities, although priests later introduced statues and images for ordinary people. According to Buddhism, suffering is the human condition because humans believe in the existence of a self and are motivated by desire. Human illusions subject us to the cycle of births and rebirths. Yet, through spiritual enlightenment, individuals can end their ignorance and achieve Nirvana (Enlightenment).

However, enlightenment is accessible only to scholars and monks of the Chinese Zen (Dhyanist, Thiền) School, which is an amalgamation of Buddhism and Taoism. The Vietnamese Zen Buddhist School advocates transcendence through the intellect, communion between master and disciple without speech and scriptures as intermediaries, and meditation until enlightenment. We can see here the syncretism of Buddhism, Taoism, and Confucianism. For ordinary Vietnamese, Buddhism brought not only consolation during feudal exploitation and oppression but also provided the hope of achieving earthly wishes. For this reason, Vietnamese worshipers often invoke Buddha Amitabha (A Di Đà) and Bodhisattva Avalokitesvara (Quan Âm), who are thought to rescue the deprived.

Vietnamese Culture: Southeast Asian Roots Facing Chinese Confucianism

Two French scholars, Pierre Huard and Maurice Durand, have aptly remarked on the nature and evolution of Vietnamese culture:
"Vietnamese culture over the centuries has never absorbed any foreign element (Hindu, Chinese, or Western) without trying to imprint on it a Vietnamese cultural stamp. That trait guarantees that Vietnamese culture has sufficient cohesion to resist external pressure."

Over time, Vietnamese culture has always preserved its Southeast Asian roots while enriching itself with different grafts. During the 2,000 years before French colonization in the 1870s and 1880s, Việt Nam evolved in the cultural orbit of East Asia and, like Korea and Japan, was imbued with Confucianism. Chinese cultural influence came during two different periods—the Chinese occupation (179 BCE – 938 CE) and then Vietnamese emulation during the first era of independence (939–1884). The relations between Vietnamese and Chinese followed a particular dynamic. On one hand, the Việts rejected the aggressor's culture and aspired to preserve their Southeast Asian roots. On the other, they were attracted to Chinese culture, which seemed richer. The Vietnamese borrowed from Chinese culture the elements that could enrich their own culture. Rejection and attraction characterized this ambiguous relationship, just as it does today.

In general, what have these Confucian and Chinese grafts brought to Việt Nam's Southeast Asian roots?

In terms of lifestyle in ancient times, Chinese influence brought extensive use of iron, domestication of the horse, intensive cultivation of rice (iron plows, buffaloes, oxen, irrigation, fertilizers), enameled ceramics, the development of weaving and wicker ware, the manufacture of paper and glass, great progress in river and sea navigation, the Spice Road between China and Southeast Asia, and trade with Java, Burma, and India.

In terms of intellectual and spiritual development, adoption of Chinese ideograms made possible the propagation of Confucianism, the official doctrine that radiated throughout all domains but particularly in general ideology and education. Confucianism endured because it suited Asian feudal societies, which were agricultural, autarchic, stationary, and subject to a monarchic regime, which decreed that all land was the king's private property. Confucianism was the moral and political creed of the learned man, the intellectual, the "superior man" (*quân tử*), who followed the principle: "Perfect oneself morally, manage one's family, govern the country, and establish order in the world." Confucianism had very strict rules about social behavior in order to maintain order and harmony in a strongly hierarchical society.

Confucianism took root easily in Việt Nam because the Vietnamese community spirit that Confucianism enshrined was highly compatible with the spirit prevailing at the Vietnamese nation's birth, when peasants faced the permanent threat of aggression from the north and the Red River's floods. However, after penetrating Việt Nam, Confucianism lost many of its original concepts, including the strictures of filial piety, absolute fidelity to the monarch, and many of the complicated rites.

Thus, two parallel and complementary cultures took shape on Vietnamese soil—the popular culture anchored in the villages and more faithful to the roots of the Việt and the scholarly culture marked by Confucian-Chinese grafting. The Confucianized Vietnamese intelligentsia had several strata: orthodox scholars (the Court and the mandarinate); those faithful to the king but also concerned with the well-being of the people (e.g., Nguyễn Trãi, 1380–1442); those resolutely siding with the people against the king (e.g., rebel Cao Bá Quát, 1809–1853); and those integrated into the life of the people (e.g., village school teachers).

The brutal intervention of French colonizers in the late 1800s compelled enlightened scholars to make a painful revision of their Confucian values.

French Culture in Việt Nam Today

When the BBC interviewed me by phone about the role of French culture in today's Việt Nam, I was reluctant to answer because, with a subject so large, one can say nothing about this third facet of Vietnamese culture in three minutes. Still, I couldn't refuse the invitation made so graciously by the interviewer, an ethnic-Vietnamese woman who seemed very young, judging by the sound of her voice.

I had the impression that she was raising the question more on the level of French language than of French culture. Of course, language is an important element of culture, but it isn't everything. Such a misunderstanding is not surprising. The world "*Francophonie*," with its root "*phone*," makes one think more of the language than of the culture. Given the decline of French-language teaching in Việt Nam, some might think French culture no longer has the least importance to Vietnamese culture. It's true that in Việt Nam, as in other Asian countries, young people are going crazy for English, although not to master Shakespeare or Hemingway but, above all, to secure a job, particularly one involving foreigners.

French (which is to say, Western) culture has made important contributions to Vietnamese culture. Naturally, this leaves aside the crimes of colonialism. The BBC interviewer was astonished that I would compare the one-hundred-year influence of French culture to the impact of Chinese culture covering two millennia. But I think we shouldn't measure cultural influence by duration. The truth is that each of those two cultures had its own impact on our Vietnamese culture. The introduction of French culture in the mid-1800s brought Việt Nam its first stage of modernization (or Westernization). The second stage came after the August 1945 Revolution and especially since *Đổi Mới* (Renovation or Renewal) in late 1986.

Many cultural triumphs illustrate Franco-Vietnamese cultural integration: the adoption of Romanized script to replace Chinese *Hán* and Vietnamese *Nôm* characters in social, political, and literary activities; the Revolution's successful literacy campaign, which was built on that foundation; the creation of a scientific vocabulary in Vietnamese to enable higher education in our national language; integration of the ideal of liberty from the 1789 French Revolution in our Vietnamese struggle against feudalism and for our own national liberation; creation of new genres in painting (lacquer, silk), architecture (the Indochinese style), theater (*kịch* or spoken theater, *cải lương* or reformed theater), music (pop songs), the humanities (new disciplines, including historical science, archeology, sociology, ethnography, and literature).

This brief review shows that French (or Western) culture is an integral part of Vietnamese culture. It is our responsibility, along with the people of France, to preserve and develop this heritage in the interest of our two peoples. Our researchers should guard against two extremes—considering the French (Western) contribution as the only culture of value on one side and, on the other, completely rejecting the French contribution in favor of a traditional, Confucian culture. Moreover, in this era of globalization, we should open ourselves to all the world's cultures and absorb the best qualities from each one.

Franco-Vietnamese Karma

A French stamp sealed our forced marriage with the West at the beginning of Việt Nam's modern history. Then, after nine years of war (1945–1954), reconciliation led step-by-step to a remarriage based on free consent. This included Việt Nam's Francophone participation heightened by the Seventh Summit of French-Speaking Countries held in Hà Nội in 1997. French colonization had brought Việt Nam face to face with modernity. That conflict between our traditional culture and modern French culture enabled us to reap fruits, which at times upset the colonizers' calculations. Vietnamese culture, while modernizing (Westernizing), also preserved itself.

Our political culture modernized from contact with the French. At the end of the 1800s, ideas from Montesquieu (1689–1755), Rousseau (1712–1778), Voltaire (1694–1778), and others captivated many Confucian scholars, who had read the French authors' works in Chinese translations. Phan Châu (Chu) Trinh (1872–1926), a famous patriotic scholar, espoused ideas from the French 1789 Revolution, advocated abolition of the monarchy, and encouraged pursuit of national independence through education.

Many Vietnamese arts reflect Western (French) cultural grafts onto Vietnamese cultural stock. For example, French dramatic arts impacted traditional Vietnamese musical theater in the creation of two new genres: spoken theater (*kịch nói*) and renovated musical theater (*cải lương*). Stage directors Bửu Tiến (1918–1992) and Tào Mạt (1930–1993) analyzed French dramaturgical and scenographic influences on popular opera (*chèo*) and classical opera (*tuồng*). French music influenced modern songs, including revolutionary songs. Musician Nguyễn Xuân Khoát (1910–1993) combined Western and Eastern music. Georges Sadoul (1904–1967) exerted a profound influence on newly emerging Vietnamese cinema. Students at the Indochina Fine Arts College assimilated Western painting techniques, transformed lacquer art, and renovated painting on silk. French architecture produced the Indochinese style pioneered by Ernest Hébrard (1875–1933). The French

Institute for Far-East Studies (École française d'Extrême-Orient)—with eminent researchers Georges Ceodès (1886–1969), Léopold Cadière (1869–1955), Louis Bezacier (1906–1966), Henri Maspéro (1883–1945), Madeleine Colani (1866–1943), Louis Finot (1864–1935), and Léonard Aurousseau (1888–1929)—began modern Vietnamese Studies.

Franco-Vietnamese acculturation appeared in literature, arts, and social science. The greatest Western contribution to Vietnamese culture is individualism, which was missing in the Eastern cultures that emphasized community. Individualism filtered into Việt Nam through the French romanticism of Alphonse de Lamartine (1790–1869), Victor Hugo (1802–1885), and Alfred de Musset (1810–1857). This explains the emergence in the 1920s and 1930s of Vietnamese romantic literature, which abandoned Vietnamese classical poetry's impersonal style for lyricism in the first person. Modern Vietnamese literature could also reach unprecedented popularity thanks to a concomitant movement to encourage the Romanized Vietnamese script (*Quốc Ngữ*), which European missionaries, notably the French Jesuit Alexandre de Rhodes (1591–1660), had developed in the 1600s as an evangelical tool.

Poet Xuân Diệu (1916–1985), an early proponent of the New Poetry (*Thơ Mới*) Movement of the 1930s, noted, "Our fathers and grandfathers said '*ta*' (I, we) to speak of themselves; they did not specify that they were individuals. Rather, they existed as the king's subjects, their masters' pupils, and their fathers' sons—always as inferiors to the trinity holding all spiritual and material power. Our forefathers spoke of human destiny in general. But in the 1930s their sons and grandsons began to use the word '*tôi*' (I, me). Adoption of the Romanized script further aided the individual in literature and in social activities, especially in urban areas. There appeared new literary genres—journalism, the modern novel, and literary criticism. Immediately after independence, we used the Romanized Vietnamese script to develop an educational system from primary school through high school."

This brief account gives an idea of the legacy of Franco-Vietnamese acculturation.

"Asian Values" and "Family Values"

For some years, researchers, politicians, and economists tried to explain the Asian economic miracles first in Japan and then in the little dragons (Republic of Korea, Taiwan, and Singapore) by referring to Asian cultural values. In the early 1990s, Lee Kuan Yew (1923–2015) of Singapore and Mahathir bin Mohamad (1925–) of Malaysia drew attention to the importance of Asian values. Western researchers have also attributed these countries' economic successes to these Asian cultural traditions: a strong work ethic, thrift, family stability, a strong sense of community, and a paternalistic government.

When the 1997 financial crisis struck down these booming economies, some Western researchers found it opportune to rebuff earlier explanations as far-fetched commentaries, which served only to camouflage authoritarianism. They condemned Asian values for the abuses that these values had allegedly engendered, including nepotism and a lack of transparency. Citing German political-economist Max Weber (1864–1920), these commentators claimed that Asian economies could prosper only when Asian nations and businesses adopted the European ideas of private property, scientific rationalism, and modern governmental institutions. In other words, Asia must renounce its own values and embrace Western values.

My first impression is that "Asian values" is too vague a term because it is so vast. There is so much difference among Asians (Eastern, Southeastern, Southern, Central, and Western), not to mention differences between national cultures and between ethnic minorities within national cultures. Many commentators attribute the initial successes of Việt Nam's economic reforms to commonly shared Asian values—patriotism, national pride, a strong sense of community, diligence, and thrift. In fact, the Vietnamese nation and culture have affirmed themselves through two parallel historical processes: mixing of indigenous populations and acculturation with foreign cultures, particularly Chinese culture and then French (Western) culture. An essential characteristic of Vietnamese culture is its preservation of national identity while enriching itself with contributions from foreign cultures.

Let me conclude by citing a typical Vietnamese example— the family. Despite the changes that have come from national and international development, our institution of the family remains quite strong, thanks to efforts to uphold traditional values. These include the importance of community, parental authority, the worship of ancestors, the rituals surrounding birth, marriage, death, and the anniversaries of the deceased, and to say nothing about the spirit of family life. However, the family must modernize by relieving itself of Confucian constraints while adopting selectively some Western values, such as gender equality and authentic rights for the individual.

Vietnamese Culture and Đổi Mới

We can divide Việt Nam's recent history into two periods: 1) internationalization and 2) globalization and regionalization. Two wars fundamentally of national liberation involving foreign nations characterized internationalization. Vietnamese patriotic movements during the French colonial period had ended in failure, which led Vietnamese to think they could not regain independence through their own efforts but must seek international aid for national liberation. After the League for the Independence of Việt Nam (**Việt** Nam Độc Lập Đồng **Minh** Hội or Việt Minh) seized political power in 1945, President Hồ Chí Minh tried in vain to negotiate with the French. However, France, which was supported by the Western bloc led by the United States and Great Britain, rejected his proposals. As a result, Việt Nam joined the socialist bloc to continue the fight for independence. During the two decades our country was divided (1954–1975), North Việt Nam embraced socialism, while South Việt Nam embraced capitalism.

A brief period of recovery following the end of the American War (1975) lasted until the end of the 1970s, when Việt Nam experienced two more wars—with Cambodia and China, with the United States politically backing the genocidal Khmer Rouge and the Chinese invasion of six Vietnamese border provinces. Việt Nam simultaneously experienced a fifteen-year economic crisis, which placed the country on the brink of bankruptcy. The situation improved with the *Đổi Mới* (Renovation or Renewal) policy in late 1986. Those reforms had some similarities to *perestroika* in Russia. However, the former succeeded, while the latter failed.

In order to introduce *perestroika* effectively, the Russians needed capital, modern technology, and industrial expertise. However, tensions between Russia and the West limited international assistance. Việt Nam's situation was simpler. More than 80 percent of Vietnamese lived in the countryside. To address our economic problems, first, we had to change production methods. The government kept the state-owned sector but encouraged a competitive private sector by returning land to the farmers while encouraging trade, the arts, crafts, and private industry. The export in 1989 of two million tons of rice and nearly two million tons of oil and oil products signaled the beginning of economic recovery.

Đổi Mới has been characterized by Việt Nam's participation in globalization through increasing integration into world markets and participation in regionalization through membership and participation in ASEAN (Association of Southeast Asian Nations) and the International Organization of Francophone Countries. *Đổi Mới* sanctioned the market economy and introduced an open-door policy toward all countries willing to establish normalized diplomatic relations. These changes revitalized our economy and enriched our culture. However, we have seen negative effects, since the market economy encourages competition but, at the same time, encourages individualism, greed, and rejection of traditional values, especially among the young. There are those who hold that Việt Nam's open-door policy has introduced some Western values in opposition to our national, community-oriented spirit.

Globalization has engendered a social and ecological crisis, which has harmed poorer people and poorer countries. An ever-increasing gap between rich and poor has created an elite group with growing power. The world also faces an ecological crisis, which, unless steps are taken, may lead to the degradation of life for all species in our biosphere. In response, Vietnamese culture must develop a balance ensuring the harmonious development of our culture and our economy. Modernity must evolve alongside preservation of our identity. Thus, Việt Nam has chosen the slogan: "[Let us work for] prosperity of the people and strength of the country to build an equitable, democratic, and cultured society." This pragmatic formula without ideological overtones is a vision Vietnamese of all strata—both at home and abroad—can adopt.

Việt Nam's
Confucian Heritage

How to Translate "Văn Miếu"

Hà Nội's Văn Miếu Temple, which is devoted to Confucius (551–479 BCE) and his disciples, was built in 1070. The official translation of *"Văn Miếu"* in French is *"Temple de la Litterature"* and in English is "Temple of Literature."

But are these translations correct?

This is not a question of linguistic quibbling but, rather, of semantics.

Functionally, this temple is devoted to the worship of Confucius with a view to glorifying the doctrine of the Chinese philosopher who exerted the most profound and durable influence on Eastern Asia. Việt Nam has a network of Confucian temples; these are called *"văn miếu"* in the capital city, *"khổng miếu"* in provincial towns, and *"văn từ"* or *"văn chỉ"* in districts, communes, and villages. There are only two *văn miếu* temples. The one in Hà Nội was inspired by the original Chinese model in Qufu (homeland of Confucius in southwestern Shandong Province, China), while the one in Huế was built in 1809 following the capital's transfer in 1802 from Hà Nội to Huế.

Translating *"văn miếu"* is not easy. The Sino-Vietnamese term, *"miếu,"* means "a temple to the genies and spirits," "a temple where the tablets of ancestors are kept," or "a small temple." *"Văn"* can mean: "line," "vein," "tattoo," "ornament," "letters," "writings," "literature," "culture," "civilization," and "beautiful." In *Ancient Tonkin* (Le Tonkin Ancien, 1937), Claude Madroll translated *"Văn Miếu"* as "Temple of Culture," which I think is closer to the real meaning than "Temple of Literature." *"Văn"* might evoke Confucian culture, the doctrine of the Master (*nho*), which is expressed mostly by writings, that is, by literature in the most general sense as well as by culture in general and not only the humanities.

In his *Annamese-Chinese-French Dictionary* (Dictionnaire Annamite-Chinois-Français, 1937), Gustave Joseph Hue considers synonymous the terms *"văn," "văn minh," "văn hiến,"* and *"văn hóa"* as meaning "culture." But we should consider two points: First, ancient tradition did not distinguish between literature, culture, philosophy, and history. Second, all cultures of Eastern Asia dominated by Chinese influence have a literary character. According to Vietnamese literary historian Dương Quảng Hàm (1898–1946), "Chinese culture was introduced into our country through different channels, but essentially through the channel of literature, that is, through Chinese ideograms and works in Chinese characters. Since then, Chinese literature has governed thought, erudition, morality, politics, and the customs of our people."

Cao Xuân Huy (1900–1983), a Taoist scholar, wrote, "Confucius believed that the object of knowledge and history is not natural phenomena but, rather, is poetry, rituals, and music, that is to say, religion and the traditional culture of the Western Zhou."

The Vietnamese placed their own stamp on Hà Nội's Văn Miếu Temple by worshiping the Vietnamese scholar Chu Văn An (1292–1370), by installing eighty-two stone steles engraved with the names of Vietnamese doctoral recipients from 1442 to 1779, and by establishing Quốc Tử Giám, Việt Nam's first university, which opened in 1076. Given these Vietnamese additions, instead of translating *"Văn Miếu"* as "Temple of Literature," wouldn't it be more apt to say "Temple of Culture," "Temple to Confucius," or "Temple of Confucian Culture?"

Confucius Set Free

The Temple of Culture (Temple of Confucian Culture, Temple to Confucius, or Temple of Literature, known as Văn Miếu in Vietnamese) epitomizes the acculturation from the marriage of our ancient Việt culture with Chinese culture, a marriage imposed by over ten centuries of Chinese domination (179 BCE – 938 CE) followed by voluntary, diligent study of Chinese culture during the independent Vietnamese dynasties (938 CE – 1800s). The teachings of Confucius, to which the Temple of Culture was devoted, left a deep imprint on Vietnamese social life, as it also did in other East Asian countries. The temple's architecture—its straight lines, right angles, symmetry, and harmony—expresses a philosophy based on reason, which inspired a patriarchal society with a strict hierarchy. Confucianism was an ethical system (rather than a religion) serving the sovereign, who reigned from the social pyramid's apex. Mandarin officials, who had been recruited through examinations, occupied the intermediate levels.

Văn Miếu's third courtyard contains eighty-two stone steles with the inscribed names of over a thousand scholars, who earned doctorates in literature at the 124 examinations given between 1442 and 1779. Under the ancient regime, scholar-mandarins imbued with Confucianism helped build a solid, prosperous Vietnamese kingdom. However, during the second half of the 1900s, most Confucian scholars ignored the Western colonial onslaught and shrank from the reforms needed to prevent loss of national independence.

Because of this conservatism, for many decades after the 1945 Revolution, the statues of Confucius and his four closest disciples were banned from the sanctuary of the Temple of Culture. After *Đổi Mới* (the policy of Renovation or Renewal, which began in late 1986), the statues were removed from the recesses, where they had kept company with cockroaches. They were beautifully refurbished. The Confucian doctrine's humanistic qualities received due recognition, while the philosophy's repressive aspects remain condemned.

Hồ Chí Minh was the founder of the modern Vietnamese state, a revolutionary, a humanist scholar, and a wise politician. He adopted a flexible attitude toward Confucianism. As a child and youth, he had studied Confucian classics, from which he learned the ethics, ideals, and ideas that later went well with his Marxist values—rationalism, concern for social morality, and the overriding importance of action. While in France, Hồ Chí Minh used the name Nguyễn Ái Quốc (Nguyễn the Patriot). In 1921, Nguyễn Ái Quốc wrote a short introduction to Confucianism in "Indochina" (Đông Dương), an article published in *The Communist Review* (La Revue Communiste). On his birthday (May 19) in 1965, while on a visit to China, President Hồ Chí Minh made a pilgrimage to Qufu, homeland of Confucius in southwestern Shandong Province.

During that visit, President Hồ told a journalist, "Confucius, Jesus Christ, Marx, and Sun Yat-sen had many qualities in common. They all worked for society's good. Were they still alive and living side by side, they would understand one another perfectly as good friends."

To mobilize the Vietnamese people, Hồ Chí Minh adapted Confucian concepts to new conditions in service of the Revolution. It's a pity that Hồ Chí Minh's openness of mind and heart failed to register with the Vietnamese politicians who could not differentiate between the wealth of Confucian humanism and the negative, conservative, and even retrogressive aspects of the Master's doctrine.

Filial Piety

In ancient Việt Nam, only males were considered fit to uphold the familial responsibilities of Confucian ethics. The father –son relationship was one among three mainstays of social order (*tam cương*), alongside the king – subject and husband – wife relationships. Filial piety (*hiếu*) was a basic virtue.

However, the Chinese concept of filial piety was too mystical for Vietnamese. Children in Chinese antiquity martyred themselves to express filial piety toward their parents, whom they venerated much as the Catholic Church venerates its saints. Edifying stories abound in classical Chinese literature. In our Vietnamese eyes, actions of characters in these tales verge on madness: A child of four abstains from food whenever a parent falls ill. A youth willingly submits to his father and stepmother's frequent, unjust beatings. A thirteen-year-old girl drowns herself in the river after crying seven days for her father, who had drowned in the same river.

Yet traditional Vietnamese education also cultivated filial piety. Even during French colonization, the first lesson in the first-grade primer depicted a child's duty to his parents. The father's word was the family's law. Children, whatever their age, were their parents' possessions. However, parents' possessive attitudes declined sharply following the August 1945 Revolution and especially during the thirty years of Resistance War (1945–1975), when civic instructions exalted patriotism and placed less emphasis on familial obligations.

Now, with the return of peace, long-suppressed individualism has found an excellent breeding ground in a burgeoning consumer lifestyle. Not a few children have completely abandoned their parents. Using a selective approach, Việt Nam is returning to old moral values yet without reviving absolute parental authority, which would be impossible anyway. It would be ideal if children could blend the great respect that people in the East feel toward their parents with the democratic spirit of the West to create affectionate bonds based on mutual understanding and mutual love.

Confucian Scholar-Administrators

For nearly nine centuries, the Vietnamese royal dynasties held multi-level scholastic examinations to recruit mandarins for the Royal Court. The first such examination was held in 1075, while the last national examination was in 1913, when the French colonial rulers forced closure of the national-level exams. Local examinations continued through 1918. The examinations had three stages or levels: a triennial examination (*thi hương*) in various regions determined by the Royal Court, a national examination (*thi hội*) in the capital for a doctorate, and the Royal Court examination (*thi đình*) presided over by the king in the capital to choose the top-placed, first doctor.

The examinations encouraged education based on Confucian humanities and on historical and literary knowledge rather than on common knowledge and science. The written tests were in Chinese ideograms, although pronunciation was based on Vietnamese. One of the most important examinations was the literary dissertation (*văn sách*). Originally, the king posed questions to learn the candidate's views on political and economic issues and to judge how much the candidate wanted to improve the people's lives. Eventually, this genre became an exercise glorifying the monarch and the Royal Court.

In dissertations, parallelism in style (ideas, phrases, tonality) was obligatory, but no rhyme was necessary. Take, for example, a literary dissertation composed by Vũ Kiệt, a twenty-year-old laureate doctor at the royal examination in 1472 during the reign of Lê Thánh Tông (life: 1442–1497; reign: 1460–1497). In his dissertation, Vũ Kiệt stressed the importance of education if a country is to thrive. He wrote:

> Sire, Your subject has heard people say that in the old times the teacher was a necessity. The teacher propagates the doctrine of Confucius, shows the mistakes, and explains controversial points. . . . There are, however, teachers of disputable quality not versed in literary style. What students need is erudition, but these teachers have only superficial knowledge. . . . Teachers must pass a rigorous selection process. Education of students must be severe.... The quest for talent must take morality into account.

Vũ Kiệt condemned corrupt mandarins:

> Sire, the question put by Your Majesty aims at the purity of mandarin customs. The treatise, *The Annals of Spring and Autumn*, says that the integrity or crimes of mandarins creates a state's prosperity or decline. In my humble opinion, if misappropriations of public funds are brought to light, there will be no place for corruption.... Sire, I have heard that Your Majesty is severe in the judgment of dishonest persons and generous in the reward of honest persons, but Your Majesty has not accorded enough attention to petty mandarins. *The Analects* say, "If the high mandarins do not breach rules, petty mandarins will be righteous. It is necessary to order royal inspectors to

accomplish their task of control in order to encourage and honor upright mandarins. . . . Corrupt mandarins must receive the punishment they deserve."

Today, five hundred years later, this scholastic text makes us smile. How beautifully it captures the *Zeitgeist* of both Vũ Kiệt's time and ours! In the mid-1880s, the French completed their conquest of Việt Nam. The colonial administration began to replace Chinese characters with the French language and the Romanized Vietnamese script (*Quốc Ngữ*). Nevertheless, the French allowed the old system of national mandarin examinations to continue until 1913 but with some modifications, in particular, adoption of dissertations in Vietnamese. The following two examples from the mandarin examinations highlight the changing times:

From an assignment in 1907:

> Expand the following Vietnamese saying and give some examples: "A man jealously keeps his field but takes his cows to graze in others' fields."

From an essay in 1907:

> Back from traveling within Indochina, a professor gave a lecture to his students on communication. He showed them that commerce is useful for a country's development and that communications influence a country's expansion and facilitate exchanges. We may classify various means of communication in the order of their utility.

Confucius and Machiavelli

Without being pessimistic, I tend to think that politics and ethics are not well-suited to each other and that a policy based solely on ethics risks being utopian. That explains the failure of Confucius (551–479 BCE), a philosopher whose influence can nevertheless be felt even now in more than one East Asian political figure. At its base, Confucianism is more an ethic than a religion because it does not address metaphysics. The Master lived when the Zhou Dynasty (1046–256 BCE) emperors had lost authority. Rival lords were tearing the country asunder. Confucius traveled from one principality to another, offering his services in vain to petty kings. During the Master's lifetime, no one practiced the ideas summarized in *The Analects* and *The Annals of Spring and Autumn*.

The Confucian doctrine's social mores preach the restoration of a government similar to administrations early in the Zhou Dynasty. These regimes owed their success to the monarchs' virtue, for a good government relies more on the people's confidence and adequate food for the people than on the army because "death has been and can be there any time, but a people cannot survive if they do not trust their sovereign." The basis of such a regime must be humanism, as expressed in these teachings: "Let your eyes, ears, tongue, and everything in you be kept within the rules of honesty." "Do not do to others what you would not do to yourself." "In the principality, let there be nobody who is not pleased with you; in the family, let there be nobody who complains of your conduct."

For two thousand years, Confucianism inspired successive generations of Vietnamese scholars. The most illustrious of these scholars, Nguyễn Trãi (1380–1442), interpreted the Master's teaching in his own way by emphasizing love for the people. He expressed his humanism through original concepts, such as, "Winning hearts is more important than storming citadels in waging resistance war and in ending war between two countries." After helping King Lê Lợi (life: 1385–1433; reign:1428–1433) drive out the Chinese occupier following ten years of struggle, Nguyễn Trãi proclaimed: "Peace and happiness for the people are the foundation of humanity and justice."

Opposing Confucian principles is *realpolitik* with its objective of effectiveness overshadowing morality and principle. Typical in this regard are the views of Niccolò Machiavelli (1469–1527), an official responsible for political and military affairs in the Republic of Florence. Machiavelli is famous for having subordinated morals to the needs and interests of the state. In *The Prince,* Machiavelli holds that he who governs must constantly resort to trickery and deception to disguise his thoughts and behavior in order to serve the homeland's superior interests. It is better to be cruel when necessary than to show useless mercy; it is better to inspire fear and respect than to be insufficiently respected. A prince, according to Machiavelli, should know how to be simultaneously a fox and a lion. He should be known *not* to act on his word (oath) when this could harm him and when his reasons for the oath no longer exist. It could be necessary for him to show mercy, faithfulness, sincerity, and piety, but he should know how to ignore those feelings. In short, he must "keep himself away from good if he should, and he should know how to commit evil if necessary."

Over the last few years, international politics continue, alas, sometimes to support and follow the considerations of Machiavelli.

Confucian Contempt for Commerce and Finance

Hà Nội, City of Refinement and Elegance (Hà Nội Thanh Lịch, by Hoàng Đạo Thúy, 1900–1994) is a small, popular encyclopedia about the capital city during its passage from the old Việt Nam with its traditional heritage to the new Việt Nam under French colonization. In this edited excerpt from "Commerce" (Buôn Bán), Hoàng Đạo Thúy shows how Confucian influences caused traditional Vietnamese scholars to avoid trade, finance, and economics:

> Confucius and Mencius recommended an ethical system, which was political, humanistic, compassionate, democratic, and not superstitious. Mencius taught, "When men quarrel about 'profit,' the nation is in 'danger.'" An interpretation held, "Regarding riches as petty shows a noble mind." Confucian scholars believed, "To trade, one must

lie." They counseled their children, "No matter what, do not become traders."

Confucian scholars also taught, "When holding your rice bowl, remember the peasants' hardships. When dressing, remember the weavers' labor." These lessons emphasized lifestyles but neglected product distribution. Confucians listed four professions: scholar (*sỹ*), farmer (*nông*), laborer (*công*), and trader (*cổ*). Young children memorized these lines in five-word meter:

> Ten thousand occupations are inferior,
> Only reading and studying are noble.

Since reading was the highest occupation, scholars were the highest social class. Nevertheless, we also have this oral folk poem (*ca dao*) in four-word meter:

> Scholars first, farmers second,
> Empty rice granary, search!
> Farmers first, scholars second.

Men strove to be scholars, since by achieving a high appraisal at the triennial examinations they might become mandarins. Anyone failing the examinations could still be a master (*thầy*, teacher). A saying characterized those professions:

> Profit for a mandarin, status for a master.

Family burdens fell on the women, who were forbidden to study and mix in company. They could only be petty traders. Guest traders—foreigners with the companies that had international branches—controlled foreign, interprovincial, and intra-provincial trade. Lack of Vietnamese commerce and the loss of authority over our seas helped create poverty, weakness, and economic decline.

Confucianism and the Vietnamese Revolution

Việt Nam's August 1945 Socialist Revolution was the outcome of an eighty-year movement for national liberation and also a break from Confucian thought, which had reigned in Việt Nam for over two thousand years. The Confucian doctrine's moral imperative—loyalty to the king—had already completely disappeared during the relentless, constantly renewed struggle against the colonial administration. The people considered the rulers whom the French installed to be puppets. The Revolution finally forced the last ruler from the Nguyễn Dynasty (1802–1945) to abdicate.

The Revolution upset the Confucian social hierarchy, since the Revolution's agrarian reforms emphasized the peasant (*tiểu nhân*, the low-level man) and not the scholar (*quân tử*, the gentleman). Likewise, within the family, respect and affection replaced filial piety. Meanwhile, women achieved the freedom to love and choose a husband as well as to participate in social activities and in the war. In addition, the Revolution emphasized science and democracy, notions absent in Confucianism and Eastern culture in general.

But did the Socialist Revolution completely sweep away Confucianism?

Some militants attempted to wipe out Confucianism, arguing that its rigid conservatism had sapped national independence. During the 1960s and 1970s, the Philosophy Institute adopted an anti-Confucian attitude. However, well-balanced Marxists took a more cautious approach. They placed a high value on Confucianism's humanist ideals yet condemned the negative side of Confucianism's political and social ethics. Scholar, writer, and historian Nguyễn Khắc Viện (1913–1997) remarked that Confucianism had trained Vietnamese for centuries not to speculate on the Other World; thus, Marxism found easier acceptance in Việt Nam than would have been possible in an Islamic or a Christian culture.

Revolutionary Confucian Scholars

Many Vietnamese towns have a street named for Phan Bội Châu. Indeed, it is an unspoken rule that any town with a Phan Bội Châu Street will have a street named for Phan Châu (Chu) Trinh. Both men were eminent Confucian scholars, contemporaries, and great patriots. The French colonial administration had quashed the Save-the-King (Cần Vương) Insurrection (1885–1896) led by Confucian scholars loyal to the king. By the end of the 1800s, the French had firmly established colonial rule across Việt Nam. Then, in the early 1900s, there appeared two nationalist movements— a legal struggle represented by Phan Châu Trinh and an armed struggle represented by Phan Bội Châu.

Phan Bội Châu (1867–1940) was born into a family of poor scholars in central Việt Nam's Nghệ An Province. The anti-French Save-the-King Movement excited him when he was a child. At age nineteen, he gathered some sixty students into an insurgent organization, which, however, soon disintegrated. Then for ten years, until he was thirty-one, he refused public and political commitments in order to tend his ill father, as an orthodox Confucian would. Nevertheless, he used those years to expand his classical knowledge, read progressive Chinese authors, evaluate the country's situation, and liaise with patriotic scholars while simultaneously preparing for the Huế Royal Court's triennial literary examination. He knew that to pursue militant politics he needed the prestige that only a degree from the mandarin examinations could confer.

Phan Bội Châu was honored as the first laureate in the Regional Examinations of 1900, the same year his father died. These two events freed Phan Bội Châu to devote his efforts to militancy. Between 1900 and 1905, he scoured the country to rally supporters following an abortive uprising in Nghệ An. In 1906, he founded the Renovation (Duy Tân) Movement to send Vietnamese revolutionary students to Japan to study. The following year, he went to Japan, where he campaigned against French colonizers in Việt

Nam. As an advocate of armed struggle, he sought foreign aid and alliances with progressive people in other Asian countries.

Expelled from Japan in 1909, Phan Bội Châu went to China and then to Thailand. After the success of the 1911 Chinese Revolution, he founded the Association for Restoration of Independence for Việt Nam (Việt Nam Quang Phục Hội) in 1912. The French sentenced him to death *in absentia* in 1913, but then the Chinese jailed Phan Bội Châu from 1913 to 1917. In 1918, Phan Bội Châu made a tactical error by advocating "Franco-Vietnamese harmony" (*Pháp-Việt đề huề*), which the French administration exploited. After October 1917, Phan Bội Châu leaned toward world revolution. In 1925, the French arrested Phan Bội Châu in Shanghai, a French concession, and brought him back to Việt Nam.

The French-Vietnamese court condemned Phan Bội Châu to forced labor for life, but then a vast protest movement spread across Việt Nam, forcing the colonizers to release Phan Bội Châu from that sentence. The French confined Phan Bội Châu to house arrest in Huế, where he nevertheless met weekly with students, including young Võ Nguyên Giáp, later Việt Nam's most famous modern general. Until the end of his life, Phan Bội Châu never ceased writing to keep alight the flame of patriotism. He described his own life as "the story of innumerable defeats without a single success." However, Phan Bội Châu, the soul behind nationalist revolts in the early 1900s, inspired younger generations with his literary works and exemplary devotion to nationalism.

Phan Châu Trinh (1872–1926) led the other method of resistance. Born in central Việt Nam's Quảng Nam Province, he was the son of a military mandarin of low rank and a well-educated mother, who introduced him to classical literature. After earning a diploma as doctor of humanities, second rank, he accepted an appointment to the Ministry of Rites in 1903. Two years later, he resigned after being influenced by progressive Chinese authors and French thinkers, including Charles-Louis Montesquieu (1689–1755) and Jean-Jacques Rousseau (1712–1788), whom he had read through Chinese translations. Phan Châu Trinh traveled up and down Việt Nam for five years, seeking a way to save the nation. He met guerrilla leader Hoàng Hoa Thám (1858–1913) in the jungles of Yên Thế (Bắc Giang Province) and later went to China and Japan, where he met Phan Bội Châu, with whom he had long discussions without reaching common ground.

Phan Châu Trinh did not believe in armed violence or in the disinterested aid of other Asian countries. His plan for regaining national independence involved abolition of the monarchy and the mandarinate, assurance of democratic freedoms, educational reforms to raise the people's cultural standard, and development of industry and commerce. He naively thought one could exploit the colonial administration's promises of a civilizing mission.

In 1906, Phan Châu Trinh sent a letter to the French governor-general of Indochina, denouncing the excesses of mandarins:

> For a score of years now, the high-level dignitaries of the Royal Court have indulged in luxury and have neglected public affairs. The mandarins in the provinces care only for strengthening their positions while extorting money from the rural populace. People of some education vie in servility and flattery at the cost of their dignity. The people have been bled white and can hardly survive. Everything is going to ruin, the people are disunited, customs and habits are loosening, and morality has fallen very low. A nation of twenty million souls has been forced back almost to the age of barbarism.

In 1907, Phan Châu Trinh encouraged his province to open schools directed by the reformist scholars from the Eastern Capital School for the Just Cause (Đông Kinh Nghĩa Thục, also known as the Tonkin Free School). The strike in 1908 against heavy taxes in Central Việt Nam (Annam, Trung Kỳ) triggered massive French repression. Phan Châu Trinh was arrested and exiled to Poulo Condor (Côn Đảo) Prison Island. Released in 1910 thanks to the intervention of the French Human Rights League, he went into self-exile in Paris, hoping to appeal to liberal French politicians and, with their assistance, win reforms from the French government. But this effort failed. In 1922, when King Khải Định (life:

1885–1925; reign: 1916–1925) went to France, Phan Châu Trinh wrote the king a letter openly condemning the king's vices and accusing him of treason. In 1925, Phan Châu Trinh returned to Sài Gòn, where he wrote treatises on political theory and organized conferences on political and social issues. Those meetings left a profound impression on young intellectuals. Phan Châu Trinh died of illness a year later at the age of fifty-four.

Hồ Chí Minh, founder of the modern Vietnamese state, knew both patriots. Phan Bội Châu was friends with Hồ Chí Minh's father and knew President Hồ when he was a boy using the name Nguyễn Tất Thành. Their relationship continued. As for Phan Châu Trinh, President Hồ told Mme. Nguyễn Thị Bình (1927–), the only living signatory to the Paris Agreement on Restoring Peace in Viet-Nam (1973), that Phan Châu Trinh (her maternal grandfather) had been one of his mentors in Paris during the early 1920s.

Confucian Scholars and Modernization

In Việt Nam—and I think this is also the case with all Asian countries—"modernization" is synonymous with "Westernization." Our country felt the need for Westernization in the late 1800s, after the French invasion. The few Confucian scholars who had come in contact with the outside world broke away from old concepts and advocated reforms in education and the economy. Between 1863 and 1871, Nguyễn Trường Tộ (1830–1871) proposed judicious reforms, in particular, reforms in education. "Even today," he wrote, "many people do not realize that the current situation has evolved through centuries. They admire unreservedly the ancient times, which, in their view, later epochs cannot equal. In everything they do, they want to return to the past. The experts in the Confucian doctrine of the Song Chinese Dynasty have misled our country, weakening it and undermining its ability to prosper."

However, Nguyễn Trường Tộ's appeals for renovation did not find echoes among the conservative kings and mandarins.

The French had begun their conquest in 1858 and completed it with the Treaty of Huế (Patenôtre Treaty) in 1884, when the Huế Royal Court capitulated. However, scholars launched an armed resistance, "Save the King" (Cần Vương), because their Confucian ethics identified the king with the Homeland. Their struggle lasted until the end of the century. After the French finished their military pacification, they started a program of economic exploitation (1897–1914), which they euphemistically called "bringing forth the country's value." Following World War I, this policy created two new urban social strata: a petit bourgeoisie and workers. This internal evolution alongside modernization movements in Japan and China impacted Vietnamese political thought. Some Vietnamese Confucian scholars adopted Western bourgeois concepts. The Vietnamese patriotic movement diversified into two paths: armed insurrection and socio-economic reform.

The Eastern Capital School for the Just Cause, sometimes called the Tonkin Free School (Đông Kinh Nghĩa Thục), was part of the second path; it came into being in Hà Nội in March 1907 as a private school run by modernist scholars, whose orientation was a compromise between Confucianism and Western bourgeois thought. Their long-term goal was national liberation. They looked to preserve Confucianism's moral and political doctrine with its fundamental principles, which they respected. The school's moral code emphasized loyalty to the king and filial piety, as expressed in this point: "Loyalty to the King and filial piety have the same origin. To be loyal to the King means to be pious to one's parents and vice versa." However, these scholars replaced Confucianism's image of the absolute monarch with a concept of the king as "representative of the people." The school's textbooks presented Confucian teachings, including the Master's lesson for disciples "to perfect themselves to make virtue radiate." Regardless, the movement's foremost concerns were patriotism and the struggle against colonialism, as shown in one of its patriotic songs:

> Through all five watches of the long night
> Never does love for our country leave us.

One of the movement's tracts, "Song of Exile in the Southern Sea" (Nam Hải Bô Thần Ca, sometimes called Á Tế Á Ca) openly denounced colonial extortion by relentlessly repeating lines beginning with "Taxes" to tabulate colonial exploitation. This famous treatise was attributed to several possible authors until fairly recently, when scholars examined the original text, which had been sent to Hà Nội from Japan in 1906. This examination limited the writer to one possibility—Phan Bội Châu. (For an essay on Phan Bội Châu, see p. 74.)

Scholars in this movement began to repudiate Chinese ideograms, which had been the provenance of saints and sages. That step in itself was a revolutionary act. The scholars' classes covered new subjects—hygiene, mathematics, common knowledge, civic rights, industry, and trade.

Despite these reformers' moderation, the colonial authorities viewed the school as a dangerous breeding ground for subversion. The French banned the movement in December 1907 after barely nine months of activity, and then the French dismantled the organization. They arrested the school's principal, Lương Văn Can (1854–1927), six months later but released him. In 1908, they arrested Nguyễn Quyền (1869–1941), the other key organizer, and imprisoned him at Hỏa Lò (called the Hà Nội Hilton during the American War), and then sent him to Côn Đảo (Poulo Condor) Prison Island south of Sài Gòn.

In 2010, during the thousandth anniversary of the founding of Hà Nội, Vietnamese scholar Chương Thâu highlighted the work of these patriots with publication of *The Eastern Capital School for the Just Cause and Its Literature* (Đông Kinh Nghĩa Thục và Văn Thơ Đông Kinh Nghĩa Thục) in two volumes. Each volume consisted of one thousand pages.

Buddhism in Việt Nam

The Layout of a Vietnamese Buddhist Pagoda

In a Vietnamese village, the visitor will generally see three kinds of religious buildings: the communal house (*đình*) dedicated to the community's tutelary god; the pagoda (*chùa*) reserved for Buddhist worship; and various temples, such as the *đền* for the worship of heroes or genies, the *điện* for the Taoist-tinged worship of spirits and immortals, and the *văn từ* for the worship of Confucius. The village pagoda hides behind age-old trees and is surrounded by a wall. It comprises a central building and several outbuildings. Visitors enter the grounds through a gate with three entrances (*tam quan*) topped by a bell tower. The general design of the pagoda is:

A. The central building with the main sanctuary (*tam bảo* or *chính điện*), which is preceded by a Hall of Ceremonies (*bái đường*), where rituals are conducted. The main sanctuary features rows of statues rising in tiers.

+ Nearest the roof is the first tier with the Trinity (Tam Thế) representing the Past, the Present, and the Future, or the Three Bodies of Buddha.

+ In the second tier sits Amitabha (A Di Đà) and the Buddha of Pure Land of the Western Paradise (Tịnh Độ), whose statue is even larger than that of Shakyamuni, the historical Buddha. The Buddha of Pure Land of the Western Paradise is flanked by two candidate Buddhas or Bodhisattvas (Bồ Tát).

+ From the third tier down, the arrangement of statues varies, the main ones being:

  - the historical Buddha or Shakyamuni (Thích Ca Mâu Ni), who lived in India between the sixth and fourth centuries BCE. He may be represented in several forms:

as a newborn baby surrounded by nine dragons; as an ascetic, emaciated monk sitting on Snow Mountain (Himalaya or Tuyết Sơn); or as a reclining figure resting on his left side, his head supported by his left hand on his folded left arm (Entering Nirvana).

- the Bodhisattva Maitreya (Di Lặc), the future successor of Shakyamuni, represented as a fat man with a bare chest and a happy smile showing that he is free from human cares and worries

- the female Bodhisattva Avalokitesvara (Quan Âm or Quan Thế Âm), the Goddess of Mercy. She is represented standing at the side of Amitabha or sitting by herself as a deity "with a thousand eyes and a thousand arms"

- the Guardian Spirit of the Land of the Pagoda, who may also be placed in the Hall of Ceremonies

- the Taoist deities, who somehow stray into the pagoda: the Emperor of Heaven (Ngọc Hoàng), the Nam Tào (presiding at births), and Bắc Đẩu (presiding at deaths)

- eight Vajrapanis (Kim Cương), the terror of evil spirits

B. The outbuildings:

+ Side buildings: Here, there are sixteen to eighteen statues of arhats (Buddhist monks who have not attained Nirvana) and representations of scenes in Hell, where wrongdoers are judged by magistrates and tortured by demons. There may be figures representing the Ten Kings of Hell.

+ Back buildings: These are reserved for the cult of Buddhist leaders, among them Bodhidharma (Bồ Đề Đạt Ma, with Indian features, a beard and a dark complexion) as well as for the worship of deceased abbots from the pagoda and various spirits and immortals (*chư vị*), including the divine mother goddesses (*mẫu*) from popular beliefs tinged with Taoism. Here, there are also little shrines installed by people for their deceased parents against payment of a certain sum (*hậu*). The back buildings also house the monks' living quarters.

The Buddhist Goddess of Mercy

In one of his letters, my late friend, German journalist Erwin Borchers (a.k.a. Chiến Sĩ or Militant), told me of a comment made by Goethe, that a man of culture should begin his day by contemplating a work of art. During his time in Việt Nam, Borchers meditated every morning before a plaster reproduction of the statue of Bodhisattva Avalokitesvara (Quan Âm) of One Thousand Eyes and One Thousand Arms, which was housed at Bút Tháp Pagoda in the Red River Delta's Bắc Ninh Province. The Fine Arts Museum in Hà Nội has a plaster cast of this masterpiece. Louis Bezacier (1906–1966), a French expert on Vietnamese art, attributes the original to the 1600s.

Of all the women's faces I've observed in Việt Nam, none surpasses the beauty of the Quan Âm sculpture that captivated my friend. Its regular features, half-closed eyes, and chaste lips create the impression of womanly gentleness and Buddhist serenity. Further, the hair tied into a knot looks quite modern. The Goddess Quan Âm (Kwan Yin in Chinese and Kannon in Japanese) was called Avalokitesvara in Sanskrit and Lokeshvara in the ancient Khmer and Chăm Pa Empires. "*Quan Âm*" literally means "attentive to all sounds," which is to say, "sensitive to any complaints from mortals." A *Quan Âm* is a Bodhisattva or a future Buddha. This deity has a masculine nature in India, the country of origin, but became feminine through metamorphosis in the Far East. Quan Âm sits on a giant lotus supported by a dragon, a positive symbol in Việt Nam. The dragon's head and paws appear among undulating waves.

Why is Quan Âm represented with one thousand eyes and one thousand arms?

Some people say this shows her incessant activity and vigilance, while others argue this better equips her to fight demons. Bodhisattva Quan Âm is wrongly called the Buddhist Virgin Mary. As Goddess of Mercy, she is believed to be in attendance when a child is born. Sterile women turn to her, seeking fertility. Every spring, they make pilgrimages to the famous Perfume Pagoda (Chùa Hương) near Hà Nội, which has grottos dedicated to Quan Âm. There, they stroke any stalactites, stalagmites, or rocks resembling a child's head.

The Bearded Indian in Vietnamese Village Pagodas

Việt Nam's major ethnic group, the Việt, lives mainly in tens of thousands of villages in the plains. These villages, the nation's repositories of its culture, all have one or two Buddhist pagodas.

A pagoda may have several structures. The central building is shaped like an inverted T. The hall of ceremonies (*bái đường*) is the horizontal top of the T, while the principle sanctuary (*chính điện* or *tam bảo*) is the vertical stem. The main sanctuary houses the idols in the pantheon of Mahayana Buddhism (School of the Great Vehicle), which is widely practiced in China, Japan, Korea, and Việt Nam. The most common among the statues are Amitabha (A Di Đà, Buddha of the Infinite Light), Shakyamuni (Thích Ca, the historic Buddha), Maitreya (Di Lặc, Buddha of the Future), and Guanyin (Quan Âm, Goddess of Compassion). It should be noted that Buddhism's metaphysical nature does not admit the existence of divinities since everything is only *maya* or illusion. Thus, originally, Buddhism denounced all forms of idolatry.

In addition to the central building, the pagoda has a Chapel Room of the Patriarchs (*nhà tổ*) for worship of the deceased bonzes who lived in the pagoda. However, there is always a statue or picture of a patriarch with bronze complexion and a beard.

Who is he?

The female clergy (*chư bà*) and the elderly faithful (*già lam*) often visit pagodas, but they are at a loss for an answer.

The bearded patriarch is, in fact, the Indian Bodhidharma, or Bồ Đề Đạt Ma in Vietnamese and Ta Mo (Patriarch of the West) in Chinese. His presence is rather curious on the altar where the rest of the patriarchs are Vietnamese. Ordinary Vietnamese feel closer to the Buddha statues in the central building because, despite their Indian origin, these statues appear more Sinicized and therefore look more Vietnamese than the patriarch in the Chapel Room.

Bodhidharma (470–543), an Indian Buddhist master, was founder of Chinese Chan Buddhism (also called Zen or Dhyana Buddhism and known in Vietnamese as Thiền) and the twenty-eighth patriarch after Shakayamuni. A scion of a Brahmin royal dynasty in South India, he left for Canton (now Guangzhou), China when he was sixty at the bidding of his master, Prajnadhara. Bodhidharma was the guest in Nanking of Emperor Liang Wu Ti (life: 464–549; reign: 502–549) of the Liang Dynasty (502–557). He realized that Wu Ti was not interested in propagating Buddhism. According to legend, Bodhidharma crossed the Yangtze River on a leaf, went north, and took up residence at Shaolin Temple. He spent nine years meditating before the wall of a cave. Only then did the image of the way to Chan Buddhism emerge.

Chan Buddhism is a mixture of India's Dhyana Buddhism and Chinese Taoism. Chan meditation draws from the philosophic and religious thoughts of ancient India but was shaped by the Chinese school of Bodhidharma, which in turn had been heavily influenced by the Sutra (religious book) of the Buddha and techniques to attain Enlightenment. In Japanese pagodas, Bodhidharma is worshipped in a special room with an oil lamp, which is always kept lit. Bodhidharma advocated transcontemplation until Enlightenment.

The message of Bodhidharma might be summarized as a special transmission outside the Scriptures, no dependence on words, directly pointing to the human mind, looking into oneself, and attaining Buddhahood.

Mount Yên Tử: The Cradle of Vietnamese Zen

Lines from oral folk poetry (*ca dao*) tell us:

> Whoever has decided to adopt the faith of Buddha
> Will find peace of mind only after visiting Yên Tử.

On a bright winter morning in 2002, local people and visiting dignitaries held an inauguration ceremony for Lân Pagoda and the Zen Bamboo Forest (Trúc Lâm) Ashram at Yên Tử Mountain in Quảng Ninh, Việt Nam's coastal province along the border with China. Lân Pagoda, named for the hill on which it stands, is an important link in the eleven Buddhist pagodas from the mountain's foot to its summit (elevation: 1,068 meters). Work on this pagoda had begun during the 1200s. Atop the peak is the famous Chùa Đồng (Bronze Pagoda), which was built in the 1600s or 1700s but was destroyed. In 1930, it was replaced by a concrete pagoda and then by a bronze version in 1933.

Yên Tử Mountain, which is part of the Đông Triều Mountain Range, is about a hundred kilometers east of Hà Nội and fifty kilometers west of Hạ Long Bay. In the past, many medicinal plants grew on Yên Tử Mountain. During the third century BCE, Taoist priest An Kỳ Sinh, also known as Master Yên Tử, gathered medicinal herbs, which he made widely available. Some people think he may have also been a Chinese magician and geomancer. In gratitude for his cures, local people called him An Tử Master, hence the mountain's name, Yên (An) Tử.

During the Trần Dynasty (1225–1400), Yên Tử Mountain became particularly famous as a Buddhist sanctuary because of King Trần Nhân Tông (life: 1258–1308; reign: 1278–1293), who was a hero from our Wars Against the Mongols as well as a diplomat, poet, Buddhist theologian, and one of the most endearing figures in our history and culture.

By the mid-1200s, the Mongol Empire stretched from Beijing to the Volga. In 1285, Mongol Prince Toghan (Thoát Hoan, ? – c. 1301), son of Mongol Emperor Kublai Khan (1215–1294), invaded

Việt Nam with five hundred thousand troops. The Vietnamese employed a strategic withdrawal and then launched a guerrilla war. Then, after some months, the Vietnamese staged a counteroffensive and routed the Mongols. However, in 1287, another half million Mongols invaded Việt Nam, this time with a formidable river fleet. The Vietnamese enticed the Mongols up the Bạch Đằng River near Hạ Long Bay and ambushed them. The Mongols fled, only to impale their ships at low tide on stakes the Vietnamese had hidden in the river. King Trần Nhân Tông was present at that decisive Vietnamese victory in 1288. He was thirty years old. Five years later, he retired to a monastery at Yên Tử, where he founded the Bamboo Forest Zen Buddhist sect (Trúc Lâm Thiền). Trần Nhân Tông named his sect after the magnificent Yên Tử bamboo groves.

Buddhism had been introduced into Việt Nam during the third centruy CE. Its form and nature were closer to Chinese Buddhism than to Indian Buddhism. The Zen (Thiền, Dhyana) sect is one of ten Chinese Buddhist sects. Before Trần Nhân Tông, Việt Nam had known three Thiền schools with three founders: Vinitaruci (?–594), an Indian monk who came from China in the 500s; Wu Yan Tong (Vô Ngôn Thông, c. 759–826), a Chinese monk who arrived in the 800s; and Thảo Đường (Chinese name not known, ?–?), a Chinese monk whom a Lý king brought from Chăm Pa in the 1000s.

Trần Nhân Tông's Bamboo Forest sect teaches the immanence of Buddha and introduces special techniques of meditation to achieve enlightenment. It advocates intuitive rather than discursive intelligence without taking the sacred scriptures into consideration and suggests that by watching clouds float by, one can comprehend the Buddhist concept of Being and Non-Being.

Trần Nhân Tông's extant works include *In a Community of Bonzes* (Tăng Già Toái Sự) and two poetry books, *Collected Poems about the Great Perfume Sea* (Đại Hương Hải Ấn Thi Tập) and *Collected Poems by Trần Nhân Tông* (Trần Nhân Tông Thi Tập). Trần Nhân Tông's quatrain, "Spring Discerned" (Xuân Hiểu), an early poem written with Chinese ideograms (*Hán*) in five-word meter, is particularly famous:

Awakening, I open the window,
Spring arrived without my knowledge.
A pair of white butterflies
Flutters about among the flowers.

Exemplary Vietnamese

The Trưng Sisters (Hai Bà Trưng)

The Chinese conquest of Việt Nam was in 111 BCE.

Old annals say that the rebellion led by Trưng Trắc (?–43 CE) was a response to the assassination by Chinese Pro-Consul Su Ting (Tô Định) of Trưng Trắc's husband, Thi Sách. In 40 CE, Trưng Trắc, the daughter of a Vietnamese lord, raised the standard of revolt, assisted by her younger sister, Trưng Nhị, and Lạc lords. Trưng Trắc's troops stormed sixty-five Chinese-occupied citadels. Su Ting, the cruel Chinese proconsul, fled. Trưng Trắc proclaimed herself queen. However, in 41 CE, the Chinese Royal Court sent battle-hardened General Ma Yuan (Mã Viện) against Queen Trưng Trắc. After winning several battles, the Trưng Sisters were defeated. They died in 43 CE. That much is historical fact. Legend has it that the sisters drowned themselves in the Hát River in Hà Tây Province, now a district of Hà Nội.

The story of the Trưng Sisters is engraved on the minds and hearts of all Vietnamese. The sisters were symbols of patriotism during French colonialism and during the American War, just as they were during Chinese domination.

What is the origin of the Vietnamese veneration and affection that makes the Trưng Sisters unique among Vietnamese heroes of national independence?

First, timing. The Trưng Sisters were the first historical (as opposed to legendary) heroes to use armed force to assert national identity for the Việt of the Red River Delta. Second, they were women. At that time, matriarchy had not yet disappeared under patriarchal Chinese rule. The popular imagination blazes with the image of these two women taking arms to avenge Trưng Trắc's husband. Yet the Vietnamese combatants were not only the two sisters but also their mother and the sisters' female commanders, whose names appear in historical records.

Hà Nội and three neighboring provinces have two hundred temples dedicated to the Trưng Sisters. According to legend, when Trưng Trắc and Trưng Nhị threw themselves into the Hát River, their bodies floated downstream as far as Đồng Nhân (now part of Hà Nội), where villagers erected a temple in their honor. A flood ruined that temple, which was moved in 1819 to Đồng Nhân Village, now Hà Nội's Đồng Nhân Street. Each year, local residents organize a festival to honor the Trưng Sisters at Đồng Nhân Temple on the Third Day of the Fifth Lunar Month.

Lady Triệu (Bà Triệu)

In ancient Vietnamese society, which had been strongly marked by Confucianism, daughters of orthodox families bound their breasts so people of good breeding would not brand them as indecent. The very use of the world "breast" (*vú*) was taboo. However, even the most prudish did not hesitate to mention the voluminous breasts of national heroine Lady Triệu (225– 248 CE). Confucian scholar Phan Điện (late 1800s) wrote these lines in a eulogy, using seven-word meter:

> The enemy arrived, she had to fight
> Flag raised, breasts tossing, her elephant charging.

> *Phải đánh vì chúng giặc đến nhà,*
> *Phất cờ, vắt vú, cưỡi voi ra.*

Popular imagination crystallized around this image, which is part history, part legend. Lady Triệu (Triệu Ấu, with "Ấu" being an old Vietnamese form of address for esteemed elders) was born Triệu Thị Trinh or Triệu Trinh Nương in the mountainous region of Quân Yên (in modern-day Thanh Hóa Province). Orphaned as an infant, she lived with her brother, Triệu Quốc Đạt, a local chieftain. She was spirited, independent, and skilled in martial arts. At age twenty, she could not bear her cantankerous sister-in-law and fled to the forest. Her brother urged her to marry, but she replied, "I want to ride the tempests, tame the waves, and behead the sharks in the East Sea. I want to exterminate the enemy, protect our borders, and save our people from the misery of slavery. I do not want a life of bowing my head and bending my back as a concubine." This determination so impressed Lady Triệu's brother that he joined her insurrectionist army to fight the Chinese invaders.

By the mid third century CE, the Chinese had subjugated Việt Nam for nearly five centuries. The Wu rulers' colonial policy was particularly harsh. The Vietnamese paid triple taxes—tributes to the Chinese Royal Court as well as taxes to the local Chinese administration and the local Chinese military apparatus. In addition, the Chinese demanded forced labor from the peasants. A separatist revolt plotted by a former Chinese Governor, Shi Xie (Sĩ Nhiếp), provided a pretext for the bloody Chinese repression that killed tens of thousands of Vietnamese and exiled thousands more to China as slaves to build a new Wu capital.

Lady Triệu's insurrection broke out in 248 CE. Supported by the population, she assaulted one Chinese post after another, forcing the enemy to flee. The Wu soldiers said to each other, "It's easier to defend oneself with a lance against a tiger than to confront the 'Queen.'" Then the Wu sent General Lu Yin against Lady Triệu. Legend has it that the Chinese general ordered his men to advance stark naked. This shameless offence caused Lady Triệu and her soldiers to recoil. She took her own life on Tùng Sơn Mountain. Her grave lies on the mountain's peak, while a temple devoted to her stands at its foot in Hậu Lộc District, Thanh Hóa Province.

Lý Thường Kiệt

The given name of Lý Thường Kiệt (1019–1105), a brilliant general, is Ngô Tuấn (Tuấn of the Ngô clan), but in recognition of his military exploits, he received permission to use the family name of the Lý Royal Dynasty (1009–1225). As a young man, Lý Thường

Kiệt showed a passion for literary studies and martial arts. At age twenty-three, he became a eunuch mandarin (*nội giám*). A great strategist inspired by ardent patriotism, he served three kings. In 1069, at age fifty (a very old age in those days), he commanded an expedition against the turbulent kingdom of Chăm Pa to establish peace on Việt Nam's southern frontier. He secured Vietnamese authority over the territories (present-day Quảng Bình and Quảng Trị Provinces) that Chăm Pa had ceded, thereby advancing Viet Nam's southward expansion.

However, Lý Thường Kiệt's reputation rests primarily on his victories over the Chinese Song (Tống) aggressors.

The Việt formed their first state during the first millennium BCE, but then the Chinese empire annexed the Việt state for more than a thousand years, until 938 CE. During the following seventy years, short-lived Vietnamese dynasties failed to establish national stability. Only beginning in the 1000s did the Lý Dynasty and then the Trần Dynasty (1225–1400) consolidate national independence, build a prosperous country, and endow it with Thăng Long Culture. Indeed, "Thăng Long" (Rising Dragon) is an old name for Hà Nội.

However, the Song Chinese Royal Court would not renounce its claims on Việt Nam. Prime Minister Wang An Shi prepared a great expedition to rob Việt Nam of its wealth. In 1075, General Lý Thường Kiệt was regent for the ten-year-old Lý king, Lý Nhân Tông (life: 1066–1127; reign: 1072–1127). Lý Thường Kiệt launched a preemptive attack against the Song with two armies totaling a hundred thousand men. One army under Tôn Đản, a chief from the Nùng ethnic minority, approached by sea and attacked several Chinese districts. The other army under Lý Thường Kiệt traveled overland and won support from the many Chinese unhappy with Wang An Shi's reforms.

Lý Thường Kiệt withdrew after destroying the bases the Chinese army had established for its invasion. The Song Royal Court prepared a counter-offensive, forming a coalition with the Chăm and Khmer kingdoms. In 1077, Chinese troops crossed the border and reached the northern bank of the Như Nguyệt (Sông Cầu) River about thirty kilometers northeast of Hà Nội. Lý Thường Kiệt waited on the southern bank. The bitter fighting that ensued prevented the Chinese from crossing the river. Decimated by tropical diseases, the Chinese made peace in return for Vietnamese cessation of five border districts, which the Việt took back two years later.

Hoàng Xuân Hãn (1908–1996), author of a book on Lý Thường Kiệt, notes:

> There is unanimity in attributing to Lý Thường Kiệt extraordinary merits with regard to the destiny of our nation—the expansion of our territory to the north and the south, the victorious struggle against foreign invasions, and the consolidation of our frontiers. All this led to respect from our neighbors. . . . Lý Thường Kiệt knew how to overcome force by surprise, oppose his strong points against the enemy's weak points, pitch his well-rested troops against the enemy's weary soldiers, apply patience to arrogance, and, particularly, how to rely on our people's determination to survive.

The following stanza from "Mountains and Rivers of the Empire of the South" (Nam Quốc Sơn Hà) in seven-word meter contains the only extant lines by Lý Thường Kiệt:

> The Southern King rules the Southern Land
> As the Book of Heaven has recorded.
> How dare you strangers invade our land?
> Waiting, you will see your army annihilated.

Legend has it that Lý Thường Kiệt boosted morale with a clever ruse in the battle on the Như Nguyệt River, when the odds were against the Việt troops. A man with a stentorian voice secretly entered a nearby shrine dedicated to a national hero. The cantor shouted the lines above, making them sound like a supernatural voice. This terrified the enemy and galvanized the Việts.

Many regard this quatrain as Việt Nam's first written Declaration of Independence. The second Declaration of Independence is "The Proclamation of Victory over the Ngô [Ming Chinese]"

(Bình Ngô Đại Cáo), which Nguyễn Trãi wrote in 1427. (For essays on Nguyễn Trãi, see p. 102 and p. 137.) The third Declaration of Independence is the one written by Hồ Chí Minh and read by President Hồ on September 2, 1945.

Chu Văn An: Spiritual Master

The name Chu Văn An is frequently heard on Hà Nội's streets because there is a Chu Văn An Street (called Van Vollenhoven during French colonialism), which runs between the Ministry of Foreign Affairs and the Temple to Confucius (Temple of Literature). Chu Văn An is the only Vietnamese scholar to have his own altar in that temple. Chu Văn An High School on the bank of West Lake is Hà Nội's most prestigious school and is comparable to Lycée Henry IV or Louis le Grand in Paris.

The reputation of Chu Văn An (1212–1270) as a model master-teacher and as symbol of intransigence about moral uprightness has radiated across the centuries. Generations of Confucian scholars praised his broad knowledge of the humanities and his unrestrained contempt for riches and honors.

Born in Quang Liệt Commune of Hà Tây Province, Chu Văn An devoted his life to education. While still young, he opened a school in his native village to train disciples, including Phạm Sư Mạnh (?–?, a talented diplomat, administrator, and military man) and Lê Quát (famous for his erudition and moral qualities). After Chu Văn An earned his doctorate (*thái học sinh*) in the mandarin examinations, King Trần Minh Tông (life: 1300–1357; reign:1314–1329), one of Chu Văn An's former students, appointed him vice-rector of the Royal College for Sons of the Nation (Quốc Tử Giám), Việt Nam's first university. The Royal College, which predates the Sorbonne by two centuries, was founded in 1076 within the walls of the Temple for Confucius. Initially, the university was to serve princes, but then opened to mandarins' sons chosen by the king and eventually opened to students from a wider social range.

During the reign of King Trần Dụ Tông (life: 1336–1369; reign: 1341–1369), Chu Văn An submitted a motion for the execution of seven mandarins, who were flatterers and instigators of court plots. When his request was denied, he withdrew to Chí Linh District (Hải Dương Province), where he lived as a hermit until his death.

Chu Văn An wrote many works in Chinese *Hán* script, including *Abridged Commentaries on the Four Classical Books* (Tứ Thư Thuyết Ước) and *Poems by a Hermit Woodcutter* (Tiều Ẩn Thi Tập). He also wrote *Poems in the National Language by a Hermit Woodcutter* (Tiều Ẩn Quốc Ngữ Thi Tập), where "*Quốc Ngữ*" (National Language) as used here refers to *Nôm*, the Vietnamese ideographic script. Only a dozen of his poems in Chinese script have survived, including these two, the first in seven-word meter and the second in six-word, eight-word meter.

In the Beginning of Summer (Đầu Hạ)

Awakening in serenity at my hilltop house,
Breezes rustle the japonica in the courtyard.
Cicadas raise new voices, one following another,
Swallows flock back to their old nests.
Lotus dotting the stream show noble comportment,
Bamboo penetrating the fence show brilliant talent.
The lazy phoenix lingers on the paulownia,
Breezes rumple my book on the bookstand.

Honoring Chí Linh Mountain (Vịnh Cảnh Núi Chí Linh)

Hills like images painted on a screen,
Evening bathes half the river in light.
No one travels on the grassy paths,
A magpie's lone call haunts the mist.

Trần Hưng Đạo

Trần Hưng Đạo (1228–1300), victor over the Mongol invaders, is among Việt Nam's most illustrious military leaders. The Mongol tribes lived in Central Asia north of China and south of Siberia. These warlike nomads united under Genghis Khan (c. 1162–1227), conquered country after country, and established an empire stretching from Asia to Europe. Nothing could stop their powerful and intrepid cavalry. Genghis Khan's descendants failed in Japan in 1281, when a typhoon destroyed their fleet, and they failed in Việt Nam in 1258, 1285, and 1288 because of national resistance led by Trần Hưng Đạo.

Following Genghis Khan's conquest of northern China, his grandson, Kublai Khan (1215–1294), wanted to pursue even farther-flung conquests. In 1252, he demanded that the Việt let his troops pass through their country so he could penetrate China from the south. The Trần king refused. A Mongol army invaded and set Thăng Long (Hà Nội), Việt Nam's capital, afire after the Royal Court and the population had fled. However, Vietnamese troops cut the invaders' supply lines; before long, Việt Nam's harsh climate wreaked havoc among the Mongol troops. The Vietnamese launched a counter-offensive and forced the Mongols to withdraw.

The Vietnamese foiled two subsequent Mongol invasions in 1285 and 1288. After completing the conquest of China, the Mongols pushed southward toward Southeast Asia by occupying Việt Nam and then Chăm Pa. A Sino-Mongol army of five hundred thousand men under Mongol Prince Toghan (Thoát Hoan, ? – c. 1301), son of Mongol Emperor Kublai Khan, demanded passage through Việt Nam to attack Chăm Pa. Facing another Vietnamese refusal, the Sino-Mongol army swept into Việt Nam. Vietnamese General Trần Hưng Đạo undertook a strategic withdrawal. King Trần Nhân Tông (life: 1258–1308; reign: 1278–1293) wanted to surrender to spare his people terrible miseries, but Trần Hưng Đạo begged the king, saying, "If such is Your will, then behead me first."

Trần Hưng Đạo galvanized the people into stiff resistance; the Vietnamese drove out the invaders after six months of combat. Thirsting for revenge, Toghan staged a comeback with three hundred thousand men and a fleet of five hundred vessels. Again, Toghan managed to occupy large tracts of our country. Once again, the Mongols torched Thăng Long, our capital, but in 1288

Trần Hưng Đạo defeated the Mongols in a resounding victory on the Bạch Đằng River. He did so by repeating the strategy that Ngô Quyền had used at Bạch Đằng against the Southern Hán Chinese Dynasty in 938 CE. Trần Hưng Đạo's troops set pointed stakes in the Bạch Đằng Estuary, enticed the Mongol armada upstream and over the hidden stakes during high tide, and then ambushed the Mongol fleet. The Mongol armada fled downstream only to be trapped by the stakes revealed at low tide. The waiting Việt staged their second ambush, achieving victory.

More than seven centuries have passed. Trần Hưng Đạo resides in the hearts of the Vietnamese who have deified him. They worship him in public shrines and private homes. Popular beliefs have made Trần Hưng Đạo a demigod with miraculous powers. Women pray to him for protection against miscarriages and painful delivery caused by Demon Nhan. According to folk belief, Demon Nhan was a Mongol prisoner sentenced to death, but after each decapitation, his head grew back. Finally, Trần Hưng Đạo's magic sword squelched Phạm Nhan's demonic powers. Out of revenge, Nhan's vindictive ghost seeks to harm women at their time of delivery.

Many households have altars to Trần Hưng Đạo, who is believed to terrorize evil spirits in general and the demons of epidemics in particular. As a god with great powers, Trần Hưng Đạo is among the popular Taoist pantheon receiving special worship. The priests officiating in these rituals are male mediums (*ông đồng*, *thanh đồng*), whom family members invite to cure a man who has fallen ill. The medium goes into a trance and pierces his own cheeks with a pointed metal stick to cut his tongue. He collects the blood trickling from his wounds and smears it on amulets for the sick man to wear. Or the medium burns the amulets and has the patient swallow the ashes. The ill man enters a sleep-like trance and then starts slapping his face, beating himself with a rod, or striking himself with a mallet. All this, it is hoped, will drive evil spirits from his body. The center of this spiritualistic exorcism is Kiếp Bạc (Hải Dương Province east of Hà Nội), the site of a resistance base during General Trần Hưng Đạo's battles against the

Mongols. Each year, on the Twentieth Day of the Eighth Lunar Month, large numbers of pilgrims and priests attend a ceremony at Kiếp Bạc Shrine.

So great are Trần Hưng Đạo's supernatural powers in the minds of the populace that he often replaces the Chinese demigod Guan Yu (Kuan Yu, Quan Vũ, or Quan Công, 160–219), a famous Chinese warrior and a symbol of loyalty and uprightness. Such is the case at Ngọc Sơn Temple on an islet in Hà Nội's Lake of the Restored Sword, where Trần Hưng Đạo is worshipped.

Nguyễn Trãi: Việt Nam's Greatest Humanist?

Traditional Western humanism centers on the person as an individual, while in the East, which is characterized by Confucianism and the rural community's communal spirit, traditional humanism focuses more on the person as a social being. Considering this difference, who would be the "greatest Vietnamese humanist?"

Several names come to mind: poet-educator Chu Văn An (1292–1370), poet-statesman-strategist Nguyễn Trãi (1380–1442), poet-sage Nguyễn Bỉnh Khiêm (1491–1585), scholar-official Ngô Thì Nhậm (1746–1803), and Nguyễn Du (1766–1820), author of Việt Nam's national epic.

Among these notables, Nguyễn Trãi is prominent.

Most people consider Nguyễn Trãi—eminent statesman, famous strategist, skillful diplomat, scholar, and poet—as Việt Nam's greatest humanist. He also approaches Western humanism's norms. Nguyễn Trãi's thought may be epitomized in two words—"humanity" and "justice." Throughout his life, he worked toward those ideals for his people. In 1980, UNESCO (United Nations Educational, Scientific, and Cultural Organization) sponsored an international commemoration of Nguyễn Trãi's sixth centenary. Director General of UNESCO Amadou-Mahtar M'Bow highlighted Nguyễn Trãi's humanist vision.

I can't help drawing parallels between Nguyễn Trãi and Hồ Chí Minh regarding their attitudes toward the enemy and prisoners of war. First, let us place Nguyễn Trãi in historical context. In the early 1400s, when the Chinese Ming occupied Việt Nam, Nguyễn Trãi aided Lê Lợi during a ten-year resistance war (1418–1428), which the Việt waged from their base in the Lam Sơn Mountains in Thanh Hóa Province. Victorious, Lê Lợi (life: 1385–1433; reign: 1428–1433) founded the Lê Dynasty (1428–1788).

On behalf of Lê Lợi, Nguyễn Trãi wrote appeals to the invaders, the insurgents, and the population. These documents reveal Nguyễn Trãi's strategy—conquer the adversary's heart—as one among the three simultaneous strategic initiatives—political, military, and diplomatic—needed to achieve national independence. The Vietnamese used this tri-partite approach during the French War and the American War.

During the Ming invasion, Nguyễn Trãi wanted to persuade enemy soldiers that their military campaigns were doomed. He appealed to their respect for justice by highlighting the rights of a weaker people, and he spoke to their humanism by emphasizing the need to curtail both sides' losses. His initiative was not psychological war as conceived today but, rather, a strategy urging the adversary to end an unjust war. This extract from "New Letter to Vương Thông" (Tái Dụ Vương Thông Thư) reveals Nguyễn Trãi's thought. Vương Thông was the Ming Chinese commander-in-chief. In this text, "Southern Empire" refers to Việt Nam:

> . . . Placing myself in your position, I find six reasons for your imminent defeat:

> The floods are rising, your ramparts are crumbling, your food is running out, your horses are dying, and your men are falling ill—that's your first defeat.

> . . . By now, our most difficult mountain passes all have our soldiers and generals posted to block you. If your reinforcements arrive, they'll meet certain defeat. With your reinforcements defeated, your remaining troops will have no place to flee—that's your second defeat.

Your country has strong troops and healthy horses, but they are now all at your northern border, defending your country against the Yuan and leaving you no means to fight us in the Southern Empire—that's your third defeat.

You have fomented constant war and punitive expeditions against smaller nations, thereby overburdening your own people and driving them into restless despair—that's your fourth defeat.

Dishonest mandarins in your administration hold the power, your sovereign is too weak to rule, while your mandarins fight and destroy one another, leaving your royal family vulnerable to change—that's your fifth defeat.

I have raised our just cause with my men. From top to bottom, we are united and ready to try our heroic best. Our troops and officers are better trained every day, and their weapons are ever sharper. Our soldiers and officers both plow our fields and fight our enemies, while your troops are besieged inside their citadels, where they grow more and more exhausted and are destined to perish—that's your sixth defeat.

Those six paragraphs might have been signed by Hồ Chí Minh. They express the essence of the people's war that the Vietnamese conducted against the French and the Americans.

Nguyễn Trãi's view of war was imbued with humanity as shown in these opening lines from "The Proclamation of Victory over the Ngô [Ming]" (Bình Ngô Đại Cáo):

Everyone, listen:
A just cause: first, peace for the people,
Our warriors' focus is to prevent violence,
As in our Great Việt since ancient times.

Nguyễn Trãi's strategy for conquering his adversaries' hearts reminds me of the philosophy of Mahatma Gandhi, whom Hồ Chí Minh admired. In Nguyễn Trãi's view, the capture of citadels was important, but no less important was making the invader ashamed of his warring actions and giving the adversary a face-saving way out of war. The aim of a war of liberation, as he tells us in this excerpt from "Ode to Mount Chí Linh" (Chí Linh Sơn Phú), written in six-word meter, is to end war between two countries:

> An upright master does not massacre,
> His virtue is great, as is his kindness.
> He thinks of protecting his nation forever,
> Releasing a hundred thousand prisoners,
> Re-establishing peace between two nations,
> Ending war for ten thousand generations,
> To secure national sovereignty and security.

After the war, Nguyễn Trãi continued to devote himself to the people's well-being. Alas, this high-minded man was the victim of a plot hatched by jealous courtiers. He was beheaded in 1442, along with his entire extended family. Twenty years later, Lê Lợi's grandson, King Lê Thánh Tông (life: 1442–1497; reign: 1460–1497), rehabilitated Nguyễn Trãi's reputation by announcing that the famous poet-statesman had been falsely accused.

Lê Lợi and Lam Kinh, Capital of an Ancient Kingdom

It's late on an April afternoon. The tropical sun slants over a corner of the forest. Age-old banyans with their knotty branches draping, entangling like snakes, dominate the landscape. Around this forest, within a radius of a thousand meters, lie scattered steles, graves, temples, and palace ruins. History and nostalgia float in the air, leading me to recall verses by Mme. Thanh Quan (For an essay on Mme. Thanh Quan, see p. 143), the eighteenth-century woman poet who mourned the ruins of Thăng Long, the royal capital of the Soaring Dragon in "Nostalgia for Thăng Long" (Thăng Long Hoài Cổ):

Time has swiftly flown, consigned to mist,
Horse-cart paths have turned into grassy wisps,
Former palace grounds rest in the twilight.

Lam Kinh in Thanh Hóa Province, which is about two hundred kilometers southwest of Hà Nội, evokes the vicissitudes of the lights and shadows of more than three hundred years of the Lê Dynasty (1428–1788). Its founding sovereign was Lê Lợi, later known as King Lê Thái Tổ (life: 1385–1433; reign: 1428–1433), a native of Lam Sơn (Thọ Xuân District, Thanh Hóa Province). He is a Vietnamese national hero because he successfully led ten years of resistance against a Chinese Ming regime marked by brutal exploitation, repression, heavy taxes, monopolization of the salt trade, slavery, forced resettlement of Vietnamese intellectuals and artists in China, and destruction of national cultural treasures, including books.

Lê Lợi, a land-owner in Lam Kinh (Xuân Lam Commune, Thọ Xuân District, Thanh Hóa Province), and a thousand followers rose up against the Chinese Ming. Following their victory, Lê Lợi established himself in the old capital of Thăng Long (Soaring Dragon), now Hà Nội, which was also called "Đông Kinh" (Royal Capital of the East), written exactly like "Tokyo" in the Chinese script. Lê Lợi built another citadel in Lam Kinh, which became known as "Tây Kinh" (Royal Capital of the West). He located the Tây Kinh Citadel on hilly terrain, with the Chu River to the north and flanked on the east and west by mountains, in accordance with the principles of geomancy for earth, wind, and water.

The Lam Kinh Citadel was re-built three times, the first after a fire caused by the Mạc usurpers in 1448, the second after destruction by rebel troops in 1788, and the third in 1994 with a systematic restoration through an initial investment of US $2 million. Only a few traces of ramparts and trenches remain to indicate where King Lê Thế Tông (life: 1567–1599; reign: 1573–1599) received the first

Catholic missionaries, who were led by Spaniard Pedro Ordonez de Cavallos in 1590.

A few stone foundations near the banyan forest hint at the former splendor of Lam Kinh Palace and the staircase decorated by the two rows of statues of mandarins, elephants, tigers, and rhinos that led to King Lê Lợi's tomb. Six kings and two queens are buried at the site. Nearby is the restored pavilion sheltering Vĩnh Lăng, one of the largest and most beautiful stone stele in Việt Nam. Nguyễn Trãi, the great humanist-strategist-poet, wrote the text summarizing King Lê Lợi's life and contributions.

Quang Trung and His Unfulfilled Vision

The legend of King Quang Trung (life: 1753–1792; reign: 1788–1792) has haunted Vietnamese memory for many generations, especially during the French colonial occupation and the American War. Quang Trung was deeply mourned at his premature death after only a few years of rule, for he had already shown abilities as a great general, a clear-sighted reformer, a well-advised politician, and a skillful diplomat. Early death robbed the Vietnamese people of a farsighted sovereign.

Born in 1753 in Tây Sơn Village, Bình Định Province in central Việt Nam, Nguyễn Huệ (Quang Trung) grew up when the country was partitioned. From the middle of the 1500s, the Trịnh lords had ruled the North, while the Nguyễn lords ruled the South, including Bình Định Province in the nation's center. (For a definition of "North" and "South" during this period of Việt Nam's history, see p. 9.) The Trịnh and the Nguyễn both claimed the mandate of the Lê kings, who reigned without ruling in their capital, Thăng Long (modern-day Hà Nội).

The story is confusing because two warring factions had the same family name, Nguyễn, the most common family name in Việt Nam.

The Lê feudal regime was in crisis. In 1771, three brothers— Nguyễn Nhạc (1753–1793, a petty functionary), Nguyễn Huệ (a.k.a. Quang Trung), and Nguyễn Lữ (1754–1787)—from Tây Sơn Village launched a peasants' insurrection, which eventually spread across the South, giving the brothers power. Then Nguyễn Ánh, a descendant of the Nguyễn lords in the South, appealed for help to the Siamese (modern-day Thai) monarch, who responded with twenty thousand troops and three hundred warships. Nguyễn Huệ lured the Siamese armada into an ambush on the Mỹ Tho River in the Mekong Delta in 1785, trouncing the Siamese. Two thousand Siamese troops survived and fled overland.

The Tây Sơn Brothers then turned to fight the northern Trịnh, who had taken advantage of the brothers' battle with the Siamese to seize Huế. In 1786, Nguyễn Huệ crossed the Pass of the Clouds (Đèo Hải Vân), occupied Huế, and, with support from the population, set out for the North, where he ended the Trịnh lords' regime. Nguyễn Huệ paid homage to King Lê Hiển Tông (life: 1717–1786; reign: 1740–1786), who gave Nguyễn Huệ one of his daughters in marriage. Then, while Nguyễn Huệ was on his way back to the South, the king's son, Lê Chiêu Thống (life: 1765–1793; reign: 1786–1788), assumed the throne. Lê Chiêu Thống resented Nguyễn Huệ's mounting fame and called on the Chinese Qing Dynasty's Sino-Manchu emperor for help. In 1788, a Chinese army of two hundred thousand men commanded by Sun Shiyi (1720–1796) entered northern Việt Nam and occupied Thăng Long (Hà Nội) under the pretext of assisting the Lê Dynasty.

Nguyễn Huệ was in Huế, while his two brothers were managing their own fiefdoms farther south. He planned a lightning march to Thăng Long. After taking ten days to recruit new troops, Nguyễn Huệ led his Tây Sơn army north in three columns. The soldiers carried glutinous rice cakes, so that they did not need to cook; they marched continuously, with two soldiers carrying a third, who slept in a hammock. Tết, the Lunar New Year and Việt Nam's major holiday, was approaching. Arriving at Ninh Bình in the Red River Delta two days before Tết, Quang Trung ordered his troops to celebrate this sacred festival in advance. To his men massed under the Tây Sơn banner, he declared, "By the Seventh Day of the First Month of the New Year, we will have entered Thăng Long and will celebrate Tết in the capital. Mark my words."

Nguyễn Huệ's column stormed the Chinese camp fifteen kilometers south of Thăng Long with an advance battalion of war elephants. The two other columns pierced the enemy's flank west of the capital at Đống Đa (now a part of Hà Nội) during a bloody, day-long battle. The Chinese post commander hung himself. The Vietnamese troops' lightning victory terrified Chinese Commander-in-Chief Sun Shiyi. He had no time to saddle his horse or don his armor before fleeing with his lieutenants. Nguyễn Huệ entered Thăng Long on the Fifth Day of Tết in 1789. His troops celebrated Tết in the capital, as he had promised. Within six days, his army had advanced eighty-one kilometers and had completely defeated the two-hundred-thousand-strong Chinese army in one of the most brilliant victories in Việt Nam's history. This tactic of a surprise attack during Tết is known as "Tết Quang Trung." The Vietnamese used a version of the same tactic during the French War and as the surprise 1968 Tết Offensive during the American War.

King Quang Trung (Nguyễn Huệ) also distinguished himself with his reforms. He reorganized the army, the government, and the educational sector with the help of talented men, whom he had won over with his military prowess and his exemplary conduct. He promulgated a judicious policy to distribute communal lands and promote agriculture, developed handicrafts as well as trade, and decreed that Vietnamese ideograms (Nôm) would replace Chinese characters for education and official documents.

Quang Trung died unexpectedly in 1792, before he could complete what he had begun. His son and brothers did not have his stature. Thus, the Nguyễn Dynasty (1802–1945) started by Gia Long (a.k.a. Nguyễn Ánh, life: 1762–1820; reign: 1802–1820), whom the Tây Sơn had defeated on the Mỹ Tho River in the Mekong Delta seven years before, replaced the Tây Sơn Dynasty (1788–1802).

Each year, Hà Nội's Đống Đa District celebrates Quang Trung's victory with a festival on the Fifth Day of Tết, that is, the Fifth Day of the First Lunar Month. In the morning, residents hold a sacrificial ceremony at the Khương Thượng Communal House.

At midday, a procession takes the palanquin with Hero Quang Trung's statue from the communal house to the temple on Đống Đa Hill, where a ceremony commemorates all those who fell on the battlefield.

Ngô Thì Nhậm:
A Confucian Scholar's Difficult Choice

No historical figure in Việt Nam has been more controversial than Ngô Thì Nhậm (1746–1803). He lived during a pivotal era of our history, when civil war between North and South rent the country for two centuries. (For a definition of "North" and "South" during this period of Việt Nam's history, see p. 9.) The North was under the nominal reign of the legitimate Lê Dynasty (1428–1788), but real power lay in the hands of the Trịnh lords. In the South, the ruling Nguyễn lords also claimed to be governing in the name of the Lê Dynasty.

The Ngô clan had served the Lê and Trịnh in the North for successive generations. At age thirty, Ngô Thì Nhậm earned his doctorate during the 1776 examinations and was appointed vice-minister of public works. Feudal exploitation and continual warfare between the Trịnh and Nguyễn lords made life for the peasants intolerable. In the South, Nguyễn Huệ and his brothers won support from peasants and laborers for a vast rebellion known as the Tây Sơn Uprising. They seized the Nguyễn lords' land in the South and overthrew the Trịnh lords in the North.

The Confucian scholars in the North had been saturated with intransigent Confucian doctrine demanding absolute loyalty to legitimate rulers. They faced an agonizing choice: Should they follow the Lê-Trịnh regime, which had discredited itself through impotence, incompetence, and corruption? Or, should they rally to the new Tây Sơn Dynasty founder, Nguyễn Huệ, the commoner who had become Emperor Quang Trung and who had been the only man able to save the country from anarchy, ruin, and the threat of foreign occupation?

Ngô Thì Nhậm supported Emperor Quang Trung, while one of his brothers followed the Lê Dynasty toward what became treason. Ngô Thì Nhậm was well versed in politics and strategy. When the Sino-Manchu Qing emperor sent an army to occupy Việt Nam under the pretext of assisting the legitimate Lê Dynasty, Ngô Thì Nhậm suggested quickly marching the Tây Sơn troops from Huế to the North. Using this lightning strike, Quang Trung expelled the two-hundred-thousand-strong Chinese army entrenched in Hà Nội.

Ngô Thì Nhậm became Emperor Quang Trung's right-hand man. Diplomacy needed to be firm and supple to placate the Celestial (Chinese) Royal Court while consolidating national independence. Quang Trung entrusted this task to Ngô Thì Nhậm, who accomplished it brilliantly. By decrees composed in literary *Hán* ideograms, he succeeded in ending the Qing thirst for vengeance and secured Chinese recognition of Quang Trung as Việt Nam's sovereign. Ngô Thì Nhậm went to China on two ambassadorial missions, which won him the esteem and respect of his Chinese hosts and heightened Việt Nam's prestige. While traveling, he wrote many poems about renunciation and commitment, the landscape, historical sites, personalities, moral torments, and love for his country.

Ngô Thì Nhậm's career with Quang Trung lasted only five years, until the emperor died. The new Tây Sơn Royal Court headed by a ten-year-old king fell into plots and intrigue. Ngô Thì Nhậm kept a distance and devoted himself to studying Buddhist doctrine. He helped reinvigorate the Bamboo Forest (Trúc Lâm) Dhyanist sect, which King Trần Nhân Tông (life: 1258–1308; reign: 1278–1293) had founded during his retirement.

In 1802, Nguyễn Ánh, a descendant of the Nguyễn lords from the South, toppled the Tây Sơn Dynasty and founded the Nguyễn Dynasty (1820–1945), ruling as Gia Long (life: 1762–1820; reign: 1802–1820). Ngô Thì Nhậm was arrested and beaten to death; his name was effaced from the stele of doctorate laureates at the Temple to Confucius (Temple of Literature). Some time ago, Ngô Thì Nhậm's gravestone was unearthed. The stone has four lines testifying to his spirit:

Constant heart: the Ganges!
Coming and going: the Universe.
Neither dissipating nor immortal,
Life and death are natural.

Hoàng Diệu

Blood-Drenched Annam (L'Annam Sanglant, 1898) by Albert de Pouvourville (a.k.a. Mặt Giời or Sun, 1861–1939) describes the fall of Hà Nội to French gunboats in 1873. This novel is bathed in the cheap exoticism common in colonial literature. Its clichés are familiar—the conqueror's courage and generosity, the perversity of subtle Asiatic cruelty, the bloodletting, sensual pleasure, and opium. Vietnamese Commander Hoàng Diệu (1828–1882) appears as a coward: "He was fearful of war, like a true sage and an egoist longing for peace." In the novel, the Chinese chief of the Black Flags, who had been sent to rescue the Vietnamese Royal Court, forces Hoàng Diệu to commit suicide by hanging in order to fan the Vietnamese people's hatred and encourage them to resist the Tây" (Western people, i.e., the French).

All that is pure fiction. A scholar of humanities with a doctorate, Hoàng Diệu was appointed governor of Hà Ninh (Hà Nội and Ninh Bình Province) in 1880. He saw the French plot as soon as the French arrived in Hà Nội in 1882 from Huế (then the capital) and asked the Court to organize the defense. King Tự Đức (life: 1829–1883; reign: 1847–1883) accused Hoàng Diệu of recommending an "ill-timed defense." Soon, early in 1882, Henri Rivière's gunboats dropped anchor at Hà Nội. Rivière pretended that he was forced to face "Vietnamese war preparations." He sent an ultimatum to Hoàng Diệu, demanding that he dismantle all defenses and withdraw his forces. Then, without waiting for an answer, Rivière launched an attack. Defeated, Hoàng Diệu wrote his "Petition of Feelings to the Court" (Trần Tình Biểu), excerpted here, before hanging himself at the Temple of Military Arts:

Your servant's education is rudimentary, yet he has been entrusted with heavy responsibilities to protect an area of our country when our borders are not yet peaceful. Your servant is only a student, who is not yet knowledgeable about frontier problems. But after ten years of negotiations, how can we believe the enemy? . . .

Your servant ventures to think that Hà Nội City is the entry-way to the throat and to our Homeland's vulnerable region. If one day Hà Nội shatters like collapsed earth, then the surrounding provinces will fall one after another like loose roofing tiles. Sire, Your servant is seized with worry. . . . Your servant has requested that Your Majesty send more troops in order to ensure timely and early success. But then, just as many times, Your servant has received imperial edicts chiding him. . . .

Your humble servant cannot but take this as discipline causing him fear like in the hearts of the ancients when worshiping the King. Every day, Your servant discussed this situation with his colleagues. Some colleagues held that we should open our gates and let the French come and go at will; some said we should disarm our troops to end French suspicions. Yet even if Your servant's bones were crushed and his flesh beaten to a pulp, he could never resign himself to such measures.

A compromise had not been decided when the French opened fire. . . . Your humble servant was ill and in bed, but he rushed out to fight at the head of a column of our troops. We killed more than a hundred enemy soldiers and held our citadel for half a day. But the enemy remained near full strength, and we were exhausted. With no reinforcements, we were desperate. Our troops collapsed. Terrified, they fled en masse. A crowd of waiting mandarins fled. Your servant's heart was shattered. How could he fight single-handedly? Unable to command, he saw his life as useless. The citadel was lost with no way to save it. Death cannot be any compensation. . . .

An anonymous poem composed a few months after Hoàng Diệu's death, circulated by word of mouth. In it, the people sang their praise of Hoàng Diệu as the symbol of uprightness and patriotism:

> With iron courage
> And a heart the color of cinnabar,
> To clear himself of all suspicions
> Born of cruel defeat
> And demonstrate loyalty to his King,
> He entrusted to the branch of a tree
> His exhausted spirit.

Trương Vĩnh Ký: A Controversial Figure

When I began to learn French at age six or seven, my first Annamite-French dictionary was by Pétrus Trương Vĩnh Ký (1837–1898). On the first page was a portrait of the lexicographer wearing our national costume for men—a long black tunic and a turban. His chest was bedecked with medals. I did not know then that the author would become the object of a long controversy, which continues more than a century after his death.

Was Trương Vĩnh Ký a collaborator with the French from the start? Or was he a scholar, who gave remarkable service to his country through his many works? Pétrus Ký's "Final Message" (Tuyệt Bút) written in seven-word meter just before his death expresses the cruel dilemma tearing at him:

> This notebook of life's achievements and faults,
> Must be submitted to a judge's evaluation.

The five-volume *Grand Larousse Encyclopédique* says this about Trương Vĩnh Ký, or Pétrus Ký (his Christian name): "Pioneer of journalism in Việt Nam, he was also the author of numerous historical, didactic, and linguistic works and a translator of Chinese classics."

We should add a few details to understand this controversial figure.

Trương Vĩnh Ký was born into a Catholic family of long standing. His father, a senior officer in the Huế Royal Court, had suffered when the Royal Court persecuted Catholics before French colonization. Petrus Ký studied in neighboring countries and was an indefatigable self-learner. He taught himself to read and speak a dozen living and dead languages, worked as an interpreter in the new colonial administration, taught in the first French schools, and directed some of the first newspapers published in the Romanized Vietnamese script (*Quốc Ngữ*).

In 1863, Pétrus Ký interpreted for the delegation that Phan Thanh Giản (1796–1867) led to Paris on behalf of Emperor Tự Đức (life: 1829–1883; reign: 1847–1883) shortly after the first French landed at Đà Nẵng. Paul Bert (1833–1886), the French resident-superior for Annam (the Central Region, Trung Kỳ), trusted Trương Vĩnh Ký and appointed him to the Royal Court's Secret Council. Trương Vĩnh Ký fell into disgrace six months after Paul Bert's death, left public service, and concentrated on cultural activities until his death.

To judge Trương Vĩnh Ký and his works, it is worth referring to the eighty-page booklet that *Catholicism and the Nation* (Công Giáo và Dân Tộc), a monthly review, published about the scholar in December 1998. There, poet and literary critic Lê Đình Bảng reviews the assessments of Trương Vĩnh Ký, describing three periods, which can be summarized as follows:

1. From Trương Vĩnh Ký's death in 1898 to the 1945 Revolution, "the period of praise": *Indochina Magazine* (Đông Dương Tạp Chí) described Trương Vĩnh Ký as "a writer and journalist having a brilliant career." Critic Thiếu Sơn (1908–1978) called him "a sage," while cultural researcher Dương Quảng Hàm (1898–1946) referred to him as "a pioneer of the new literature in Romanized script." Only writer and cultural researcher Phạm Quỳnh (1892–1945) described Trương Vĩnh Ký simply as "a compiler of textbooks for children."

2. From 1945 to 1974, "the period of criticism and praise":
The views from both sides arose mostly from political mo-
tives. The critics dwelt on Trương Vĩnh Ký's collaboration
with French colonizers. In 1933, Thanh Lam referred to
his "propagation of the spirit of capitulation," while issues of *Historical Studies Review* published in North Việt
Nam during 1963 and 1964 described Trương Vĩnh Ký as
a man "in service to the reactionary feudal class and the
enemy," who was "used by the French as a spy in his travels
to Tonkin [the Northern Region, Bắc Kỳ]," and was a proponent of "Catholic education in service to the capitalist
aggressors."

Writer and journalist Hồ Hữu Tường (1926–) came to
Trương Vĩnh Ký's defense, writing in *Encyclopedic Review*
(Tập Bách Khoa) in South Việt Nam: "Catholic education
necessarily paved the way for collaboration, all the more so
since he had to protect himself against persecution; Ký took
the right action by retiring at the right time to devote himself to cultural activities." Other articles in the magazine
refuted this argument, saying Pétrus Ký was a henchman
of Paul Bert and that the colonizers propagated Romanized
script to eliminate the influence of traditional religions and
Chinese culture.

3. After 1975, including Việt Nam's open-door policy of *Đổi
Mới*: In 1990, Nguyễn Văn Trung (1930–), a professor of
literature and foreign languages, called Trương Vĩnh Ký a
pioneer who, in light of the situation during his lifetime,
could not have acted otherwise. Bằng Giang, who published his literary criticism of Trương Vĩnh Ký's work in
1995, noted that Pétrus Ký had courage and clarity.

Father Trương Bá Cần (1930–2009), a Catholic leader, wrote
a subtle analysis of Trương Vĩnh Ký's life and work by trying to
answer three questions, summarized as:

1. Why did Trương Vĩnh Ký collaborate with the French? His thirty-eight-year collaboration seems inevitable in the context of his time. Given that training of Catholics benefited the French and that the Vietnamese Royal Court before colonialism persecuted Catholics, Trương Vĩnh Ký would have had no alternative but collaboration, especially when Catholics believed that the French presence was the Will of God. On the other hand, as a patriotic Catholic, Trương Vĩnh Ký did not believe that evangelism's purpose was to help Europeans occupy Việt Nam. Perhaps he was ill-advised politically and did not at first perceive that collaboration was synonymous with treason.

2. In what domain did Trương Vĩnh Ký collaborate with the French? Trương Vĩnh Ký never participated directly in administrative affairs. During the six or seven months that Ký worked for Paul Bert, he held a seat in the Secret Council, sincerely believing in his mission of persuasion. He wanted to tell his friends and foes that all resistance was useless, while collaboration with the French government might assure relative autonomy for the Huế Royal Court. In fact, Trương Vĩnh Ký's activities were essentially cultural, as a translator, teacher, and journalist.

3. Did his collaboration benefit only the French? It certainly served colonial policy, since the popularization of Romanized script came within the French administration's plans. That does not hide the fact that Trương Vĩnh Ký sincerely wanted to bridge the two cultures. The immense oeuvre he left us—over a hundred works—is devoid of colonial propaganda. On the contrary, it is a treasure of linguistics, geography, history, education, and national literature.

In short, it seems to me that one should not judge Trương Vĩnh Ký according to the norms of a hero ready to die for the Homeland. Like the rest of our people forced to live under colonialism, he wanted to be useful. Now that our country has regained its independence, we should profit from the cultural heritage he left us.

Nguyễn Văn Vĩnh

Opinion remains divided about Nguyễn Văn Vĩnh (1882–1936). Some have branded him a toady to the French and a seller of the Homeland. This is mostly because Nguyễn Văn Vĩnh wanted the protectorates—the Northern Region (Tonkin, Bắc Kỳ) and the Central Region (Annam, Trung Kỳ), which were under the nominal authority of the Huế Royal Court—to have the higher status of a colony under the direct administration of France, like the Southern Region (Cochin China, Nam Kỳ).

To understand this rather strange political affiliation, we must understand the conditions of Việt Nam at the beginning of the 1900s. The French had completed their military conquest by repressing the Confucian scholars' Save-the-King (Cần Vương) Insurrection. Applying a divide-and-rule policy, the colonizers split the country into three. Cochin China had been a colony since 1874. Annam and Tonkin became French protectorates. The French kept the king in Huế but only as a puppet.

Nguyễn Văn Vĩnh was born into a poor family in Phương Vũ Village (Sơn Tây Province in northern Việt Nam). He eeked out his living from age eight and educated himself in classes at the School of Interpreters. In 1906, the French sent Nguyễn Văn Vĩnh, by then a young petty clerk in his mid-twenties, to Marseilles for the Colonial Exposition. Nguyễn Văn Vĩnh returned from his sojourn in a Western democracy and called for political reforms.

But what strategy could Vietnamese adopt to regain national independence?

Vietnamese patriots had two options: armed struggle or peaceful struggle by legal means. The second choice implied revising the feudalist monarchy and raising the general population's educational level and political awareness. The key figure in that second option was Phan Châu (Chu) Trinh (1872–1926), a patriotic scholar ten years older than Nguyễn Văn Vĩnh. (For essays on Phan Châu Trinh, see p. 73 and p. 237.) Nguyễn Văn Vĩnh had been the first Vietnamese member of the French Human Rights League. When Phan Châu Trinh was arrested in 1908, Nguyễn Văn Vĩnh and several French colleagues signed a letter demanding the famous patriot's release.

Nguyễn Văn Vĩnh worked as editor and as editor-in-chief for a number of newspapers published in Vietnamese and in French but with the publishing permission held by a French colleague. Then, in 1931, he established his own daily, *L'Annam Nouveau* (New Annam), in Hà Nội. In 1932, the authorities accused him of long-time abuses against the regime and required that he cease his activities against the Court, cease writing, and return to Huế as a deputy minister. Nguyễn Văn Vĩnh refused. The authorities subjected him to a huge fine for offenses dating back five years. Nevertheless, he continued writing and publishing.

In 1926, the French repressed the nationwide demonstrations for Phan Châu Trinh's funeral. On the seventh anniversary of Phan Châu Trinh's death, Nguyễn Văn Vĩnh wrote, "Our compatriots have commemorated in a dignified manner the memory of the man whose name is from now on linked to the work of peaceful renovation undertaken by the clear-sighted minds in this country. Let us remember the life full of privations and sufferings of this patriot so exemplary and so worthy of veneration."

In 1935, the authorities changed their requirements for Nguyễn Văn Vĩnh's submission to three alternatives: 1) cessation of all writing, 2) prison, or 3) exile in Laos to search for gold to pay his fines. These demands forced Nguyễn Văn Vĩnh into bankruptcy. He lost all his possessions, including his house. During thirty years, from 1906 to 1936, he had worked tirelessly as a printer, journalist, translator, editor, and then director of several newspapers, including *Indochina Magazine* (Đông Dương Tạp Chí), *Literary News from Annam and Tonkin* (Trung Bắc Tân Văn), *Our Journal* (Notre Journal), and *New Annam* (L'Annam Nouveau).

Nguyễn Văn Vĩnh went to Laos allegedly to explore for gold. On May 1, 1936, he died in a small boat on the Sebanhieng River during a violent storm, still holding in his hand a fountain pen. He was writing the first pages of a report on gold speculation.

Nguyễn Thái Học: Hero of Thổ Tang Village

I remember when I was ten or eleven, at the time of French colonization, I would pass the Hà Nội Police Station on Phố Hàng Đậu (Bean Market Street) while en route to school. One day, I heard rumors that militants from the Vietnamese Nationalist Party (Việt Nam Quốc Dân Đảng) had hurled a bomb at the Police Station. The hand-made bomb never exploded. Nevertheless, this act of prowess filled me with admiration for the nationalists, many of whom later mounted the gallows after the Nationalist Party's Yên Bái Insurrection failed in February 1930.

Women's News (Phụ Nữ Tân Văn) published a photo of Nationalist Party leader Nguyễn Thái Học (1902–1930) in prison. That image has never left my memory. More than seventy years later, I came across that same photograph on a family's ancestral altar in Nguyễn Thái Học's native village, Thổ Tang (Vĩnh Tường District, Vĩnh Phúc Province). The family's head and owner of a traditional medicine shop was Nguyễn Khắc Nỉ, then age seventy-five. He was Nguyễn Thái Học's youngest brother. Nguyễn Khắc Nỉ had taken refuge in China to escape the Vichy French colonial police and the Japanese Kempeitai military police during Japan's occupation (1940–1945); he returned to his native village in the early 1970s.

With great emotion, I shook this Confucian scholar's frail hand.

As I walked around Thổ Tang Village, cradle of the Nationalist Party, Nguyễn Thái Học's wrenching last words before execution resounded in my heart: "Long live Việt Nam!" (*Việt Nam vạn tuế!*—literally, Việt Nam ten thousand years!).

Despite the premature conditions for revolution in 1930, the Yên Bái patriots had agreed on armed action, vowing to follow Nguyễn Thái Học's slogan, "Use iron and blood" (*Phải dùng sắt và máu*). Indeed, the bloody Yên Bái Insurrection remains a historic landmark on the path to Việt Nam's national liberation.

Teachers at Private Schools in Huế

The Second World War broke out in 1939. In May 1940, the Nazis occupied France. In September, the Japanese invaded French Indochina (Việt Nam, Laos, and Cambodia). Hồ Chí Minh founded the League for the Independence of Việt Nam (**Việt** Nam Độc Lập Đồng **Minh** Hội or Việt Minh) in May 1941 to liberate the country from its Japanese-French yoke. Then the Japanese coup d'état in Việt Nam on March 9, 1945 ended French power over our country. A month later, the Japanese installed the puppet government of Trần Trọng Kim (1883–1953) in Huế. The August Revolution broke out on August 19, 1945 in Hà Nội and on August 23 in Huế, then the imperial capital. Throughout these upheavals, until August 23, 1945, life continued on its peaceful course on the banks of Huế's Perfume River. The private schools remained full.

However, this calm concealed a tidal wave.

In 1925, public opinion had compelled the French to commute the 1913 death sentence *in absentia* for Phan Bội Châu (1867–1940) to hard labor for life. Then, after many protests, the French confined the patriot to perpetual house arrest in Huế. The French assumed they could limit the elderly revolutionary's political influence because the puppet Royal Court was devoted to the French, and the imperial capital in Huế was politically calm. However, the French did not realize that Phan Bội Châu's mere presence reminded people about the cause of national liberation. Phan Bội Châu became known as the Bến Ngự Patriarch, a reference to his house near the Perfume River's Bến Ngự Wharf. Although the Bến Ngự Patriarch had died in 1940, his literary-political works still infused Huế's atmosphere, which revolutionary poet Tố Hữu (1920–2002) further animated.

Most of the teachers at Huế's private schools opposed French colonization. Lexicographer Đào Duy Anh (1904–1988) used his Sino-Vietnamese and French-Vietnamese dictionaries to propagate Marxism. His friend, Taoist philosopher Cao Xuân Huy (1900–1983), spoke little and wrote even less. Like me, Cao Xuân Huy taught French at the Việt Anh High School. I was eighteen years his junior. Cao Xuân Huy was a graduate of the Teachers' College and had taken up teaching at a private school after being imprisoned for his activism with Tân Việt Revolutionary Party, which became one of the three predecessor communist parties to the Vietnamese Communist Party. He had a brilliant intellect, drew Taoism and physics closer together, and achieved later fame as one of our greatest scholars of ancient Vietnamese history.

Tôn Quang Phiệt (1900–1973), director of the Thuận Hóa School, had been a leader of the League for the Restoration of Việt Nam (Phục Việt) in the Northern Region in 1925. He had also graduated from the Teachers' College. He published works on Phan Bội Châu and Hoàng Hoa Thám (a.k.a. Đề Thám, 1858–1913), leader of the revolutionary uprising at Yên Thế in Bắc Giang Province in the Northern Region (Tonkin, Bắc Kỳ). After the 1945 August Revolution, Tôn Quang Phiệt served as president of the People's Committee of Thừa Thiên Province and became a leader of the National Assembly and the Fatherland Front (the umbrella for the Party's mass organizations of young people, women, elders, and other groups).

Professor Tạ Quang Bửu (1910–1986), a Paris-trained mathematician, taught English at the Catholic Providence School. He and Nguyễn Lân (1906–2003), a teacher at Khải Định High School, were prominent leaders of Huế's Boy Scout Movement. Later, Tạ Quang Bửu was Việt Nam's signatory to the 1954 Geneva Agreements and then minister of higher education and vocational training from 1965 until the country was formally re-unified in 1976. A fellow Boy Scout, my friend Cao Văn Khánh (1917–1980), taught mathematics at Việt Anh School. A likeable fellow of great honesty, he rode a racing bicycle. He later became a brilliant general of the People's Army during the Resistance War Against France and the Resistance War Against the United States.

Many of Huế's private-school teachers excelled in literature. These included Chế Lan Viên, Trần Tế Hanh, Thanh Tịnh, Nguyễn Văn Bổng, Hoài Thanh, Đoàn Phú Tứ, and Phan Khắc Khoan, all of whom also made substantial contributions to the Revolution. They were among the best known writers in the New Poetry (*Thơ Mới*) Movement during the 1930s.

Chế Lan Viên (1920–1989) won his fame when he was sixteen with his collection, *Ruins* (Điêu Tàn, 1937). He lived in poverty in Huế, seldom able to make ends meet. Tế Hanh (1921–2009) was our poet of tenderness. His verses are simple and graced with sweet music. Thanh Tịnh (1911–1988) lived in Gia Lạc Hamlet, on a bank of the Perfume River. A connoisseur of Huế, he distinguished himself with velvety poetry and moving stories. Nguyễn Văn Bổng (1921–2001) owed his fame to his novel, *The Buffalo* (Con Trâu, 1952), written during the Resistance War Against France, as well as other works written during the American War. Hoài Thanh (1909–1982) was known as a clear-sighted critic. Đoàn Phú Tứ (1910–1989) was famous for his poem, "Color of Time" (Màu Thời Gian), and his short theatrical pieces. Phan Khắc Khoan (1916–1998) was a pioneer of modern drama in verse.

Two renowned painters—Nguyễn Đức Nùng (1914–1983) and Nguyễn Đỗ Cung (1912–1977)—also taught at Việt Anh School.

Nguyễn Văn Huyên: My History Teacher

I recollect this as if it were yesterday. It was the winter of 1938, and I was in my last year at Hà Nội's Lycée du Protectorat. Việt Nam was still under French rule. My history teacher, Nguyễn Văn Huyên, rubbed his hands vigorously to drive away the cold. He looked fondly at the books that littered his desk and said to us, "Each time I see a desk loaded with books, my heart spills over with joy. Books and studies— they are my life." However, Nguyễn Văn Huyên's life took another turn. A great scholar and teacher, he served as a government minister for thirty years until his death in 1975.

Nguyễn Văn Huyên was born in 1908, when the French had firmly established their occupation. In primary schools, the Romanized Vietnamese script (*Quốc Ngữ*) had replaced Chinese script (*Hán*) in traditional education imbued with Confucianism, while French was the language of instruction in secondary schools. Higher education was not available in Việt Nam until the next decade. Nguyễn Văn Huyên belonged to the first generation of Vietnamese intellectuals to train in France and earn diplomas from major French universities.

Nguyễn Văn Huyên came from a family of scholars and traditional herbal doctors in Hà Nội's ancient quarter. His father, a low-level functionary from Lai Xá Village, died when Huyên was young. However, Nguyễn Văn Huyên's academic achievements led to scholarships in France. From 1926 to 1934, he earned bachelor degrees in literature (1929) and law (1931) and then became the first Vietnamese to defend a doctoral dissertation at the Sorbonne. His thesis, "The Alternating Songs of Young Men and Women of Việt Nam," and a supplementary thesis on stilt houses in Southeast Asia were published in 1935. They were well received throughout France, Germany, and Holland, receiving praise from specialists, such as Charles Robequain (1907–1963) and Jean Pyzyluski (1885–1944).

After earning his doctorate at age twenty-six, Nguyễn Văn Huyên refused a post in Paris so he could return to Việt Nam, where he chose teaching instead of a more lucrative career in colonial service. He taught for three years (1935–1938) at the Lycée du Protectorat, where I was among his students. Soon afterward, he gave up teaching to devote himself to the Hà Nội branch of the French Institute for Far-East Studies (École française d'Extrême-Orient), where he was the only Vietnamese participant until 1945.

Responding to President Hồ Chí Minh's invitation, Nguyễn Văn Huyên joined the Revolution and left for the jungle Resistance base to become the first minister of education in the Democratic Republic of Việt Nam (DRVN) government, which had been formally established by our first National Assembly in early 1946. From 1946 until 1975, he built an educational system suited to a country freshly delivered from eighty years of enslavement but then gripped by thirty years of war. He won the trust and affection of everyone through his simplicity, modesty, knowledge, and clarity.

No less important is Nguyễn Văn Huyên's contribution as a pioneer of modern Vietnamese Studies. Together with other Vietnamese researchers from his generation, he helped transform the old Chinese-based historical and cultural studies by steering academic research toward scientific concepts appropriate to the industrial age. Driven by patriotism and respect for the Vietnamese traditions that the French despised, these Vietnamese intellectuals introduced a new methodology in ethnography, sociology, and history. Nguyễn Văn Huyên's immense field of research focused on the cultural and social institutions that were the foundation of traditional society. He paid particular attention to the peasants of the northern delta and regions inhabited by ethnic minorities. He avidly studied Việt Nam's folk festivals and beliefs, cultural traditions, and social institutions.

Hồ Chí Minh and Western Cultural Values

*An essay honoring the hundredth anniversary
of Hồ Chí Minh's birth, May 1990*

Hồ Chí Minh was born in a poor village in Việt Nam's Central Region (Annam, Trung Kỳ) in 1890. As unusual as it may appear, Hồ Chí Minh, who symbolizes the struggle of oppressed peoples against Western colonialism, was culturally close to the West. Journalist/biographer Jean Lacouture found in Hồ Chí Minh "clear evidence of his intellectual and political links" with the American people. Gaullist Minister Edmond Michelet observed, "He was very French." According to Italian activist Michele Zecchini, Hồ Chí Minh "actively took part in strikes on a bank of the Thames River. This was a great moment in his early life."

In contrast with the lives of other famous Asian revolutionary leaders, many of Hồ Chí Minh's earliest political experiences were in Europe. He completed his education there. However, this did not make Hồ Chí Minh any less Vietnamese or any less Asian. Foreigners who met him were struck by this fact. Jean Fous, a journalist for *France Tireur*, noted that Hồ Chí Minh "combined heroism and wisdom. . . . He became a sort of Marxist Gandhi, . . . an embodiment of Asian wisdom."

The *Manila Times*, in its obituary about President Hồ, considered him "a symbol of Asia."

Ruth Fischer, the German Communist Party representative at the Comintern (**Com**munist **Intern**ational), commented on the young Vietnamese activist's wisdom in Paris during 1922 and 1923, saying, "Among the experienced revolutionaries (those difficult-to-please intellectuals), he bore himself with charming good nature and simplicity. He belonged to the good among us— to the most learned of all. . . . Thanks to this quality, he was spared internal conflicts."

To judge the extent to which Western culture influenced Hồ Chí Minh, it is important to understand his life's aim. When Hồ Chí Minh was born, Việt Nam had been a colony for a decade. How could the nation be liberated and the people's lot be bettered? Hồ Chí Minh was preoccupied with this problem until his last breath. Other Asian nations and other patriots also faced this challenge in the second half of the 1800s. Westernization offered itself as the only effective solution.

In 1911, Hồ Chí Minh sailed for France to search for a way to save our nation and to learn, as he once told Osip Mandelstam, what lay behind the French motto, "*Liberté, Equalité, Fraternité.*" Hồ Chí Minh, then twenty-one, already possessed the maturity necessary to absorb new ideas without denying himself. He would remain, as Christiane Pasquel Rageau said, "the modern man most representative of Việt Nam."

Memories of Hồ Chí Minh's childhood and adolescence remained fresh during his wanderings around the world. Those memories included the people and scenery of his homeland, Kim Liên

(Golden Lotus) Village, his family of patriotic scholars from peasant background, and local popular struggles against the aggressors. American journalist David Halberstam wrote that Hồ Chí Minh would always retain "the eternal Vietnamese values: respect for old people, disdain for money, affection for children." His Vietnamese heart was intact, with its communal sentiment, family ties, dedication to work, common sense, peasant humor, and poetic instinct.

Hồ Chí Minh had studied French culture in a Franco-Vietnamese school in Việt Nam and had studied Vietnamese and Chinese classics with his father. President Hồ's early Confucian education provided him with elements for his later choice of Marxism, which in turn gave him rationalism, faith in education, and concern for social ethics and the primacy of action. For most Vietnamese scholars, Confucianism and Taoism are contradictory complements. For Hồ Chí Minh, the combination of varying philosophies manifested itself in his desire for a contemplative life, anti-formalism, feminism, and humor. Hồ Chí Minh spoke of Shakyamuni "as the Buddha of Mercy, for his kindness is immense."

Although scholar Paul Mus's description of Hồ Chí Minh as the embodiment of Vietnamese and Asian psyche is not to be accepted out of hand, it is important to stress that a deep understanding of the cultural and ideological evolution of the future Vietnamese president would prove impossible without studying Eastern thinking as marked by the quest for cosmic unity, a recognition of the harmony of opposites, and a leaning toward intuition and synthesis.

Young Hồ Chí Minh approached the West with an unusually open mind and remained open throughout his life, as shown in this quotation from Trần Dân Tiên's *Anecdotes from the Life and Work of President Hồ* (Những Mẩu Chuyện về Đời Hoạt Động của Hồ Chủ Tịch, 1948). Young Hồ Chí Minh asks, "'What did Confucius, Jesus, Karl Marx, and Sun Yat-Sen have in common? They each held the goal of everyone's happiness, and each one sought to serve society. If these four leaders were alive today and could meet, I think they would agree that they could live very congenially with each other and would become close friends. In my own life, I try to be a beginning student of these great men.'"

Hồ Chí Minh's open-mindedness coupled with his warmth made him many friends and also helped him adapt to the West. He enriched his knowledge and experience through readings, relationships, travel in Europe, America, Africa, and Asia, as well as through social and political activities. Western thinking—with reason and science as the criteria for truth—provided Hồ Chí Minh with the analytical method that led him to Marxist dialectics. Jean Sainteny, one of the few Westerners who knew Hồ Chí Minh well, observed that President Hồ's traditional education "in combination with the general culture he had absorbed during his travels, especially in Paris, was enough to develop in him a sharp, analytical faculty, unusual subtlety, and a fervent curiosity, which he put to good use the rest of his life."

Hồ Chí Minh's style of exploring topics is at odds with Confucian scholasticism. He must have learned this from French socialists and communists during the early 1920s. Among his friends were Jacques Duclos, Marcel Cachin, and Jean Longuet. He attended lectures by the woman writer and activist Séverine, made speeches at the Faubourg Club, and engaged in discussions about astronomy, politics, literature, watercress-growing, and snail-raising.

President Hồ's gift for analysis became sharper when he branched out into journalism, where he was first encouraged to expand his writing and then to shorten it. He often wrote his poetry in the Chinese T'ang Dynasty style, with a six-word line followed by an eight-word line. Under dramatic circumstances, his language was laconic. In 1946, when the young Democratic Republic of Việt Nam (DRVN) was in danger, President Hồ had to leave Hà Nội for Fontainebleau to negotiate with the French government. He turned the DRVN government over to Interior Minister Huỳnh Thúc Kháng with this six-word instruction:

Retain immutable principles during myriad changes,
Take the people's will as your will.

Dĩ bất biến ứng vạn biến,
Dĩ chúng tâm vi kỷ tâm.

During the thirty years Hồ Chí Minh was overseas after leaving Việt Nam in 1911, he absorbed the Western revolutionary ideas of progress, freedom, and democracy. These had been circulating among modern Vietnamese scholars since the end of the 1800s, thanks to Chinese translations of works by Montesquieu, Rousseau, Voltaire, and others. At first, Hồ Chí Minh viewed these sources through the prism of national liberation. He joined the group that broke off from the French Socialist Party in 1920 to found the French Communist Party in order to ally with the Third **Com**munist **Intern**ational (Comintern) because he believed communist organizations championed the cause of colonized peoples.

French Minister of War Edmond Michelet, who was responsible for receiving Hồ Chí Minh in Paris in 1946, described the Vietnamese statesman: "He was an idealistic communist. . . . He always seemed influenced by the great author Marx and, no doubt, by Lenin. . . . But he was also influenced . . . by Jaurès. . . . He had chosen communism but with a profound humanism. . . . I believe that in the communist world he is certainly among those who commit themselves to communist revolution, yes . . . but in freedom." That observation made by an adversary brings home the point that Hồ Chí Minh effectively searched for a human-faced communism, which inherited the 1917 Russian Revolution's traditions yet retained the bourgeois revolution's achievements. President Hồ sought and created a form of communism to support the liberation of colonized peoples while respecting individuals.

In the preamble to Việt Nam's Declaration of Independence, which Hồ Chí Minh read before the Vietnamese people on September 2, 1945, he quoted the American Declaration of Independence and the French Declaration of the Rights of Man and the Citizen. He said to the French writer Jean Lacouture, "A nation like yours, which has given the world the literature of freedom, will always find in us . . . good friends. You see, I have read Victor Hugo and Jules Michelet again and again every year. No doubt, they voiced the concern of your ordinary people, who are our brothers."

British parliamentarian William Warbey commented, "Hồ Chí Minh's admiration for the historic achievements and aspirations of the American people dated from the visits he made to New York and Boston when on shore leave from French ships during the early 1900s. There, he got to know and like the American people and, through reading, to admire their statesmen. In particular, Abraham Lincoln's fight against slavery and the exploitation of laborers seemed to Ho an example for his own mission to free the Vietnamese people."

After national independence had been declared, Hồ Chí Minh wrote to Việt Nam's People's Committees at all levels across the country on October 17, 1945, saying, "We have now founded the Democratic Republic of Việt Nam. However, if the country is independent and the people do not have freedom and happiness, then independence is meaningless."

Although Hồ Chí Minh came from a community-based culture, he did not sacrifice the individual when stressing the people as a whole. Western culture with its essentially individualistic nature had left its mark on President Hồ. His class consciousness was devoid of dogmatism and was very humanistic. Hồ Chí Minh deplored the extreme measures carried out during the Land Reform Campaign from 1953 to 1955. For example, he sided with a doctor, whom extremists had accused of providing medical treatment for a cruel landlord's young son.

In his Last Will and Testament, President Hồ showed a special regard for children, the elderly, women, soldiers, and the war injured. As a young man in Paris during the mid-1920s, he had founded and edited *Le Paria*, a nationalist newspaper. From his first articles onward, his writings show compassion for the world's downtrodden, with his sensibility reflecting his first readings while in the West.

Hồ Chí Minh liked to read Shakespeare and Dickens in English, Lu Xun in Chinese, and Hugo and Zola in French. Anatole France and Leo Tolstoy were the masters from whom he learned the most. He read aloud philosopher Pierre-Joseph Proudhon and historian Jules Michelet to young Vietnamese expatriates in a basement on Marché des Patriarches in Paris. He knew Colette and admired Jean Jaurès. The common denominator among his favorite authors was their empathy for the humble and oppressed. While imprisoned in a Chinese Guomindang jail in the mid-1940s, Hồ Chí Minh sympathized with a fellow prisoner's wife, as he expressed in "A Fellow Prisoner's Wife Visits Her Husband" (Vợ Người Bạn Tù Đến Nhà Lao Thăm Chồng), Poem #38 in *Prison Diary* (Nhật Ký Trong Tù, 1942–1943). He wrote the poem in Chinese, using five-word meter:

> He is inside the bars,
> On the outside, his sweetheart;
> So close, only inches away,
> Their two lives, worlds apart.
> What their lips cannot say,
> Only their eyes can impart;
> Tears flow before they speak,
> Their plight rends the heart!

Jean Lacouture noted that Hồ Chí Minh's poetry was a "blend of Asian sensibility and French romanticism." Like all Vietnamese poets, Hồ Chí Minh felt a special communion with nature. He composed "Traveling by Boat on the Đáy River" (Đi Thuyền Trên Sông Đáy) in six-word, eight-word meter on August 18, 1949, while in the Northwest Liberated Area during the French War (1945–1954):

> The river, silent like a grave,
> Stars guide the lone sampan, the moon follows.
> All about, deserted hills and hollows,
> The only sound: the oar and oarlock creaking.
> He's consumed by his private seeking,
> Worrying how to reclaim his nation's ancient land.
> Dawn emerges, he returns by sampan,
> A fresh rose hue spreads along the horizon.

How can one explain the links between Hồ Chí Minh and Anatole France, between the man of action (who was earnest and optimistic) and the aesthete (who was skeptical and frustrated)? Hồ Chí Minh secured from his master, Anatole France, the human tenderness that made him, while serving as Việt Nam's president, the sentimental communist who wrote with sobriety and a luminosity of style.

Hồ Chí Minh's humor resulted from mixing Eastern and Western qualities. He could interplay peasant banter with a traditional scholar's caustic tone and a petit Parisien's malice. Hồ Chí Minh scorned the cult of personality and could mock himself and others. During the Resistance War Against France, soldiers welcomed Hồ Chí Minh after his long trek through the jungle, shouting, "Long live President Hồ!" (*Hồ Chủ Tịch muôn năm!*) He answered with the same phrase but modified the tones on two words, saying, "President Hồ wants to lie down!" (*Hồ Chủ Tịch muốn nằm!*)

While in Paris in 1946, President Hồ was returning from the Champs Elysées when a companion observed, "Well, Mr. President, people came out in droves to see you."

"I suppose," Hồ Chí Minh answered, "they wanted to see the Vietnamese Charlie Chaplin!"

East and West, nationalism and internationalism, action and dreams, tradition and revolution, reason and heart—Hồ Chí Minh reconciled these opposites into harmony. His life and work symbolized Pascal's concept that a person shows his greatness not by sticking to one pole but by joining two opposite poles together so that they complement each other.

Vietnamese Literature: An Expression of the Nation's Spirit

Nguyễn Du and The Tale of Kiều: The Brigand and the Courtesan

When I was small, we would play a fortune-telling game at Tết (the Lunar New Year). The source of divination was *The Tale of Kiều* (Truyện Kiều), the famous verse novel by Nguyễn Du (1766–1820). After lighting a stick of incense, its wisp of smoke communicating with the Other World, we would take a closed copy of *The Tale of Kiều* in both hands, raise it to our foreheads, and pray to the novel's characters: "I prostrate myself before you, Oh King Từ Hải, Oh Mother Giác Duyên, Oh Beautiful Thúy Kiều." Next, we would think of a relatively low number and then open the book at random, looking at the right-hand page if we were female, at the left-hand page if male. We would then count verses from the top until we reached the couplet corresponding to our selected number. A variation of this method was to close our eyes and point at random.

If you try this game and if you are party to a lawsuit, then you are likely to lose if you fall on the following couplet in six-word, eight-word meter:

> Amazed and astounded, the family panicked,
> The victims' protests of innocence shook the clouds.

However, an unhappy lover may find solace in these lines:

> A fortunate change, this unexpected encounter,
> This serendipity satisfying his heart's longed-for flower.

Nguyễn Du wrote his famous epic in 3,254 lines with six-word, eight-word meter. Here is a brief summary of the story:

Kiều is a beautiful, young girl with a gift for poetry and music. One day in spring, she and her younger sister and brother take flowers to the family's graves. Kiều weeps at the neglected tomb

135

of an unlucky courtesan, whose ghost has appeared to her. Kiều has the sense that her own life will be a sad one. She meets Kim, a handsome young man who is her brother's friend. Kiều and Kim, being well-mannered, do not speak, but nevertheless it is love at first sight. Kim creates a situation allowing them to see each other again and to swear eternal love.

Later, Kiều's father is falsely accused and arrested while Kim is away in his native province. Kiều sells herself as a concubine to a merchant to pay the bribe that will save her father. Before leaving home, she prostrates herself before her younger sister, beseeching her to marry Kim so that the sister can "pay Kiều's debt of love to Kim." However, it turns out that the merchant is not seeking a concubine. Rather, he traffics in human flesh; he forces Kiều into prostitution.

Charmed by Kiều's beauty and talent, a prestigious warlord named Từ Hải makes Kiều his wife. She, in turn, urges Từ Hải to make peace with the imperial court. He agrees but falls into a trap set by a treacherous official and dies. Desolate, Kiều throws herself into a river. A nun, Giác Duyên, rescues Kiều and persuades her to take holy orders. Meanwhile, Kim has married Kiều's younger sister in fulfillment of Kiều's wish. Nevertheless, he travels throughout the country, searching for Kiều until he finally traces her to the pagoda. Fifteen years have passed. Kim beseeches Kiều to come home, marry him, and live with him and her younger sister, polygamy being respectable at the time. But Kiều deems herself unworthy of Kim's love. Eventually, after entreaties from Kiều's parents and sister, Kiều consents to a platonic union with the man she loves.

Invoking this novel's characters shows understanding of the book's themes—revolt against feudal morals and adoption of Buddhist compassion. Such readers understand Kiều's choices and approve of her actions: Kiều's first love is for the man of her choice, not someone her parents have selected. Later, she dares to marry a brigand, as the court labels rebellious warlord Từ Hải.

Nguyễn Du, the author of *Kiều*, was a Confucian scholar, who defied ideology by siding with the rebel and also with Kiều in her role as prostitute. No wonder vigilant parents in the old days told their daughters, "Young women must not listen to *The Tale of Kiều.*" And yet, the novel's theme is quite Confucian in upholding the individual's sacrifice for the family's patriarchal head. At the same time, the theme relates to Buddhist karma, for fate is always jealous of beauty and talent. Many critics think that Kiều's destiny reflects the vicissitudes experienced by Nguyễn Du himself.

The Tale of Kiều is a unique literary and sociological phenomenon in Việt Nam. For the last two centuries, ordinary people—whether illiterate or scholarly—loved this tale. All know some passages by heart. Mothers lulled their babies by singing a few verses. Literary preferences come and go, but *The Tale of Kiều* remains on the literary scene. Old scholars find in *Kiều* the lyricism that official doctrine banned; young people regard *Kiều* as the bible of love and individual emancipation; revolutionaries like its anti-feudal flavor. No Vietnamese, not even the most Westernized of our poets, has repudiated *Kiều*. The book's lasting value comes from its reliance on genuine national traditions, the mixture of scholarly and folk literatures, use of both romanticism and realism, and poetic language of unrivaled richness and harmony. *The Tale of Kiều* makes the most of the metric unit that is Vietnamese poetry par excellence, the six-word, eight-work couplet.

One may say that *The Tale of Kiều* is the repository of the Vietnamese soul, since all Vietnamese see something of themselves in the work. As a marvelous adaptation of a second-rate Chinese novel, *The Tale of Kiều* expressed national identity when Chinese cultural influence prevailed. During the French colonial regime, *Kiều* retained its role as cultural guardian. It has been said that, "As long as *Kiều* lives on, our Vietnamese language shall live on. And as long as our language lives on, our nation will not die."

Nguyễn Trãi: One of Our Most Famous Poets

Nguyễn Trãi (a.k.a. Ức Trai, 1380–1442) made great contributions as a humanist in strategy, but he was also one of Việt Nam's greatest poets. His poems in Chinese *Hán* appear in *Collection of Poems of Ức Trai* (Ức Trai Thi Tập) with 105 poems. His *Collection of Poems in the National Language* (Quốc Âm Thi Tập) contains 254 poems in *Nôm,* the Vietnamese ideographic script. These are the first important works in the Vietnamese national script that have been handed down to us. Besides revealing a major poet, they provide interesting material for study of the Vietnamese language and script used in the fifteenth century.

With Nguyễn Trãi, the humanist tendency of Vietnamese Confucianism reached its apogee, for he believed in fidelity to his monarch and to his people yet also believed in filial piety. These qualities marked a worthy man of letters. The important services he rendered did not lead him to seek vain honors at court, where contemptible flatterers swarmed. To save the country, he had to serve a king, but he never toadied to royalty. Nguyễn Trãi can be compared to the ivory bamboo with its stalk proudly shooting upwards, often standing alone. He suffered from witnessing incessant court intrigues and social injustices. The serenity he could not find in his entourage explains his extraordinary attachment to nature, which he chose as his confidant. Yet, for Nguyễn Trãi, commitment to social obligations always prevailed over withdrawal and renouncement of the world.

The samples below introduce this man's spirit and help explain why UNESCO (United Nations Educational, Scientific, and Cultural Organization) honored Nguyễn Trãi in 1980 on the six hundredth anniversary of his birth as a "Great Man of Culture of the World."

Nguyễn Trãi wrote the following poem, "Autumn Night Far from the Family, I" (Thu Dạ Khách Cảm, I), in *Hán* Chinese ideographic script, using seven-word meter:

> A desolate inn with a mat door,
> Arms folded, I recite poems at twilight.
> The sadness of autumn winds scattering leaves,
> Showers begin; dreams tremble in the lamplight.
> After war, old enemies are simply strangers,

I send that sorrowful thought to Heaven.
In the end, everything is but illusion,
Don't speak of kingdoms gained or lost.

He wrote this poem, "Profession of Faith, Poem #10" (Tự Thuật, Bài 10), with *Nôm* Vietnamese ideograms in seven-word meter, except for the first line of six words:

He seeks neither fame nor fortune,
Whether he wins or loses, who cares?
With hills and rivers he's not bored,
Poems stock his bag; wine, his gourd.
Friends are few, his lute lies silent,
With fish as companions, he won't fish.
Behold those who seek positions and fame,
Weeds will cover their graves and names.

Hồ Xuân Hương: Eroticism and Poetry

Over time, Nghệ Tĩnh (Nghệ An and Hà Tĩnh Provinces in central Việt Nam) has been famous for its picturesque sites, miraculous temples, and the individuals who reflect our nation's pride. Among these heroes are Nguyễn Du (1766–1820), author of our national epic, *The Tale of Kiều*; Mme. Hồ Xuân Hương (1772–1822), a poet famous for her anti-Confucian feminism and avowed carnal love; Nguyễn Công Trứ (1778–1859), the renowned poet, administrator, and economist; Hồ Chí Minh (1890–1969), poet and the founder of the modern Vietnamese state; hundreds of laureates of mandarin competitions; and illustrious contemporary individuals.

In 1952, while researching works in Chinese ideograms (*Hán*) and Vietnamese ideograms (*Nôm*) in the French archives, scholar Hoàng Xuân Hãn (1908–1996) found a manuscript written in *Hán*, which was a historic and geographic study of ancient Việt Nam. In the chapter dedicated to the maritime province of Quảng Yên, he found five poems by Mme. Hồ Xuân Hương. These poems praise the beauty of Hạ Long Bay as the poet's small boat passes among the startling islands and amidst sky and water, mountains and forests, birds and fish, and the fairyland-like ambiance of the setting sun.

Almost two hundred years after Hồ Xuân Hương's visit, modern-day readers can savor the feelings and impressions of a poet from our traditional culture. Here is a translation of "Crossing Hoa Phong" (Qua Vũng Hoa Phong), one of the five Quảng Yên poems that Hồ Xuân Hương wrote in seven-word meter, using Chinese ideographic script. "Hoa Phong" is an ancient name for Hạ Long Bay.

> Under sail, we leisurely cross Hoa Phong,
> Mossy green cliffs emerge from the water,
> The sea changes colors in mountains' shade,
> Waves lap at the nearby towering cliffs.
> Dragon fish dart beneath the autumn haze,
> Gulls and egrets drift into the sunset,
> Darting into the hundreds of jade grottos.
> Where is the Water Fairy's Crystal Palace?

An inevitable question arises: Is the author of this scholarly and elegant poem in Chinese characters the same Hồ Xuân Hương who scandalized Confucian orthodoxy with her poetry quivering with sensuality and vibrating with anger against social injustice? Archives of ancient works provide an affirmative answer, sketching for us a portrait of the woman from classical letters whose amorous passion found expression in the lyrical volume, *Collection of Hương's Poems* (Lưu Hương Ký).

For some time, Hồ Xuân Hương was the concubine of the governor of Vĩnh Tường District in Vĩnh Phúc Province northwest of Hà Nội. She scandalized the hypocritical feudal society with her sharp criticism of notables and her blunt yet refined verses praising the pleasures of the flesh, as in these lines in seven-word meter from "Three-Hill Pass" (Đèo Ba Dội):

> Whether sage or gentleman, none can refuse,
> Legs weakened, they still fancy the climb.

Or, consider this, the first of two quatrains from "Night Weaving" (Dệt Cửi Đêm), also written in seven-word meter:

> The lamp lit, one sees virgin white,
> The beater tapping gently through the night.
> The treadles tamp down, up again, down,
> The shuttle nudges along, a rushing sound.

If your friends think of you as rather prudish or if risqué pleasantries make you feel uneasy, do not read "The Jackfruit" (Quả Mít) by Hồ Xuân Hương, again in seven-word meter:

> Her fate: a jackfruit on a tree,
> Rough skin, but tasty in a spree.
> If you fancy, try sneaking a taste,
> Beware! A groping hand emits a trace.

This description of a fruit evoking the female reproductive organs is not from a book of erotica. Rather, Hồ Xuân Hương, one of the greatest names in classical Vietnamese literature, wrote the poem in the 1700s, using the Vietnamese ideographic script (Nôm). The original does not shock Vietnamese readers, who are charmed by the rhythm and music of the poet's words. However, the poem runs the risk of sounding obscene when translated into an analytical European language lacking the melody of Vietnamese tones.

Hồ Xuân Hương's poems lend themselves to reading on several levels. A feminist before her time, she wrote as an independent spirit struggling to survive in the stifling atmosphere of Confucianism. She dared to claim for women the right to physical love. She criticized the insincerity of hypocrites and defended unmarried mothers.

Lê Quý Đôn

The memory of this scholar lives on in anecdotes passed down by generations. People still recall his precocious intelligence and his presence of mind, which enabled him to improvise poems according to rigorous T'ang Dynasty meters and to juggle the subtlety of poetic parallel sentences. (For parallel sentences, see p. 215-16.) His reputation is perhaps best captured by the following story:

While en route to China, a typhoon struck an embassy mission, which included Lê Quý Đôn (a.k.a. Quế Đường, 1726–1784), forcing the group to stay in a local village for several days. To pass the time, Lê Quý Đôn leafed through a notebook containing the debts owed by the inn's clients. On his way back from China, Lê Quý Đôn was saddened to see that a fire had destroyed the inn. The innkeeper complained that dozens of debtors refused to pay because the innkeeper's debt book had burned. To the innkeeper's surprise, Lê Quý Đôn recalled all the debtors' names and their obligations.

Lê Quý Đôn came from Diên Hà Village in present-day Thái Bình Province. A child prodigy born into a scholar's family, he began classical studies at the age of five. He studied diligently at home until he was fourteen. Lê Quý Đôn received many honors. At eighteen, he was dubbed the first laureate at the provincial literary competition and, at twenty-seven, was first laureate in the national competition in the capital. He earned the title of doctor of the first degree, second rank (*bảng nhãn*) at the third level of competition, the one at the Royal Court.

Lê Quý Đôn worked at the Royal Academy and participated in writing its official history. In 1760, he was sent on a mission to China. Later, tired of the intrigues at the Vietnamese Royal Court, Lê Quý Đôn withdrew from public life, but he returned to the Royal Court in 1767 under the rule of Lord Trịnh Sâm (life: 1739–1782; in power: 1767–1782). Lê Quý Đôn held many important offices at the ministries of war, finance, and public works. However, he distinguished himself as the rector of the National University in Hà Nội's Temple of Confucius (Temple of Literature) and as director of the Bureau of Annals.

Lê Quý Đôn had an encyclopedic mind and an amazing capacity to produce quality scholarship. His monumental work, only part of which survives, is a precious source about the history, geography, economics, philosophy, and traditional customs of ancient Việt Nam. His historical works include *General History of Đại Việt* (Đại Việt Thông

Sử, where Đại Việt is a name for ancient Việt Nam) and *Monograph on the Frontier* (Phủ Biên Tạp Lục, about Thuận Hóa and Quảng Nam Provinces). His bibliographical works include *Anthology of Poems of Việt Nam* (Toàn Việt Thi Lục), while his philosophical works include *Explanations for the Confucian Book of Annals* (Thư Kinh Diễn Nghĩa). He also compiled works in other fields, such as *Small Collection of Things Seen and Heard* (Kiến Văn Tiểu Lục) and *Various Texts Written While Examining My Library* (Vân Đài Loại Ngữ). His candor about moral lapses at the Royal Court brought him many enemies. He died while assistant governor of Nghệ An Province.

Madame Thanh Quan

The few extant works by Mme. Thanh Quan (1805–1848, Madame Sub-Prefect of Thanh Quan District) have an undeniable originality and give her a special place in Vietnamese literature. Mme. Thanh Quan was born Nguyễn Thị Hinh in Nghi Tàm Village, now part of Hà Nội. She married the scholar Lưu Nguyên Ôn (a.k.a. Lưu Nghị), who was appointed sub-prefect of Thanh Quan District after his success at the triennial examinations in 1821. She taught at the royal harem, but as a woman, she could not take the mandarin examinations. However, she did express herself in her poetry.

Only a few of her poems remain. "Transverse Pass" (Đèo Ngang) in seven-word meter is the most famous:

> Reaching Transverse Pass as slanting shadows fall,
> Trees and flowers flourish amidst rocky walls;
> Bending, wood cutters shoulder a day's haul,
> The few riverside ethnic houses are small.
> "Remember our nation's pain," the *quốc*[1] bawls,

---

1. *Quốc*: The *quốc* (*đỗ vũ, tử quy,* and *đỗ quyên*) is probably the gold-beaked cuckoo (*Coccyzus americanus*), a medium-sized black bird with a gold beak and a white chin and breast. Its call is "*quốc quốc.*" In Vietnamese, "*quốc*" means "country."

"Cherish our precious family," the *gia*[1] calls;
Stop! Stand still! Sky, mountains, sea—all,
This moment alone, all of us, enthralled.

Another poem, "Nostalgia for Thăng Long" (Thăng Long Hoài Cổ), uses seven-word meter to ponder the flight of time, the fragility of human existence, and implacable destiny with a poignancy evoked by the sight of ruins. Although the poet expresses sorrow, her tone is sweet. "Thăng Long" (Soaring Dragon) is an old name for Hà Nội.

Then, the Creator launched his theatrical wish,
Time has swiftly flown, consigned to mist,
Horse-cart paths have turned into grassy wisps,
Former palace grounds rest in twilight's weakness.
Still, unshaken rocks do retain their grist,
The lake water's sad shimmering still persists,
Its centuries-old mirror reflecting every tryst—
This haunting, forlorn landscape: The heart twists.

Nguyễn Gia Thiều: Poet of Destiny and Sorrow

Nguyễn Gia Thiều (1741–1798) captured inexorable fate and the mishaps that strike all humans in *Lament of a Woman in the Harem*, (Cung Oán Ngâm Khúc). He wrote his poem in 356 verses, using quatrains with an uneven meter (two seven-word lines followed by a six-word line, followed by an eight-word line). This meter, which was unusual during his time, evokes a plaintive voice trembling with constrained tears. These opening quatrains set the context for Nguyễn Gia Thiều's masterpiece:

---

1. *Gia*: The *gia* is probably the Chinese Francolin (*Francolinus pintadeanus*), which is like an American grouse. Its call is "*gia gia.*" In Vietnamese, "*gia*" means "family." Vietnamese often uses two words together to create an abstraction. "*Quốc gia*" is a common compound word, which means "state," "nation," or "country."

Cinnamon paint, yet the wind still blows,
A down jacket is cold like bronze,
Begrudged payment for the royal chamber
And misfortune: A life sleeping in the harem.
Fate lures with luck, deceives with disaster,
Who else could create such heartless plots?
Why assign her this painful plight?
She looks ahead, sees she'll become more pitiful.

The military feats of Royal Guard Captain Nguyễn Gia Thiều (Marquis Ôn Như), a grandson of Shogun Lord Trịnh Cương, earned him the post of governor of Hưng Hóa, one of the thirteen provinces in the northern part of Việt Nam at that time. During his career as a mandarin, he was the target of envious colleagues' vilification and slander, which compounded the difficulties of living in a period of dynastic changes. It's not surprising that he chose to quit the mandarinal service and lead a hermit's life.

Nguyễn Gia Thiều was intrigued by Vietnamese *Nôm* script at a time when Chinese *Hán* ideograms dominated. Although he left a collection of poems in *Hán*, Nguyễn Gia Thiều's masterpiece remains *Lament of a Woman in the Harem*, which he wrote in *Nôm*. This work was startling at the time for its reflection of one woman's fate in the harem, when societal and literary tradition stood against all expression about an individual. *Lament of a Woman in the Harem* bears the imprint of Buddhism, which holds that to desire is to suffer. The young woman had wanted to enter a pagoda but was sent to the harem. Understandably, she wanted to break open the door and flee. Nguyễn Gia Thiều captured her plight:

Her heart quivered with ephemeral existence
Like foam floating on the sea of suffering.

Nguyễn Công Trứ:
The Poet of Poverty and "The Solitary Pine"

One of the most complex and fascinating Vietnamese literary figures from before the onset of the Western colonial conquest is Nguyễn

Công Trứ (1778–1858). For several decades, planners of school curricula banned the poems of this free-thinking Confucian scholar, while those taking an orthodox position on socio-economic classes accused him of repressing peasant revolts for the feudal monarchy. A more serene assessment, which takes historical circumstances into account, has rehabilitated this great man.

Nguyễn Công Trứ was born in Hà Tĩnh Province's Nghi Xuân District, the same district as our national poet, Nguyễn Du. The son of a poor scholar, Nguyễn Công Trứ was educated in the Confucian spirit. As a young man writing "Examination Poem for Myself" (Đi Thi Tự Vịnh), he dreamed of serving the country represented by the monarch. These two lines from the eight-line poem in six-word meter illustrate that point of view.

> Once we are born into this universe,
> We all deserve recognition from the nation.

Nguyễn Công Trứ was determined to pay his share of the debt that every follower of Confucianism owed to society. But despite his brilliance, he did not pass the mandarin examinations until he was forty-one, a ripe old age at that time. Beginning in a minor post, Nguyễn Công Trứ distinguished himself as a brilliant administrator and strategist. In his eventful career, he undertook important civil and military functions. He was especially known for clearing land along the coast of Nam Định and Ninh Bình Provinces. By building irrigation-and-drainage canals, he protected Tiền Hải and Kim Sơn Districts from the sea and expanded usable land. Such an economic feat was rare among old-school scholars, who were known for their literary bent rather than for action.

Despite these services, the Royal Court did not value Nguyễn Công Trứ's independent spirit. He was blamed for court intrigues and demoted. On one occasion, the Royal Court stripped Nguyễn Công Trứ of all titles and reduced him to the rank of foot soldier. Yet nothing kept Nguyễn Công Trứ from striving for the people's welfare. At age eighty, he volunteered to fight the French forces landing in Đà Nẵng, but his offer was refused.

The decadent feudal society's vices filled him with bitterness, which he expressed with his image of the solitary pine in "The Pine Tree" (Cây Thông), a six-line poem written in six-word, eight-word meter:

> When sad, he blames Heaven's guile,
> In joy, he weeps; in sorrow, he smiles,
> Refusing manhood for Next Life's trials.
> A pine, he stands rustling in the sky
> On a treacherous cliff dangerously high,
> Those who brave the cold may come nigh.

As is true of most Vietnamese old-school scholars, Nguyễn Công Trứ tempered his Confucian rationalism with tradition and with Taoism's epicureanism and irony. His favorite genre was *ca trù*—the song girls' verses taunting those who follow the social constraints of Confucianism, as he notes in this first of two quatrains from "Friendship, Poetry, and Wine" (Cầm Kỳ Thi Tửu):

> Now that he's acquired a taste for wine
> He cannot refuse a proffered cup this fine.
> Besieged by debts to poems he's heard,
> He's doomed to a life of polishing words.

Nguyễn Công Trứ also wrote about poverty in "The Poor Scholar's Charm" (Hàn Nho Phong Vị Phú), using what we now call free verse. Here, the poet refers to the use by rural people of sealed-off sections of hollow bamboo trunks as vessels for hauling water or storing rice. A household without rice (as opposed to manioc, sweet potatoes, or corn) in its stores is considered a hungry family.

> Damn poverty!
> Damn poverty!
> Aren't only a few people talented?
> Poverty is vice.
> It's one of the six misfortunes, according to the sacred
> books,

The first of all crimes, the proverbs say.
Here is an impoverished man:
His house has four walls made from areca sheaths,
Its three rooms covered with a roof of thatch,
Its rafters eaten by woodborers carving stars into the
    wood.
Spiders hang their webs in his doorway to block the
    wind,
Bamboo wattle divides this house: half, a kitchen; half,
    a bedroom.
His bamboo vessels hold only millet and beans,
Termites decorate the head of his bamboo bed with
    sinuous engravings,
The foot of his mud walls are where the worms go to
    deposit their dung.
. . .
He eats only vegetables three times a day, while
    noblemen need never eat their fill.
He sleeps soundly all night, his door left open, for he
    enjoys peace and prosperity.
. . .
He shifts one debt to another as his lenders arrogantly
    stroke their whiskers;
Like a servant facing masters, he fears they'll appear at
    his door. He turns his face, bowing.
The women, fearful, toss their trash at his back. They
    call after him with sharp retorts.
Few villagers dare approach his house.

Cao Bá Quát: Việt Nam's Rebel Poet

In the West, when speaking of a rebel poet, people might think of
the English poet, Lord Byron (1799–1824). In Việt Nam, we think
of Cao Bá Quát (1809–1853). Lord Byron died from fevers he contracted while fighting for Greek independence from the Ottoman

Empire. Cao Bá Quát died leading a peasant insurrection against the Huế Royal Court. These two poets belong not only to two different seasons of history and to two different socio-economic classes but also to two very different cultures—the Western culture characterized by a sense of individualism and the Asian culture dominated by a sense of community.

Cao Bá Quát was born into a scholarly family in Phú Thị near Hà Nội. He earned his master of arts in humanities at the age of twenty-four but was unable to proceed to his doctorate, even though others considered him a divine poet. He received an appointment to a subaltern post in Huế, where his petty functionary's work and the monarchy's corruption bored him. Then he was appointed as an official for the mandarin examinations but was condemned to death for attempting to save the capable examinees who had been unjustly accused of crimes against the sovereign. After his death sentence was commuted, he spent many years in prison, tortured like a criminal.

Released from prison, Cao Bá Quát was sent on a trade mission to Indonesia and Cambodia. This gave him an opportunity to observe Westerners (particularly the British) at close quarters and to appreciate their power. He issued a warning to potential aggressors in "The Red-Haired Strangers' Fire Boat" (Hồng Mao Hỏa Thuyền Ca). In the lines below, "Vỹ Lư" and "Ốc Tiêu" refer to "Autumn Waters," an entry in *Zhuangzi* by Zhuangzi (or perhaps by others). Zhuangzi (370–287 BCE) was a Chinese philosopher during the Warring States. "Autumn Waters" depicts myriad rivers and streams flowing into the sea and notes that, further, the sea never runs dry, can fill Vỹ Lư Cavern, and can drown the largest monolith (Ốc Tiêu).

> Foreigners, watch out:
> Floods fill Vỹ Lư, drown Ốc Tiêu,
> Look sharp: Our fire shakes the clouds.
> Take care when sailing toward the East,
> Unlike the West, we Easterners are relentless!

Cao Bá Quát sympathized with the humiliation of oppressed peoples. With sarcastic humor in "Watching Qing Actors Perform" (Đêm Xem Người Thanh Diễn Kịch), written in seven-word meter, he depicts Chinese actors from the Qing Dynasty (c. 1644–1912) in an opera. Here, "Hổ Môn" refers to the British victory over the Chinese Qing at Hổ Môn in 1840 during the First Opium War (1839–1842).

> The stage lit with only thin darkness,
> Sudden sounds make the night wind colder.
> A soldier with thick beard and mail,
> The false general calmly mounts and sits.
> Each attribute—even angry eyes—is bogus,
> Their costumes from ancient times are fake.
> Didn't Hổ Môn teach them any lessons?
> Boring! Yet the viewers, noses aloft, laugh.

While toasting a province chief, Cao Bá Quát improvised these opening lines from "An Afternoon of Wine at Province Chief Đông Tác's House" (Trên Chiếu Rượu ở Nhà Ông Tuần Phủ Đông Tác) in Chinese ideograms, using seven-word meter except for his three-word question:

> Sir, you have prepared wine, don't hesitate,
> Pour, keep on pouring! Older Brother, drink!
> Don't you see?
> The eagle flies as high as clouds,
> The black crane sleeps on the hillside,
> The oriole seeks seeds from dawn to dusk.

Here, the eagle symbolizes those who nurture big ambitions; the black crane, those who retire into a contemplative retreat; the oriole, those concerned only with their daily rice.

A man of courage, Cao Bá Quát could not bear the injustices of his time. Neither could he find solace in Buddhism, as he expressed in "Mocking the Buddha with a Broken Arm" (Trào Chiết Tý Phật), which he wrote in Chinese ideograms using seven-word meter:

Everyone says a diamond cannot be broken,
What about Buddha with a broken arm?
He cannot save himself, how about others?
His fawning bonzes skim his altar offerings.

Cao Bá Quát's death while leading rebel troops is the logical outcome for the life of a man who, under the absolute monarchy, dared to write: "All my life, I have bowed only before the flowers of plum trees."

Nguyễn Đình Chiểu:
A Poet Blinded by Tears of Grief

The most popular classical works of Việt Nam are two novels of verse written in Vietnamese ideograms (*Nôm*): *The Tale of Kiều* (Truyện Kiều) by Nguyễn Du (1766–1820) and *Lục Vân Tiên* (Lục Vân Tiên) by Nguyễn Đình Chiểu (1822–1888). While the first work captures the poet's insights in beautiful verses, the second uses the language of ordinary people to express a Confucian scholar's fiery passion as his Homeland faces French invasion.

Born as the son of a low-ranking mandarin in what is now Sài Gòn, Nguyễn Đình Chiểu went to Huế with his bachelor's degree in hand to prepare for the examination that would give him the chance to secure a master's degree and maybe even a doctorate. However, misfortune thwarted his ambitions. As a true Confucian, when he heard of his mother's death, he abandoned his academic pursuits and returned home in mourning. It is said that he wept so deeply while en route home that he lost his sight. But that was not all. The rich landlord who had promised Nguyễn Đình Chiểu his daughter's hand broke the engagement.

Nguyễn Đình Chiểu opened a school to teach traditional medicine. He married a student's sister and lived in Cần Giuộc, his wife's village, where he taught while resisting the French. When the Huế Royal Court ceded half of southern Việt Nam to the invading French in 1862, Nguyễn Đình Chiểu retired to the Mekong Delta's

Bến Tre Province, where he lived until his death, refusing to collaborate. He remained in close touch with the patriotic scholars who continued the armed resistance.

Vietnamese have immortalized Nguyễn Đình Chiểu because of his novel, *Lục Vân Tiên*, and his "Funeral Oration for the Cần Giuộc Partisans" (*Văn Tế Nghĩa Sĩ Cần Giuộc*). Cần Giuộc District (now part of Hồ Chí Minh City) fought a violent battle against the French on December 18, 1861. Nguyễn Đình Chiểu's eulogy recounts how simple peasants—barefoot, dressed in rags, and armed with bamboo spears—joined the patriotic army defending independence. The language combines a scholar's erudition with ordinary, plain language. "Six provinces" in the excerpt below refers to the six southern provinces that the French had occupied.

> You have passed on, leaving our nation in debt, with
>   your name praised across the six provinces,
> You have passed on. Our temples will honor you, spreading the word so that ten thousand generations
>   sing your praises.

Lục Vân Tiên, an epic poem written in *Nôm* ideographic script about the misfortunes of a capable young man with strong moral values, is partially autobiographical. Upon completion of his studies, Lục Vân Tiên bids farewell to his teachers and travels to the Royal Capital for the mandarin literary examination. On his way, he saves the beautiful Kiều Nguyệt Nga from the thugs who have abducted her. She vows loyalty to Lục Vân Tiên until her life's end, but he hardly notices her and later becomes engaged to another woman. Just as he is about to take his exams, Lục Vân Tiên learns of his mother's death. He abandons the examination, returns home in mourning, and weeps until he goes blind.

Trịnh Hâm, a treacherous competitor from the exams, capitalizes on Lục Vân Tiên's grief by pushing the blind scholar into a river. Lục Vân Tiên is rescued and returns to his village, only to discover that his fiancée and her father have broken the engagement. Father and daughter abandon Lục Vân Tiên in a cave, but the spirits save Lục Vân Tiên. He goes on to earn his degree at the next triennial examination and defeats the Ô Qua barbarians. Meanwhile, Kiều Nguyệt Nga, whom Lục Vân Tiên rescued from thugs years before, has been sent as tribute to King Ô Qua by the prime minister in retaliation for her refusal to marry the minister's son. Kiều Nguyệt Nga throws herself in a river to protect her love for Lục Vân Tiên. Bodhisattva Avalokitesvara (Quan Âm) saves Kiều Nguyệt Nga and eventually returns her to Lục Vân Tiên. In the end, all the wicked characters are punished, whereas the kind-hearted are rewarded.

Nguyễn Khuyến

In my generation, almost all Vietnamese children sitting at their benches in primary schools learned by heart "Fishing in Autumn" (Thu Điếu), written in seven-word meter with rhyme:

> The autumn pond is cool and clear,
> His tiny dinghy is simple to steer;
> A gentle wind keeps the water clear,
> A gold leaf glides toward the pier.
> The clouds tumble by, stacked in tiers,
> Lonely tree-lined village paths are near;
> He quietly hugs his knees and hears
> Fish gulp his bait beside the weir.

Here, poet Nguyễn Khuyến (1835–1909) sings the pleasures of retreat and his love for nature. At the same time, he expresses his melancholy and his resignation at the fate of our country occupied by the French.

Nguyễn Khuyến was a laureate three times at the triennial examinations, hence his title Tam Nguyên (Three Doctorates). During his appointment as a mandarin at the Huế Royal Court, he lived in poverty and with exemplary integrity. Loyal to Confucian traditions, he honored the king above all. However, after the Huế Royal Court surrendered to the French, Nguyễn Khuyến's love for the people prevailed over his absolute loyalty to the sovereign. In 1883, as chief of the Annual Records Bureau, he used the pretext of eye disease to request retirement to his native village, thus refusing to collaborate with the enemy. He declined a request to serve as governor of Sơn Hưng Tuyên Province, which the French had occupied.

Nguyễn Khuyến wrote in classical Chinese ideograms (*Hán*) and also in the Vietnamese ideographic script (*Nôm*). He satirized the colonizers, the French officers' concubines, the Vietnamese who profited from commerce with the occupiers, and the mandarins who knew how to make the best of the French occupation. His best known poems are "The *Chèo* Singer's Wife" (Lời Vợ Người Hát Chèo, an attack on Tonkin Viceroy Hoàng Cao Khải, an agent of the French), "Mother Mốc" (Mẹ Mốc, a poem about a widow, who fakes insanity to keep suitors away, and also a literary allusion to the patriots who refused to collaborate with the colonizers), "The Westerners' Festival" (Hội Tây, a satire about the French National Day celebration organized in Việt Nam), and "Fishing in Autumn," (Thu Điếu, the lyrical poem quoted above).

Phạm Tất Đắc: His Incendiary Poem

Phạm Tất Đắc (1909–1935) published his poem, "Invocation for the Nation's Soul" (Chiêu Hồn Nước), in Hà Nội in 1927, when he was a seventeen-year-old high-school student. The French immediately banned the poem and threw Phạm Tất Đắc in jail.

During the first decades of the 1900s, the fight against colonialism took on a new season because of great economic, social, and political upheavals. The colonizers' two stages for developing Việt Nam (the first between 1897 and 1914 and the second between 1919 and 1929) accelerated pauperization of the peasantry. A new social class—the working class—emerged following establishment of industrial and mining enterprises, the spread of railways, and the creation of rubber and coffee plantations. At the same time, a fragile bourgeoisie and a more active, intellectual petit bourgeoisie appeared. Foreign ideas and events influencing those groups included the thinking that had led to the French Revolution (1789) as conveyed through Chinese translations of works by Charles Montesquieu (1689–1755) and Jean-Jacques Rousseau (1712–1778), the victory of Japan over Russia in 1905 (that is, of Yellow people over White people), and the triumph of the Russian Proletarian Revolution in 1917.

The patriotic movement split into two trends. One was led by Phan Bội Châu (1867–1940), an advocate of armed struggle, whom the French arrested in 1925 in Shanghai, which was at that time a French concession in China. The other was led by Phan Châu (Chu) Trinh (1872–1926), a partisan of democratic reforms and political struggle, who went into self-exile in France from 1911 to 1925. The funeral of Phan Châu Trinh in 1926 led to nationwide demonstrations attended by tens of thousands of people.

Phạm Tất Đắc wrote "Invocation for the Nation's Soul" in that setting. The Protectorate Secondary School expelled him for participating in the students' walk-out honoring Phan Châu Trinh's funeral. Then, in 1927, the authorities arrested Phạm Tất Đắc for publishing his poem. He was imprisoned at Tri Cụ Detention House for Young Delinquents in Bắc Giang Province in Việt Nam's far north and then at Hà Nội's Hỏa Lò Prison, which was known during the American War as the Hà Nội Hilton. He was released in 1930 but died five years later from illness.

The beginning of Phạm Tất Đắc's long "Invocation for the Nation's Soul" evokes the unfortunate fate and shame of a nation without a Homeland. Here, "*quốc*" is the yellow-beaked cuckoo, a small black bird with a white face and breast and a gold beak. Its call is "*quốc, quốc.*" "*Quốc*" in Vietnamese means "country."

> Alone through the watches of the deserted night,
> He wants to pour out his blood, dye our rivers and peaks.
> A gust of wind enters, the stricken lamp quivers,
> The sound of the *quốc* impels him to ardent heroism.

The poem mobilized nationalists with its melancholic tone and invocation of souls of the dead, for Phạm Tất Đắc invited the soul of the Homeland to return. In the lines cited below, he mentions Hồng Lạc, where "Hồng" refers to Việt Nam's legendary founding dynasty, Hồng Bàng, while "Lạc" invokes the legendary Âu Lạc Kingdom, antecedent of modern-day Việt Nam.

> Come back, Ancient Soul, and help us,
> Descendants of Hồng Lạc, now Việt Nam.
> What greater happiness, what greater glory
> Than my corpse wrapped in my war horse's hide.

The anti-colonial movement took firmer shape between 1925 and 1936, leading to creation of several organizations: the Association of Revolutionary Vietnamese Youth (Việt Nam Thanh Niên Cách Mạng Đồng Chí Hội, established by Hồ Chí Minh in 1925), the New Việt Nam Revolutionary Party (Tân Việt Cách Mạng Đảng, 1925), and the Việt Nam Nationalist Party (Việt Nam Quốc Dân Đảng, 1927). The French crushed the last organization in 1930 after the Yên Bái Uprising, while Hồ Chí Minh united the first two with other communist organizations in early 1930 to create the Vietnamese Communist Party.

Romantic Literary Currents in the 1930s

The New Poetry (Thơ Mới) Movement dominated legally published literature during the 1930s. For many years, magazines such as *Southerly Wind* (Nam Phong) had printed long columns of poetry written in conventional forms with linguistic clichés describing the same old themes of autumn, nostalgia, tears over a friend's death, and solitary souls gazing at the moon. These old themes and their old poetic forms no longer satisfied young intellectuals in Việt Nam's burgeoning towns.

The first literary clashes came at the end of the 1920s over whether to abandon meter from the Chinese T'ang (Đường) Dynasty (816–907). Traditional poets considered T'ang meter a perfect form. Its rigid rules demanded strict correspondence between tone and rhyme, absolute symmetry in certain verses, and only depersonalized expression. T'ang poetry may have approached its perfection in classical Chinese and Vietnamese literature, but it was the poetry of a bygone era, which had effaced individual sensitivity in service of primary truths portrayed in their essence rather than with specificity. This refined poetry was comprehensible only after mature assimilation of the entire poetic tradition. Consequently, average poets—that is to say, the majority of poets—were condemned to imitating masterpieces and repeating clichés. Rare were those who produced sincere and original poems.

The polemicists favoring old forms lost out to adherents of New Poetry. Those favoring New Poetry were not better polemicists or theoreticians, but they did represent the substantial number of young poets who were bringing new vigor to Vietnamese poetry. Young urban intellectuals welcomed those new poets: Thế Lữ (1907–1989), Lưu Trọng Lư (1912–1991), Phạm Huy Thông (1916–1988), Xuân Diệu (1916–1985), Chế Lan Viên (1920–1989), Huy Cận (1919–2005), Hàn Mạc Tử (1912–1940), and Tế Hanh (1921–2009).

These newcomers had youth on their side; some had published their first poems at age sixteen. Above all, they depicted changes in a society, which had congealed into dry ritualism. Their repudiation of T'ang poetry's rules dealt more with content than form by introducing the first-person pronoun "I" into literature. Previously, Vietnamese writing had used "we" or the even the more general "one" or the third-person pronouns—"he," "she," and "they."

Poetry expanded beyond the traditional, depersonalized generalities of joy, sadness, and despair into specificity in all of its intimate, quivering, flesh-and-bones nuances. With vibrating, sharpened, almost pathological sensitivity, New Poetry unveiled previously hidden aspects of how people suffer, rejoice, feel, and savor experiences. For example, Thế Lữ characterized Tản Đà (1889–1939) as a poet from the preceding generation, whose verses were lyrical compared with those of the ancients, but in his poetry, one feels neither anguish nor bitterness nor full joy. Tản Đà pays no attention to the hidden corners of our sensitivity but, instead, remains placid, serene, like a soft breeze brushing branches in a well-kept garden. Thế Lữ wrote this about Tản Đà:

"We poets of today do not want to feel and cannot feel and be moved the way he was. Our deep feelings are far more complex. We suffer, we feel more, and when we burst with joy, that joy takes on unusual colors and nuances."

Xuân Diệu declared that the poet "listens for hidden voices, lights up even the heavy mist of our entrails, distinguishes thousands of ways to love and to express desire, and is constantly searching for the most delicate vibrations."

Each poet of this new generation had a particular style, an individual way of expressing feelings through verse and language. This sharpened sensitivity resonated with the urban petit bourgeois intellectuals whom the feudal and colonial regime had been suffocating and who were avid for new horizons but who were powerless to overthrow the regime. They sought answers to their most intimate aspirations in the artistic expression of individualized feelings.

This period does not have the vigor of the preceding generation's patriotic poets. The petit bourgeoisie did not foment widespread political movements. They confined their love for the Homeland to love for the countryside by describing corners of rural landscape or village markets with their intoxicating visual, auditory, and olfactory sensations. Facing the spectacle of life and the universe, these poets overflowed with nostalgia, the despair of unrequited love, and boundless, senseless melancholy. This was unquestionably an expression in specifically Vietnamese forms in a specific social stratum of Vietnamese society at a specific stage. Nevertheless, the influence of French poets is evident, including Alphonse de Lamartine (1790–1869), Victor Hugo (1802–1885), and, above all, Charles Baudelaire (1821–1867), Arthur Rimbaud (1854–1891), and Paul Verlaine (1844–1896).

The *belle époque* of New Poetry did not last long. This fragile flower withered at the beginning of the Second World War. Poetry rapidly became abstruse in its search for form without content. Nevertheless, this movement marked a stage of Vietnamese poetry and created new forms, particularly the eight-word line. New Poetry made poetic meter supple, and it refined the use of words, giving them colors and nuances. Over time, most poets from this generation changed their political thinking and joined the patriotic, revolutionary movement.

In addition to poetry, the short stories and novels that appeared between 1930 and 1939 (and blossomed largely between 1932 and 1936) reflected the vibrant sensitivity of the urban petit bourgeois writers who were avid for life but unable to shake the colonial, feudal regime. The Self-Reliance Literary Group (Tự Lực Văn Đoàn) and its leaders—Nhất Linh (1906–1963) and Khái Hưng (1896–1947)—are closely connected with the birth and evolution of romantic fiction, which was popular for several years.

Withdrawing from political and social problems too sensitive to handle, the Self-Reliance writers at first concentrated on the individual's revolt against feudal rules, particularly regarding love and marriage. Hoàng Ngọc Phách (1896–1973) addressed this theme first in Việt Nam's Northern Region (Tonkin, Bắc Kỳ) in 1925 with his novel, *Tố Tâm* (Tố Tâm). Fiction writers affected by the New Poetry Movement in the 1930s explored the same themes as the poets did but with greater vigor and more drama. The title of Nhất Linh's novel, *Breakaway* (Đoạn Tuyệt), is significant. The novel eloquently denounces a feudal family, which marries off its daughters only for social prestige, without considering the daughters' feelings: "By all means, safeguard the family," a character says, "but this must in no way be taken as the maintenance of a system of slavery!"

Many character types from antiquated feudalism—shrewish mothers-in-law, rich villagers, and mandarins who misappropriate public funds and property—appeared in the least flattering ways. Love, which had been liberated from financial interests and family prestige, became a basic and passionate demand. Fictional characters were young people with new ideas opposing a society bogged down in outmoded ceremony and rules. Narratives swelled with conflict, drama, and feelings from real life. The writers did not construct these novels like traditional stories, with their episodes strung together in a chronology of their heroes' exploits. Instead, they traced their characters with delicacy and described the most private aspects of their characters' emotional lives.

As in New Poetry, these writers of fiction painted nature with vibrant descriptions. Authors tenderly evoked the mossy roofs of an old pagoda, the plume of an areca palm trembling in the wind, or the colors of the sky reddening at dawn. They no longer bent their author's will toward developing a thesis. Rather, they relied on the natural logic of characters, on conflicts between characters, and on conflicts between characters and their social environment. The language was more natural and supple and followed the characters' psychological development amidst descriptions of nature and social environments. These romantic works represented a new step in Vietnamese fiction. However, weaknesses arose from content and ideology. Although the urban petit bourgeoisie was in revolt, these authors' individualism lacked perspective and yielded to personal adventure, religion, and art for art's sake.

Khái Hưng's *A Butterfly Dreams of Fairies* (Hồn Bướm Mơ Tiên, 1933) was among the first novels by an author from the Self-Reliance Group to come into vogue. It reflects an obsession with the sight of peaceful pagodas, the perfume of incense, and the long, monotonous sound of bells in the evening mist. Unfortunately, those revolting against the feudal order had no action plan for overthrowing that order and building a new society. Their heroes faded away like mysterious shadows detached from social reality and without definite action. This romanticism presented heroes who, above the crowds, scorned not only the rich and newly rich but also humble people broken by poverty and life's daily worries.

Some writers threw themselves into activity for the pleasure of action because they could not affect the established system. The years 1931 to 1936 saw the blossoming of romantic literature but also marked the death of the bourgeois nationalist parties. Writers created dreamy heroes whose "hair trembled in the winds from the four corners of the horizon" at a time when colonial repression pitilessly attacked the revolutionary militants whose political and social actions could lead to prison and the gallows.

Faced with these conditions, writers from the urban intelligentsia found consolation for their despair in romanticism through their heroes' endless, aimless trips for the pleasure of changing places. The last refuge for these men, who were so avid for action but who dared not risk action, was love. An example is the hero of Nhất Linh's *Two Friends* (Đôi Bạn): "He did not dare think of living far from Loan or of dying one day in foreign parts and lying in a dark coffin, only to have Loan lean over his grave, the hem of her gown floating in the wind."

Should Nguyễn Tuân rank among these romantics?

The question is difficult to answer because Nguyễn Tuân (1910–1987) carved out an independent place. Travel mania was prominent in his works. He described himself as "seized by an indefinable regret each time he reached his goal, as though he had lost something infinitely precious." We must also note other themes of Nguyễn Tuân's works: his nostalgia for the splendors and refinements of the past and an accentuated, romantic character.

Events rapidly overtook these authors' narrow romanticism. While some authors evolved and participated in the great mass movement that developed after 1936, the Self-Reliance Group, particularly Nhất Linh and Khái Hưng, turned first to reformism. Their novels began to praise so-called progressive landlords but then openly turned to adventurous action. But then the romantic vein dried up; these writers' subsequent works lacked their earlier books' inspiration. After 1936, the shift toward realism gradually secured dominance.

Tản Đà and Quang Dũng: Two Poets of the West Country

The region west of Hà Nội has the traditional name of Xứ Đoài (West Country). Two of its lyrical poets, Tản Đà (1889–1939, described as old-school in the essay above about New Poetry) and Quang Dũng (1921–1988), are among the most prominent writers of our recent literature. Tản Đà, the pen name taken by Nguyễn Khắc Hiếu, marks the poet's attachment to his native province, where "*Tản*" is an abbreviation for Mount Tản Viên and "*Đà*" comes from the Đà River. Tản Đà is regarded as a link between traditional poetry and New Poetry (*Thơ Mới*). After failing the mandarin examinations twice, he set aside his study of classical Chinese and earned his living as a journalist, essayist, and poet.

Tản Đà's verses, which are sprinkled with metrical audacities, are those of a man tired of living, who wants to escape modern life, seek sensuous enjoyment, and relish the company of wind and clouds, hills and streams. All his life, Tản Đà lived and worked in poverty, caring neither for wealth nor honors, as "Separation" (Tống Biệt, 1922), which he wrote in free verse, indicates. This poem builds on a Chinese legend, where two men lost in the woods meet two spirits, who take the young men to live as their husbands in the Land of Fairies. Homesick after six months, the men ask to return to the World of Mortals, but then are bereft because they can never go back to the Land of Fairies:

> Peach leaves lie scattered on the byway leading to the
>   Land of Fairies,
> The stream murmurs farewell to the oriole carrying their
>   message of loss.
> Half a year in the Land of Fairies,
> One step: This misery in the World of Mortals.
> Their oaths of fidelity are all that remain,
> A few flagstones covered with moss,
> The water flowing, a flower drifting,
> A crane ascending in open sky.
> The separation between Heaven and Earth is forever:
> The opening to the cavern,
> The mountain peak,
> The ancient pathway—
> The two search in vain in the shadows of the moon.

Tản Đà had a soft spot for wine, as appears in the first two lines from the eight-line "Poem for a Spring Day's Wine" (Ngày Xuân Thơ Rượu):

Heaven and Earth gave us wine and poetry
Without poetry and wine, how can we live?

Tản Đà also drew inspiration from folk songs, as shown in the opening couplets from several different folk poems (*ca dao*) in "Collected Songs – Oral Folk Poetry" (Hát Tạp – Lối Phong Dao) in six-eight meter, with a six-word line followed by an eight-word line:

Autumn night breezes rustle the areca:
Her husband away, who can relieve her sorrow?
Autumn night breezes twitter to her:
Do night breezes know where her husband is?
Autumn night breezes flutter the curtains:
Her husband away, why does wind dare enter?

Whereas Tản Đà heralded New Poetry, Quang Dũng (1921–1988) carried the torch forward. A participant in the August 1945 Revolution and the Resistance War Against France, he devoted his life to the ideal of sacrifice and the need for dreams and love. Typical in this respect is his poem "Westward March" (Tây Tiến), which he wrote in seven-word meter to portray young volunteers in the Resistance during the 1948 Northwest Campaign. He depicts soldiers inspired by staunch courage and tender memories as they face death in forested hills infested with malaria-carrying mosquitoes. These men, who were poorly clothed and poorly equipped, had no medicine and so little food that they lost their hair:

They march westward, scalps bare of hair
Leaf-green uniforms, faces fierce like tigers,
Their eyes sending dreams beyond the border,
Their nightly dreams of Hà Nội maidens.
Despite the graves scattered along the border,
Approaching the front, they sacrifice their youth.

Soldiers knew Quang Dũng's verses by heart. Young women repeated to themselves his poems of love, nostalgia, and fantasy. In "Eyes of a Sơn Tây Girl" (Đôi Mắt Người Sơn Tây, 1949), the poet evokes an encounter with an evacuee from his native province, beginning in seven-word meter and building to a stanza of five-word lines:

> Your brow like our native village sky,
> Your eyes like our village well water
> I miss the West Country's white clouds,
> How long have you yearned for me?
> . . .
> The Sơn Tây woman's eyes,
> Despondent during an afternoon adrift,
> Longing for her ancestral fields.

Hàn Mặc Tử: Finding Poetry in Suffering

Hàn Mặc Tử (1912–1940), known as the Leper Poet toward the end of his tormented life, occupies a place apart in the 1930s New Poetry (*Thơ Mới*) Movement. His childhood name was Pierre-François Nguyễn Trọng Trí. He came from a Catholic family in Đồng Hới, Quảng Bình Province in the Central Region (Annam, Trung Kỳ), lost his father in infancy, and was raised by his mother, who was the daughter of a medical doctor at the Royal Court. Nguyễn Trọng Trí was introduced to poetry by his brother, a witty man of letters. At age fifteen, Trí began composing poems. At twenty, he took a job at the local land office, but for only two years. He then took up journalism in Sài Gòn but at age twenty-four contracted Hansen's Disease and was sent to the Quy Hòa Leprosy Center in Bình Định Province. He died four years later of what was then an incurable disease.

During the 1600s, Jesuit missionaries created the first Catholic communities in Việt Nam. However, the Catholic Church developed only after the French conquest in the mid-1880s. Nevertheless, Catholicism did not integrate into the national culture, as had Buddhism, Taoism, and Confucianism. Those belief systems were also imported, yet even though Jesuit missionaries had developed the Romanized Vietnamese script (*Quốc Ngữ*) to facilitate evangelization, they faced the following obstacles: Christianity conflicted not only with Confucianism but also with Việt Nam's traditional worship of ancestors and mother goddesses. Other challenges to evangelization came from colonial politics because the Catholic clergy—especially the hierarchy—allied itself with the colonizing French.

Nevertheless, Christianity sowed the seeds of individualism among intellectuals and artists, including Hàn Mặc Tử. His encounters with French poetry gave him a sharpened sense of self and led to his conclusion that classical poetry was fruitlessly impersonal. Hàn Mặc Tử adopted the free verse of French poetry in his earliest poems. He praised life but with the anguish and despair of a soul thirsty for human and divine love. Never before had a Vietnamese poet written with such a personal style in eight-word meter as Hàn Mặc Tử did in "Ave Maria":

> I bow before You, Oh Our Holy Mother,
> Let my love blossom full, like the moon,
> Let my poetry flourish pure, like my heart
> Eternally singing, throbbing in my soul and veins.
> Let my poems spread, like the myriad stars,
> Let my poems enchant with music and perfume.

After he contracted leprosy, Hàn Mặc Tử wrote about the horrors of the disease and the specter of death. Particularly famous is his collection, *Poems of Madness* (Đau Thương – Thơ Điên, 1938). These lines in seven-word meter come from "Unwilling to Part, II" (Lưu Luyến, II) in the second volume of *Poems of Madness*:

> I'm crazy, speaking like a mad man,
> Imploring the Great Void: Erase these days!
> These days, great sadness tinges my suffering,
> These days, clouds in the azure sky,
> These sounds of golden music all about,
> These secret tremblings in nights of love.

Dương Quảng Hàm:
The First Modern Literary History of Việt Nam

A symposium in July 1993 commemorated the ninety-fifth birth anniversary of Dương Quảng Hàm (1898–1946), an expert on Vietnamese literature. He had participated in the August 1945 Revolution and died while college rector in 1946, during the early days of the Resistance War Against France. The conference papers brought back my fond memories of a teacher I greatly admired. Dương Quảng Hàm's erudition, dignity, and, above all, the integrity he showed while teaching French and Vietnamese at the Lycée du Protectorat in Hà Nội made him an example for many of us.

Dương Quảng Hàm belonged to the generations of traditional scholars born during Việt Nam's monarchy (900s through 1800s), which founded Việt Nam's first university. That first university, established in 1076 behind Hà Nội's Temple to Confucius (Temple of Literature), instituted a comprehensive examination system to screen professional administrators for functions previously performed by the aristocracy. Feudal education focused on morality, philosophy, and *belles-lettres*. Beginning in the 1400s, Confucianism stressed absolute loyalty to the monarch.

When the French conquered Việt Nam at the end of the 1800s, patriotic scholars rallied to the Save-the-King (Cần Vương) Movement since, for them, the king symbolized the Homeland. Their royalist cause disintegrated at the turn of the century. Old-school scholars, who had become modernists, launched new patriotic movements. These scholars included Phan Bội Châu (1867–1940), with his anti-imperialist stand; Phan Châu (Chu) Trinh (1872–1926), who tried to win support from French democratic forces; and Hồ Chí Minh (1890–1969), who placed the anti-imperial struggle in the broader context of internationalism.

Meanwhile, many modernists not directly engaged in revolutionary activities worked in the colonial administration without abandoning their patriotic stance. Among these staunch patriots was my Lycée teacher, Dương Quảng Hàm. His father and brother had been sentenced to Poulo Condor (Côn Đảo) Prison Island because of their involvement with the Eastern Capital School for the Just Cause, sometimes called the Tonkin Free School (Đông Kinh Nghĩa Thục), an underground revolutionary organization. Dương Quảng Hàm trained at the Pedagogy College in Hà Nội as a scholar of Vietnamese, Chinese, and French classical literature. He taught Vietnamese and French at the Lycée du Protectorat for more than two decades, intriguing us with our mother tongue and vernacular literature, whereas colonial education relegated these subjects to the background. He emphasized the importance of folk literature as the foundation of our national culture and showed that Vietnamese literature followed an independent course while benefiting from adoption of new forms from foreign cultures.

Dương Quảng Hàm staged a one-man cultural battle, a patriotic act of faith, by writing *Literary History of Việt Nam* (Việt Nam Văn Học Sử Yếu, 1941). This first Vietnamese literary history, which was published under strict censorship, is famous for clearsighted analysis, as shown here in the book's conclusion:

> Our people are endowed with a vitality, which has withstood every test. We have not been subjected to assimilation despite centuries of Chinese domination. What is more, we have succeeded in exploiting Chinese culture to build a wellorganized society and a literature which, without being extraordinary, does not lack in originality. It is certain that in the future, our people will find in French literature what it has as its best . . . [and] build a literature, which responds appropriately to modernity and to the need to preserve tradition.

Those lines written under Franco-Japanese censorship are a statement of national dignity, pride, and modesty. They apply to independent Việt Nam today.

Women Writers Give Vietnamese Literature Some Oooh La La

Confucian prudery reigned supreme in Vietnamese classical literature, until Nguyễn Du and Hồ Xuân Hương came along in the eighteenth century to spice things up. Woman poet Hồ Xuân Hương is thought to have written some sixty highly erotic poems. Although Nguyễn Du is the author of our epic poem, *Tale of Kiều* (Truyện Kiều), another part of his legacy is the creation of Vietnamese literature's first nude scene, where heroine Kiều is described while bathing:

> Luminescent as jade, pale as ivory,
> Rounded, full, luscious, a sculpture created by Heaven.

During French colonialism, writers flirted with libertinism but never ventured beyond timid experimentation. During the thirty years of war following our Declaration of Independence in 1945 and especially during the partition of Việt Nam from 1954 to 1975, patriotic duties outweighed personal interests in North Việt Nam. Moral rectitude reigned. The slightest misstep raised eyebrows all around.

Since *Đổi Mới* (Renovation or Renewal, which began in late 1986), a more personal and more critical trend has emerged in literature. Its latest product—eroticism—is causing strong reactions. At the forefront are women writers, among them Đỗ Hoàng Diệu (1976–), Y Ban (1961–), and Nguyễn Ngọc Tư (1976–).

Đỗ Hoàng Diệu's short story, "Nightmare" (Bóng Đè), describes a young wife haunted by her deceased Chinese father-in-law, whose photograph she has seen in a clan temple at her husband's native village. The first night of her visit to the village, the father-in-law's ghost rapes the young woman, plunging her into a nervous breakdown. The story's explicit description of sexual acts shocked many readers.

Y Ban's "I Am . . . a Woman" (I Am . . . Đàn Bà), the title story in one of her collections, describes a Vietnamese woman, who has been hired to nurse a rich man in Taiwan. When the young woman unwittingly arouses her lethargic master's libido, she is accused of sexual harassment, punished, and fired.

Perhaps best known among Nguyễn Ngọc Tư's many short-story collections is *Endless Rice Paddies* (Cánh Đồng Bất Tận), with its title story, where a duck breeder lives in sullen silence with his son and daughter. Day in and day out, he plies a maze of canals on a small sampan, which is also their home. After his beautiful wife elopes with a dealer in dry goods, he seeks revenge by seducing one woman after another. Without love, his children become mentally disturbed. The philandering father finally takes hold of himself, but it is too late. His son, who had run away, returns with a gang of wild boys and forces his father to witness the rape of his own daughter.

Nguyễn Ngọc Tư writes with simplicity, always against the backdrop of her native Cà Mau Province at the southern tip of Việt Nam. In her narratives, misery co-exists alongside resignation, compassion, and hunger for love and beauty. Whatever she describes flows naturally in light touches, creating the prose that average readers find easily palatable. However, her stories are not to the taste of some local officials, who brand them as "sexually-oriented, obscene, and mud-slinging."

Culture and the Arts

Vietnamese Lacquer:
All Tradition Is Change through Acculturation

For several decades, the ambiguous relationship in Việt Nam between tradition and revolution—between the past and modernity, between the preservation of ancestral heritage and elaboration of the future, and between our national identity and international influences—has caused much ink to flow among social scientists, cultural-policy strategists, artists, and scholars of aesthetics. Some obsessively attempt to square the art circle, asking: How can we make national tradition blossom when a world culture exerts pressure from a distance to make everything uniform? How do we avoid chauvinistic formalism caused by clinging to unchanged values?

The solution seems to lie in this maxim: "All tradition is change through acculturation."

I believe cultures have always faced the challenge of change. Even Paleolithic and Neolithic cultures had to modernize themselves, if that term may be used. To survive, all cultures must evolve through endogenous and exogenous factors while maintaining their foundations. An example from Vietnamese culture is lacquer, which comes from sumac sap. Sumacs grow in the northern uplands, particularly in Phú Thọ Province, a cradle of the Việt people's Đông Sơn Culture, which blossomed during the Bronze Age (first millennium BCE). Sumac sap is transparent, but after treatment it turns black or takes on the brown hue of cockroach wings.

Since 1961, archaeological excavations have found funerary objects of lacquered wood and leather as well as tools used in lacquer work. These artifacts, although not numerous and of little variety, prove the existence of lacquer skills among the Việt in the northern Red River Delta as early as the fourth century BCE. However, no documentation on Vietnamese lacquer work during the subsequent thousand years of Chinese domination of Việt

Nam is available. Handicrafts from independent Việt Nam's first major royal Vietnamese dynasties—the Lý (1009–1225) and the Trần (1225–1400)—are scanty, but our archives and museums do have samples of those dynasties' lacquered objects used for worship and funerals.

Vietnamese lacquer flourished between the 1600s and 1800s, mostly at religious sites, where we have lacquered statues, palanquins, wooden panels, and architectural decoration, particularly on columns in temples and pagodas. Lacquer also appears on Buddhist mummies. Đậu Pagoda in Thường Tín District, Hà Tây Province (now part of Hà Nội) contains the red-and-gold-lacquered mummies of two bonzes sitting in Zen (Dhyanist, Thiền) meditation. These well-preserved mummies date from the 1600s or 1700s.

During the 1600s and 1700s, Vietnamese artists used Chinese innovations in lacquer to improve their own techniques, strengthening their lacquer's resistance to our tropical climate and widening background materials so they could apply lacquer to wood, baked earth, stone, copper, rattan, and plaited bamboo. Lacquered articles for everyday use were few; artisans reserved their production for objects used in worship and rituals.

Vietnamese lacquer work underwent renewal during the 1920s and 1930s following contact with Western art imported after establishment of the Indochina Fine Arts College in 1925. Two French artists, Joseph Imguimberty (1896–1971) and Évarste Jonchère (1892–1956), encouraged transformation of the old lacquer handicraft, which had become essentially decorative. They helped shift lacquer into a modern art expressing many shades of thought and feeling.

Thanks to young Vietnamese students, the Indochina Fine Arts College established the Hà Nội School of Lacquer Work. Before long, Vietnamese artists developed pumiced lacquer and then enriched their art's materials, colors, subjects, and styles. Vietnamese modern lacquer work began with Bronze-Age traditions and enriched itself during several seasons of acculturation to become an example of dynamic and evolutionist faithfulness to national cultural identity.

What Do Vietnamese Water Puppets Say?

We are not sure whether water puppets also originated in other countries or whether they appeared only in Việt Nam, but we do know that their reputation continues to spread across the world. However, if you want to see water puppets in their true environment, you must watch them where they began, in the open air in a village of the Red River Delta. I had the good fortune to see such a performance in Đào Thục, a village of two thousand people about twenty-five kilometers from Hà Nội. It was drizzling that day. The pagoda stage rested in a pond in the midst of a green rice paddy. Villagers sat all around on three sides of the pond. The fourth side was reserved for the stage, which had been set in the water.

The villagers had organized the performance to celebrate Tết, the Lunar New Year. The performers were not professionals but, instead, farmers, who had made their own puppets and practiced with them whenever they could be free from the demands of farming. As I watched the audience, I saw how moved the villagers were at the deep meaning in this artistic profession of ordinary people, which dates back two thousand years. And, of course, everyone laughed when the sly fox nabbed a duck and scuttled with it up a palm tree.

Water puppets emerged in the Red River Delta, a humid area filled with rivers. There, every village has a pond or lake, which can be used as a theater. The weather must be warm, since the performers stand in water for hours. During French colonialism, urban Vietnamese did not know about the existence of water puppets because only local villagers in the countryside saw the performances. As a result, water puppets do not reflect urban life. The scenery is entirely rural: rice paddies, bamboo gates, fish ponds, banyan trees, wells, and village temples.

In order to enliven the show, the performers add action—cultivating with water buffalo, buffalo fights, boat races, kids playing water games, swimming fish and frogs, cavorting dragons, and farmers transplanting, irrigating, harvesting, and winnowing rice. Aside from farmers, the puppet characters may also be village workers (sawyers, blacksmiths, and carpenters) as well as fairies, dancing unicorns, turtles, and phoenixes. A favorite scene is a triumphant scholar's return to his home village after passing the triennial mandarin examination.

The water-puppet stories arise from Vietnamese traditional theater (*chèo* or *tuồng*) performed in the countryside or from history (heroes who have resisted invaders). Water puppets probably began as a ceremony to pray for sufficient water for the rice crop. For that reason, the dragon characters are particularly important, for dragons are a positive presence in Vietnamese culture. Water-puppet performances have a lively philosophy, which fits the wishes and needs of Red River Delta farmers, who make their living from wet-rice cultivation. In addition to their labor in the paddies, rice farmers must struggle against floods and foreign invaders. Since farmers love nature and the rice fields' intimacy with earth and water, the water-puppet performances praise the labor, perseverance, and optimism such a life requires.

The script of a water-puppet performance praises hard labor, the village, and the family, yet there is no lack of double meaning and satire. Good and evil are part of the performance, with good bringing happiness, and evil bringing its own lessons. Water puppets incorporate influences from Buddhism, Taoism, and, most of all, Chinese Confucianism but also display the local culture's animistic beliefs. When spectators see water puppets performed in the rice paddies, they can perceive that the water-puppet characters and animistic spirits exist together in a shared ambiance of pantheism.

Ancient Graphic Arts of Việt Nam

In general, popular imagery appearing in ancient, non-religious Vietnamese graphic arts comes from two sites: Đông Hồ Village in Thuận Thành District, Bắc Ninh Province, and from Phố Hàng Trống (Drum Market Street) in Hà Nội. These two represent different styles. Artists in Đông Hồ Village are famous for their images created especially for Tết, the Lunar New Year. In the past, during the Eleventh and Twelfth Lunar Months, Đông Hồ villagers sold woodcut prints at their village communal house to traders, who came from all parts of the Red River Delta.

Although Đông Hồ villagers may have been inspired by *nian hua*, the popular Chinese Lunar New Year images common after the 1500s, their prints are unique to Việt Nam. Their images reflect Vietnamese history, folk tales, and country life, including field work, festivals, domestic animals, and coconut-picking. Villagers engrave their images on wooden blocks and reproduce the prints on *dó* paper (sometimes called Nepal paper), which they make by hand from poonah (*Rhamnoneuron balansae*) shrubs. Then they coat the paper with a white powder made from sea shells. Printing involves several blocks, each one for a specific color. The artists use natural colors, including black dye produced from burnt straw, blue from indigo, and green from verdigris (a pigment obtained by adding acetic acid to copper).

The art from Hàng Trống Street may date back to the 1600s, when Chinese immigrants faithful to the Ming Dynasty (1368–1644) inspired the more urban imagery found in these prints. The Hà Nội engravers had come from Liễu Chàng and Hồng Lục Villages in Hải Dương Province southeast of Hà Nội. Their technique is different from that of Đông Hồ Village. The artists use brushes soaked in liquid paints to add color to their woodblock designs. Most of their images are artistic, religious (tigers, saints), or literary (illustrations of folk tales).

Apart from these two main sources of ancient graphic art, there are popular images on colored paper from Huế and from Kim Hoàng, Hà Tây Province (now part of Hà Nội). The most important collection of these works is the 4,577 images gathered by a French civil servant, Henri Oger, during the early 1900s. (See the sample of drawings collected by Henri Oger at the end of this book.) This encyclopedia of wood engravings has great ethnographic value. The magnificent photographs published in *Ancient Vietnamese Art* (Đồ Họa Cổ Việt Nam, 2000) by Phan Cẩm

Thượng, Lê Quốc Việt, and Cung Khắc Lược has also enriched our knowledge of Việt Nam's traditional graphic arts.

Until the introduction of the Western press at the end of the 1800s, Vietnamese engravers used xylography (woodblock engravings) to print Buddhist and other religious texts, Royal Court documents, popular images, and, on rare occasions, stories, essays, and poems by a handful of writers. Scholars copied by hand most classical texts in Chinese ideographic script (*Hán*) and Vietnamese ideographic script (*Nôm*). No xylographic text survived the thousand years of Chinese domination (179 BCE to 938 CE), except in Luy Lâu (Bắc Ninh Province), which was the center of Buddhism in Việt Nam from the fifth to the tenth century CE. There, Indian and Chinese bonzes preserved boards engraved in Chinese ideograms and Sanskrit. Xylography in Vietnamese ideograms developed later with the growth of different Vietnamese Zen (Thiền) sects across successive dynasties, whose kings ordered the printing of historic records, encyclopedias, and classical works. Epigraphy (the study and interpretation of ancient inscriptions) in popular imagery on wood, stone, and metal made great strides after the 1500s and 1600s.

In 1960, thousands of xylographic boards were preserved in pagodas; however, most of those created during our country's literary history had already been ravaged by weather, insects, and war. These days, the books that date from the 1600s, 1700s, and 1800s are crumbling. Those from the end of the 1800s and the beginning of the 1900s are fairly well preserved thanks to efforts from writers and scholars.

Tradition and Revolution in Handicrafts

I met a famous silver chaser (a silver master craftsman), Nguyễn Đức Chính, at #35C Mai Hương Lane, the small house that also serves as his workshop. At age seventy, with his emaciated face, he had a thoughtful air and a serious voice, creating the impression of a Confucian scholar from the old school rather than the ambiance of a craftsman. In fact, Chính remembers the works of the Master (Confucius) and can engrave ideograms in silver, for he was born in Đại Bái Village (Gia Bình District, Bắc Ninh Province), which is as famous for its laureates from the triennial competitions as it is for its craftsmen in copper. In his youth, Nguyễn Đức Chính received a traditional education under his grandfather and several old-school licentiates.

During the War of Resistance Against France (1945–1954), Nguyễn Đức Chính fled from his village when the French troops occupied it and then wandered until he eventually settled in Hà Nội. He had learned the silver chaser's trade from a fellow villager and practiced it with love and devotion.

Đại Bái Village, which is about fifty kilometers north of Hà Nội, has a tradition of copper engraving, which dates back five centuries. The trade's patron saint was Nguyễn Công Truyền, who was elevated after his death to become the community's tutelary spirit. From generation to generation, the village craftsmen have been fashioning objects for everyday use (such as pots and trays) together with religious objects (gongs, incense burners) and curios. During the last century, the village has practiced two other trades—sliver chasing and assembling decorative objects made from three metals (*tam khí*): bronze, copper, and silver.

Nguyễn Đức Chính is a master. His motto, which he has written in ideograms, reads: "A trade is learned through unfailing persistence." With pleasure and admiration, I watched his delicate chisel, which under the strokes of his tiny hammer caused chrysanthemum leaves and the faces of fairies to appear on sheets of silver. Each of his products is a work of love. Once, the wife of the Thai vice-premier bought from him a silver box weighing one kilogram and decorated with the twenty-eight stars, a classical astrological motif used before the twelve signs of the zodiac. A Japanese customer purchased a hexagonal jewelry box, each side of which was decorated with an episode from Nguyễn Du's eighteenth-century novel-in-verse, *The Tale of Kiều* (Truyện Kiều). In 1989, Nguyễn Đức Chính received the title, Master Craftsman (Nghệ Nhân), for his series of silver decanters engraved with dragons.

However, Nguyễn Đức Chính's golden hands have not brought him the wealth one associates with silver and jewelry. He does not sell directly to customers, for he has no shop. For a jewelry box handed to a merchant, he receives only a few dollars, after a week's work. All members of his family practice this trade. But Nguyễn Đức Chính has no complaints. He lives as a philosopher and an artist, finding pleasure in doing fine work, training disciples, engraving ideograms, and composing poems.

While Chính represents the traditional scholar-artisan of the past, his fellow villager, Nguyễn Viết Lâm, is a business craftsman of the present. I visited his gift shop at #102 Minh Khai Street in Hà Nội and was promptly handed a business card noting his credentials and skills. Whereas Chính sticks to tradition, Lâm swims with the tide, especially since Việt Nam's adoption of the market economy. Yet Lâm still honors the traditions of Đại Bái Village. His father, Nguyễn Viết Pháp, now deceased, was a master copper engraver. He left his son a precious legacy. Lâm continues to fabricate ancient-style objects, especially copper plaques engraved with old poems. But his training also comes from outside the village. He studied at the Higher School of Industrial Arts, then studied for a year at a jewelers' school in Hungary, and worked for a long time in a government department overseeing handicrafts. In cooperation with lacquer specialists, he has produced copper panels on a background of lacquered wood to depict historical sites and scenes of village life.

Ca Trù: *Classical Arias—An Ancient Art Threatened with Extinction*

One might be fortunate enough to hear *ca trù*, a centuries-old art in which poetry is allied with music, at Bích Câu (Emerald Stream) Pagoda on Hà Nội's Cát Linh Street. This art, particular to the Red River Delta, may die out because *ca trù* performers must have a solid classical education, knowledge of traditional music, and endure a long apprenticeship. *Ca trù* (with *"trù"* pronounced like "chew") is also known as *ả đào*, when referring to the singing by the girls of former times who call to mind Japanese geishas.

In *ca trù*, the singer—who is always a woman—marks the rhythm by beating a little wooden block called a *phách* with two small bamboo sticks, while a man accompanies her on a *đàn đáy*, a three-stringed lute with a very long fret board. The *đàn đáy* is particular to *ca trù* and seldom heard in any other context. A member of the audience follows the singing attentively. When he finds a passage to his taste, he strikes a little drum on its face or side, either once or several times, depending on how he feels. By expressing his appreciation in this way, he shows he is a connoisseur of *ca trù*.

Ca trù is said to have been created centuries ago by a woman named Đào. It was sung at the Royal Court and at ceremonies and festivals. Before long, *ca trù* grew to be a favorite entertainment of old-school scholars. *Ca trù* has several forms, of which the most typical is *hát nói*. "*Hát*" means "to sing," while "*nói*" means "to say or speak." Thus, *hát nói* is a kind of recitative in which singing is interspersed with quotations from vernacular poetry, oral poetry (*ca dao*), and scholarly poetry written in classical Chinese ideograms with Vietnamese pronunciation. The prosody is based on a musical pattern, which is both fixed and flexible. A classical song (*đủ khổ*) comprises three stanzas, including two quatrains and one tercet. The performer may insert additional stanzas between the first quatrain and the final tercet. The song also has a prelude and a conclusion, called *mưỡu*, both written in distichs of a line of six words followed by one of eight—a common Vietnamese form of versification.

The poetic and musical structure of *hát nói* is so supple that songwriters could express themselves and voice veiled criticism of the feudal regime. Artists could also use *hát nói* to express a personal philosophy of life, as we see in "The Power of Money" (Vịnh Đồng Tiền) by Nguyễn Công Trứ (1778–1858). Or *hát nói* can also be used to meditate on the futility of great historical events, as in Nguyễn Công Trứ's "The Xích Bích Front" (Vịnh Tiền Xích Bích) and "The Xích Bích Rearguard" (Vịnh Hậu Xích Bích). Inside each Confucian scholar lurked an epicurean, who was more or less Taoist. The scholars' repressed feelings found outlets in *hát nói*, with its beauty of nature and its adoption of the Buddhist state of indifference regarding things of this world. For example, "Song for Perfume Pagoda" (Hương Sơn Phong Cảnh Ca) by Chu Mạnh Trinh (1862–1905) praises the charm of ruins and the pleasures of drinking and idle leisure.

In "O Rose, O Snow" (Hồng Hồng, Tuyết Tuyết), one of the best known pieces of *ca trù*, a scholar makes light of an adolescent girl's affection for him by regarding her as a mere child. Time passes, and they meet again. The hair at his temples has greyed, while she has reached the height of beauty. He sighs with regret, trying to convince himself that love can ignore the barriers of age, which is not exactly an orthodox Confucian belief.

Tuồng: *Việt Nam's Classical Opera*

Tuồng is a scholarly genre, which was practiced by the Royal Court, the aristocracy, and learned men. This, however, did not prevent *tuồng* from becoming very popular. In many villages, roving professional troupes and family-based amateur groups still perform *tuồng* on festive occasions. *Tuồng* divides into two branches: *tuồng chính*, a classical opera featuring noble personages of the Royal Court, and *tuồng pho*, the people's opera born in the southern part of Việt Nam at the end of the 1700s or the early 1800s. That branch is a genre of satirical comedy, which used popular language to castigate the upper classes in the feudal society.

Tuồng chính is also known as *hát bội* or *hát kỳ*. Some researchers claim that *tuồng* is purely Vietnamese and has borrowed nothing from Peking Opera. They want to rid *tuồng* of all Chinese influence and preserve the Vietnamese art form's purity and independence. However, whether *tuồng* comes from Peking Opera or is influenced by Chinese theater is not important because, regardless of its origins, *tuồng* has become an integral part of Vietnamese culture. During the past seven hundred years, generations of Vietnamese have performed and enjoyed *tuồng*.

Under the Lý Dynasty (1009–1225), the Royal Court maintained troupes of professional actors. But Chinese opera arrived only in the 1200s under the Trần Dynasty (1225–1400), thanks to a prisoner-of-war, who introduced it to the Vietnamese Royal Court. *Tuồng* quickly caught on, but its development slowed during the 1400s after the Royal Court began discriminating against comedians. During the three centuries (1500s through the 1700s) when civil war divided Việt Nam, *tuồng* blossomed in the territory that the Nguyễn lords controlled in the South, especially thanks to Đào Duy Từ (1572–1634), an eminent statesman and scholar adept at *tuồng*. The golden age for *tuồng* arrived during the Nguyễn Dynasty (1802–1945) because King Minh Mạng (life: 1791–1841; reign: 1820–1841) and King Tự Đức (life: 1829–1883; reign: 1847–1883) were passionate *tuồng* enthusiasts. They built theaters for their royal troupes in the imperial capital of Huế, thereby creating a sub-genre known as *tuồng Huế*.

Classical Vietnamese *tuồng* borrows its subjects, themes, and its Confucian philosophy from Peking Opera. Nevertheless, it is profoundly Vietnamese, since local Vietnamese scholars and theatrical producers "Vietnamized" the Chinese qualities by placing their characters in Vietnamese history. Nevertheless, the virtues most lauded in these plays are the Confucian values of loyalty to the king and filial piety. The king represents the country and state, while the father is the family's supreme authority. In a typical *tuồng* play, the king is old, ill, or dying. The Royal Court is divided into two camps—the traitorous mandarins (who support a usurper) and the loyal mandarins (who support the heir prince—often a child—and who eventually restore the legitimate heir to the throne). A happy ending is obligatory, although the lot of some key characters is often not enviable. In fact, tragedy and heroism are the essence of *tuồng*.

Tuồng creates an abnormal, mythical world inhabited by extraordinary people, words, songs, and dances. For instance, decapitated Khương Linh Tá walks about, holding his head in his hands, while his torch represents his soul. An actor might grasp a whip and act as if he is riding a horse. Monarchs and loyal subjects have pale or scarlet faces, while warriors' faces are painted black, white, or red. Audiences easily recognize the traitor by his pasty face, sparse beard, and sly look.

The *tuồng* repertoire includes hundreds of plays. Among the most popular are: *The Base Behind the Mountain* (Sơn Hậu), *Becoming a Fox* (Hồ Nguyệt Cô Hóa Cáo), and *The Four Mollusks* (Nghêu Sò Ốc Hến), which is a people's *tuồng* play. The music, songs, tunes, and dances have an unmistakably Vietnamese flavor, to say nothing of occasional borrowings from Chăm culture.

During the French colonial administration (1884–1945), *tuồng* continued to enjoy popularity in the countryside but was forced to modernize in the towns and cities; these changes caused *tuồng* to slip out of fashion. The 1945 Revolution restored the traditional role of *tuồng*, with historical plays written to exalt patriotism. Yet in 1950, a conference on *tuồng* concluded that the genre was too archaic to serve the Resistance War Against France. Since reunification of the country on April 30, 1975 (formally on July 2, 1976), *tuồng* has regained its reputation among scholars and critics. However, more recently, the genre has lost its place in our people's hearts because of competition from radio, television, movies, and the Internet, plus *tuồng*'s failure to adapt to contemporary psychology.

Chèo: *Popular Opera—*
An Art Unique to the Red River Delta

Chèo, a folk opera originating in the Red River Delta, is normally performed in the open court of a communal house. These events usually take place in the spring, when rice farmers want to propitiate the rice crop's spirits. This genre of performance art was first developed during the 1000s. Like *tuồng, chèo* became infused with theatrical qualities during the 1200s under the influence of a prisoner-of-war, a talented actor. The genre grew in popularity until the 1400s, when Confucian King Lê Thánh Tông (life: 1442–1497; reign: 1460–1497) banned *chèo* at the Royal Court.

Nevertheless, like popular novels written in Vietnamese ideographic script (*Nôm*), *chèo* reached its peak during the 1700s and continued to develop right up to the establishment of the French colonial regime in the late 1800s. During French rule, *chèo* had to modernize to meet the tastes of new audiences, who came from the petit bourgeoisie. Nguyễn Hữu Tiến (1875–1941) introduced a sense of realism and Western-style dialogue. In the towns, *chèo* adapted to the closed space of theaters, while *chèo* in rural areas remained the chief attraction at village festivals and is still performed in the courtyards of communal houses.

Following the 1945 Revolution, people attached great importance to the restoration of traditional values. In this spirit, the Committee for the Study of *Chèo*, which was established in 1957, undertook the serious work of preserving *chèo*. However, *chèo* went into visible decline following the return of peace and particularly after *Đổi Mới* (Renovation or Renewal in late 1986). Nevertheless, the unexpected success of the Hạ Long *Chèo* Festival in 2001 revealed the public's attachment to *chèo* and the possibility of resurrecting this popular art through development of new, modern plays while following *chèo* traditions. Examples are plays by Tào Mạt (1930–1993), whose work demonstrates the attributes of traditional *chèo* adapted for modern times.

Chèo has no theatrical set and only minimal accessories. The narration, through lyrics, songs, gestures, dances, and music allows audiences to imagine the setting and historical context. For instance, a boat rower's song and gestures evoke crossing a river, while a second song may describe the river's other bank. The movement of the actors' hands, especially their wrists, is of prime importance, since those gestures reflect the principle of correspondence (body and soul; symmetry and asymmetry; horizontal and vertical).

Chèo's minimalist orchestra includes a moon-shaped zither (*đàn nguyệt*), a violin (*đàn nhị*), a flute, and percussion instruments (a drum, cymbals, and wooden bells). Performances begin with a drum roll, which the crowd answers by shouting, "*Dạ!*" (pronounced as "Ya!"), meaning "Yes, we're ready!" Then the music rises, calling on the villagers to come and watch. Two jesters dance, urging any unruly spectators to move back from the stage (several reed mats spread in the courtyard) and yield the space to the actors. As a prelude, an actor sings a tribute to the reigning monarch, thereby assuring the audience of peace and summarizing the play in a few words. Whereas in a Western opera vocalists must learn their lyrics by heart, *chèo* singers (along with the accompanying musicians) modify popular tunes according to the development of emotions and particular situations. The performance may last a few hours or the whole night, depending on the actors' improvisation and the spectators' enthusiasm.

Many characters in *chèo* are stereotypes. These include the old drunkard, the school-master, the student, the coquette, the prime minister, and especially the Royal Court jester, who is essential because comedy is a characteristic of *chèo's* mingling of laughter and tears. The jester's jokes echo the latent ridicule the populace feels toward mandarins and notables. In a *chèo* play, the comical gives way to the lyrical and to the passionate expression of individual feelings, such as love and friendship. However, the man-wife-lover relationship (a common Western literary subject) rarely appears in literature from ancient Việt Nam because Confucian edicts had established strict family values.

One exception is *Lưu Bình and Dương Lễ* (Lưu Bình và Dương Lễ), which became a popular *chèo* play. Lưu Bình and Dương Lễ were classmates. Dương Lễ, the plodder, passed the triennial examinations and became a mandarin. Lưu Bình had devoted himself more to pleasures than academic pursuits; he failed the exam and fell into poverty. In despair, Lưu Bình asked his friend for help but received only a few bowls of moldy rice and several pickled eggplants, which were tiny and rotten. Humiliated, he left, but then luck smiled on him. He met a beautiful woman, Châu Long, who promised him another chance, but Châu Long insisted that intimacy was impossible unless Lưu Bình passed the next examination. Lưu Bình studied hard and passed, but when he went to tell Châu Long about his success, he found she had left him. A heart-broken yet successful Lưu Bình sought out Dương Lễ and was humiliated to discover that

Châu Long was his friend's wife. Dương Lễ had drafted her for his scheme to prick Lưu Bình's ego.

Chèo *and* Cải Lương *(Renovated Theater): Conversations with Tào Mạt and Bửu Tiến*

I met Tào Mạt (1930–1993) by chance at the home of a woman painter. This author of popular *chèo* opera was particularly famous for his trilogy, *Three Operas of National Salvation* (Bài Ca Giữ Nước, 1986) about King Lý Thánh Tông (life: 1023–1072; reign: 1054–1072), King Lý Nhân Tông (life: 1066–1127; reign: 1072–1127), and Queen Mother and Regent Ỷ Lan (life: 1044–1117). Before long, my conversation with Tào Mạt drifted toward theater:

Hữu Ngọc: It seems to me that French theater contributed to modernizing our traditional drama. What is your opinion about this?

Tào Mạt: The essential characteristics of French theater and, more generally, of French culture are clarity, harmony, and sobriety. These characteristics influenced our renovated *chèo* comic opera. Take, for instance, the buffoon. Since this character easily conquers the public's affection, his role is often prolonged to the detriment of the play's general effect. For example, the tragic tone in the legend *Từ Thức Meets a Fairy* [Từ Thức Gặp Tiên] could shift too easily to the comic. And so, inspired by French modernization, we have shortened the buffoon's role. Of course, French modernization has also affected the structure of our dialogue and our use of language.

Hữu Ngọc: Have there been cases of inappropriate Vietnamese imitations of the French stage?

Tào Mạt: I won't talk about the plays that are slavish copies or those with the ridiculous character of a hybrid. I would rather emphasize the fundamental difference between the language of the French theater and that of our traditional drama. This difference makes adoption of elements from French drama very delicate because French drama is more literary, involves psychological analysis, and often depicts action through words. Its language evokes paintings. The language of our traditional theater is closer to sculptures. Our traditional theater combines music, gestures, and speech to create strong impressions. That explains why some *tuồng* and *chèo* plays, which were written according to French criteria, read rather well on the page but suffer when presented on stage. Let us mention another difference. Generally speaking, French drama is more realistic, while our theater is more conventional and symbolic.

*

Bửu Tiến (1918–1992) lived in the "hamlet of stage artists," the name given by residents of Hà Nội's peaceful Nguyễn Bỉnh Khiêm Street to a modest building allotted to a group of artists. Bửu Tiến's room of about thirty square meters served as his living room, studio, dining room, and bedroom. Although the space was simply furnished, it evoked a house in Huế, the ancient imperial capital, where Bửu Tiến was born. The tiny tea set had been made from ocher terra cotta, and there were large, red Chinese ideograms. Mostly, I was impressed by the master of the house, a man with a broad forehead, a stately way of speaking, and gentlemanly manners suggesting connection with the Royal House of Nguyễn. Sipping the cup of tea he offered me, I began asking about the influence of French drama on Vietnamese theater:

Hữu Ngọc: You have told me more than once that your grandfather and father, both of whom were Confucian scholars, took you to the theater when you were a small child so you could watch Vietnamese classical opera [*tuồng*]. You studied in French schools during the colonial period and acted in French plays, which had been translated into Vietnamese. After the August 1945 Revolution, you were a major player in Vietnamese drama for forty years. If I am correct, your *tuồng* opera, *Đề Thám* [Đề Thám, 1974], ran for more than five hundred performances. *Plots and Consequences* [Âm Mưu và Hậu Quả, a spoken drama—*kịch nói*—written with Nguyễn Hoàng Mai, 1971] would have had a two-year run, but production stopped because of American bombing. With such successes, you should be familiar with both ancient and modern Vietnamese theater.

Bửu Tiến: Yes, I can say that I have had the chance to experience both genres.

Hữu Ngọc: Is it true that French plays came to Việt Nam through the press?

Bửu Tiến: Quite true. The French conquered our country in 1858, but their culture began exercising a profound influence only in the late 1800s and 1900s, after the colonial administration had laid the foundations for its Franco-indigenous education. The popular press in *Quốc Ngữ* [Romanized Vietnamese script] had a wide distribution in urban centers. *Indochina Magazine* [Đông Dương Tạp Chí] printed *The Bourgeois Gentleman* [Le Bourgeois Gentihomme by Molière, 1670], *The Imaginary Invalid* [Le Malade Imaginaire by Molière, 1673], *The Miser* [L'Avare by Molière, 1668], and *Turcaret* or *Le Financier* [Turcaret or The Financier by Lesage, 1709]. *Southerly Wind* [Nam Phong] *Review,* which Phạm Quỳnh [1892–1945] had founded in 1917, printed a translation of *Le Cid* [1637] and *Horace* [1640], both by Corneille [1606–1684]. During the early 1900s, the French built large theaters in Hà Nội, Sài Gòn, and Hải Phòng.

Hữu Ngọc: But of course those buildings were for the French colonizers, not for native Vietnamese audiences. Yet wasn't it true that Vietnamese audiences could buy tickets to watch performances by touring French companies during the 1930s.

Bửu Tiến: Those plays performed in French were of interest only to a small circle of well-off Vietnamese intellectuals. The Claude Bourrin Troupe presented Vietnamese adaptations of Molière and achieved great success. Some Christian organizations performed plays in Vietnamese acted by local believers. For example, the Southern Believers Society [Nam Thanh Giáo] performed *The Passion of Jesus* [Le Passion de Jésus].

Our modern theater began during French colonialism. *Cải lương* [renovated theater] and *kịch nói* [spoken theater] started in the cities and were performed in permanent theaters to satisfy the needs of the Vietnamese employees of the state and the Vietnamese petit bourgeoisie. They wanted to watch plays with new content, not the old plays imbued with Confucian morals. *Cải lương* came into being in Cochin China [the Southern Region, Nam Kỳ], while *kịch nói* began in Tonkin [the Northern Region, Bắc Kỳ]. Both appeared after World War I. By then, many people in the Vietnamese bourgeoisie had studied in French schools. They had become an important sector of our population.

Hữu Ngọc: Was Cochin China, as the only Vietnamese region to be a colony instead of a protectorate, the pioneer modernizing our theater?

Bửu Tiến: That was the case for *cải lương*. A group of state employees in Long Xuyên Province adapted and performed Molière's *The Miser* at a village communal house in 1915. Three years later, Lê Quang Liêm pulled together a group of state employees to perform *Prince Cảnh Goes to France* [Hoàng Tử Cảnh Du Tây]. It was a flop because, until then, the Vietnamese public had been accustomed to watching sung drama. Audiences found it outlandish to have spoken drama performed without music. *Cải lương* became popular because it combined French and English music with Vietnamese folk tunes.

Hữu Ngọc: In contrast, spoken theater achieved immediate popularity in Hà Nội.

Bửu Tiến: Yes. In 1920, the public applauded *Who is the Murderer?* [Ai Giết Người by Tô Giang, based on a short story by Nguyễn Mạnh Bổng, a.k.a. Mân Châu,1897–1951] and *The Cost of Being Choosy* [Già Kén Kẹn Hom by Phạm Ngọc Khôi, 1920]. Both were performed at the Quảng Lạc Theater. The next year, Nguyễn Hữu Kim established a full-fledged theatrical troupe called Uẩn Hoa. The first play to mark the maturity of Vietnamese spoken drama was *The Cup of Poison* [Chén Thuốc Độc, 1921] by Vũ Đình Long [1896–1960]. *Kịch nói* reached its apogee in 1937–1938, thanks to the Thế Lữ and Tinh Hoa Companies. The work of Đoàn Phú Tứ [1910–1989] is very close to that of Alfred de Musset [1810–1857], while several Vietnamese dramatists took their inspiration from contemporary French authors, especially Sacha Guitry [1885–1957] and Henri-René Lenormand [1882–1951].

Cải lương also adapted French plays. I remember how intoxicated we were by the *cải lương* performances of *The Lady of the*

Camellias [La Dame aux Camélias, Trà Hoa Nữ] and *Le Cid*. To think that this was the 1930s, yet Alexander Dumas had published *La Dame aux Camélias* as a novel in 1848, and then the novel had been adapted to the French stage in 1852. But Pierre Corneille's five-act tragic-comedy, *Le Cid*, had premiered in Paris in 1637! Those dates did not matter to us. We felt very modern!

Hữu Ngọc: Do you think the French stage also influenced our traditional theater?

Bửu Tiến: Of course it did. As early as the 1920s, Nguyễn Đình Nghị [1883–1954] applied to our traditional theater the principles of Western drama by restructuring our old plots into acts and scenes to make the content more logical and by using everyday language to make our plays more attractive. Our *tuồng* [classical opera] and *chèo* [popular opera] still paid more attention to traditional setting and staging than the more modern *cải lương* [renovated theater] and *kịch nói* [spoken theater]. Writers and directors more or less modernized their *cải lương* and *kịch nói* compositions, language, staging, and performing techniques.

Hữu Ngọc: In your view, is our theater—the old and the new—drawing close to French theater by way of the tragic or the comic?

Bửu Tiến: Rather more by way of the comic, mostly because of Molière's influence. We saw this right in the beginning with *The Idiot* [Chàng Ngốc, 1930] by Nam Xương [1905–1958] and then in his *The French Annamese* [Ông Tây An Nam, 1931]. We have a long tradition of the comic in *chèo*, where stimulating laughter signals a shift from an impasse in the plot toward resolution of a social or political situation that is incongruous or deadlocked.

"Pre-War" Romantic Music Captures the Mood of an Era

The term "pre-war" in English refers to the period immediately before either of the two world wars. However, in Việt Nam, "pre-war" (*tiền chiến*)—which is not yet accepted by linguistic purists—evokes the rather ambiguous period preceding the August 1945

Revolution and the War of Resistance Against France (1945–1954). Thus, "pre-war" generally refers to the pre-revolutionary period. This distinction is important when speaking of the arts and letters because the August Revolution constitutes an ideological and sentimental delineation between two periods of history.

Vietnamese music and particularly romantic songs illustrate this definition.

New Music (Tân Nhạc) or Renovated Music (Nhạc Cải Lương) began around 1936 and lasted until the August Revolution. During this time, many intellectuals and many in the petit bourgeoisie, in particular the young people, refused to bear the dual yoke of Confucian traditional morality and colonial servitude. They thirsted for freedom for their motherland and for themselves. Except for those involved in revolutionary groups and associations (for example, the Việt Minh), most people in the intelligentsia chose social struggle (for example, the first campaign against illiteracy) and discreet patriotism filled with epic accounts of ancient battles against Chinese aggressors.

Individualism—which the communal ideal had long constrained— arose in Việt Nam after contact with French (i.e., Western) culture. The Vietnamese Boy Scouts, which were founded by Hoàng Đạo Thúy (For an essays mentioning Hoàng Đạo Thúy, see p. 71-72 and p. 216-17), responded to the aspirations of young people by providing ideals that did not worry the colonial authorities because the Boy Scout Movement was also a French institution. Further, the ideals were vague enough (love for country, nature, and humanity; service to society; self-discipline and courage; and do-it-yourself practical actions) to border on the non-committal.

Before long, the young demanded that love leading to marriage of mutual consent replace arranged marriages. The New Poetry (*Thơ Mới*) Movement of the 1930s exalted this new thrill.

The thirst for national and individual freedom found expression in New Music created in the wake of French songs by Maurice Chevalier, Josephine Baker, Tino Rossi, and Rina Ketty, who were introduced to Việt Nam through films and recordings. Before long, Vietnamese were writing Vietnamese lyrics for foreign melodies.

This cacophonic blending of two cultures antagonized delicate ears. Soon, by the mid-1930s, self-taught Vietnamese musicians were composing melodies for their own lyrics, launching modern Vietnamese music. This group was active particularly in Hà Nội, Hải Phòng, and Nam Định. It included Nguyễn Xuân Khoát (1910–1993), Lê Thương (1914–1996), Lê Yên (1917–1998), Doãn Mẫn (1919–2007), Thẩm Oánh (1916–1996), Dương Thiệu Tước (1915–1995), Đặng Thế Phong (1918–1942), Văn Cao (1923–1995, composer and lyricist for Việt Nam's national anthem), Hoàng Quý (1920–1946), and his brother, Tô Vũ (1923–2014, given name: Hoàng Phú).

Some researchers divide the New (or Renovated) Music into four tendencies: romantic, historical (struggles against Chinese invaders), youth-oriented, and revolution-oriented action. In my view, a romanticism lightly tinged with Byronism characterizes all these currents even as late as the first years of the War of Resistance Against France, when composers wrote both patriotic songs about self-sacrifice and passionate songs about love. But then, beginning in the 1950s until the end of the American War in 1975, the entire country was locked into a fight for survival. The languorous songs exulting love for love's sake, melancholy, and despair were no longer performed in public recitals or on the radio.

However, on October 8, 1997, a musical retrospective sponsored by Tô Vũ, who had been a member of Echo Group (Đồng Vọng), allowed an enthusiastic public of septuagenarians and young students to hear the two kinds of romantic music from Việt Nam's pre-war period. Echo Group had included Hoàng Quý (the founder), his brother Tô Vũ (a.k.a. Hoàng Phú), Văn Cao, and Phạm Ngữ (1920–1986). Their individualistic romanticism found its expression in songs such as Tô Vũ's "Bells on an Autumn Evening" (Tiếng Chuông Chiều Thu), which inspires nostalgia for one's native village and sweetheart.

Hoàng Quý's "The Neighbor Girl" (Cô Láng Giềng) depicts a man arriving home after a long time away to find his beloved marrying another man. Hoàng Quý could thrill listeners with his patriotic and even revolutionary romanticism in songs, such as

"Death Volunteers" (Cảm Tử Quân), which many liberation fighters sang before mounting an assault. His music evoking our ancestors' battles against invaders—for example, "On Bạch Đằng River" (Trên Sông Bạch Đằng) and "Rivers and Mountains of Lam Sõn" (Nước Non Lam Sơn)—created similar emotions.

Nam Sơn: A Meeting of East and West

Nam Sơn (1890–1973) was born into a scholarly family in Yên Lãng, Vĩnh Phúc Province in northern Việt Nam. His early education was traditional, with his first years spent studying Chinese ideograms, which gave him a love of drawing. Following his Franco-Vietnamese secondary schooling, at age eighteen, Nam Sơn became a low-level official in the French administration. He simultaneously perfected his painting in Chinese ink and enriched his book-learning about Western art. A self-taught artist, he made his name with his classical sketches, which emanated spirituality.

A turning point came in 1923, when Nam Sơn was thirty-three. He met French painter Victor Tardieu (1870–1937), who had arrived in Hà Nội. The two worked on a plan to establish the Indochina Fine Arts College. Tardieu took Nam Sơn to France to make the necessary contacts. French experts in art held that, in the framework of the meager university education available in French Indochina at the time, the proposed Fine Arts College, like any other cultural institution, must cater first to the needs of colonialism. Despite this stricture, the two artists—Tardieu (director) and Nam Sơn (organizer and teacher)—established the Indochina Fine Arts College in 1925 and turned it into a center for creating modern Vietnamese art.

In Paris, Nam Sơn assisted at the workshop of Jean Pierre Laurens (1875–1932), took courses at the Decorative Arts School, and tutored himself in the blending and application of colors. He later distinguished himself with drawings in Chinese ink and portraiture in red chalk; his prizes included the Paris Salon Award in

1930, an honors diploma at the Rome Salon in 1932, and a silver medal at the Paris Salon in 1932.

Nam Sơn taught at the Indochina Fine Arts College until the August 1945 Revolution, when he hoped to serve the Hồ Chí Minh government, which had secured the country's independence. However, in 1946, Nam Sơn was stranded in Hà Nội following the outbreak of the Resistance War Against France in the North. He refused to collaborate with Hà Nội's pro-French administration, preferring instead to teach drawing.

In 1952, in response to a charity's request, Nam Sơn created *Mountains and Forests of Việt Bắc* (Núi Rừng Việt Bắc) in India ink. This painting may be considered a manifestation of Nam Sơn's patriotic dedication. Even though he was in French-occupied Hà Nội, he expressed his absolute commitment to the Revolution in this work dedicated to Việt Bắc (Northern Liberated Area), the base for the Hồ Chí Minh government and the Revolution. The painting was auctioned to benefit orphans. The French-backed puppet government bought the painting to adorn the reception room in the Palace of the French high commissioner. Perhaps the buyers did not perceive the work's hidden meaning. Or perhaps they did.

Let us point out another of Nam Sơn's Resistance enigmas—the oil painting titled *The Northern Confucian Scholar* (Sỹ Phu Bắc Hà, 1928). An old man with a worn face and thoughtful eyes showing pain and determination wears a white mourning turban. Who is he? And why the mourning turban?

The portrait's subject is Nguyễn Sĩ Đức, the master of Confucian humanities who introduced Nam Sơn to classical culture and Oriental art. In 1907, the French colonial administration closed the Eastern Capital School for the Just Cause, sometimes called the Tonkin Free School (Đông Kinh Nghĩa Thục), a disguised anti-colonial organization. The colonizers subjected the school's leaders to harsh repression, including prison. Nguyễn Sĩ Đức, a partisan, mourned the death of the school and of his Homeland by wearing a white mourning turban. During the French occupation of Hà Nội, Nam Sơn displayed the painting but then protected the portrait from French police by placing it on his family's ancestral altar.

After Hà Nội's liberation in 1954, Nam Sơn openly expressed his sentiments toward President Hồ with *Dream during the Resistance* (Giấc Mơ Kháng Chiến), *The Soul of the People* (Hồn Dân Tộc), and *Troops on the March* (Kỳ Đội Hành Quân). The first of these paintings shows a schoolboy dozing atop a history textbook as he dreams of national liberation. Nam Sơn joined the Việt Nam Fine Arts Association's Executive Committee, on which he served until his death in 1973, at the age of eighty-three.

The Four Pillars of Vietnamese Painting

We Vietnamese have a long history of ceramics, sculpture, architecture, and art objects made from bronze, stone, wood, and lacquer, but we do not have an ancient pictorial tradition, with the exception of the engravings on the Bronze-Age drums. However, since establishment of the Indochina Fine Arts College in 1925, artists have brought tradition into modernity to express Vietnamese pathos on canvas, paper, and silk.

We have four generations of painters. The first established itself before the August 1945 Revolution; the second matured during the War of Resistance Against France (1945–1954); the third emerged during the War of Resistance Against the United States (1954–1975); and the fourth has been developing during the postwar period. Generally speaking, art circles in successive Vietnamese generations have chosen four painters as pillars (*trụ*), as in the four pillars (*tứ trụ*) of a traditional Vietnamese house or the four official courtiers (*tứ trụ triều đình*) of the Royal Court.

The four pillars of the first generation are Nguyễn Gia Trí (1908–1993), Nguyễn Tường Lân (1906–1946), Tô Ngọc Vân (1906–1954), and Trần Văn Cẩn (1910–1994). The four in the second generation are Nguyễn Tư Nghiêm (1922–), Dương Bích Liên (1924–1988), Nguyễn Sáng (1923–1988), and Bùi Xuân Phái (1920–1988). A consensus has yet to settle on the third and fourth generations, since it is difficult to decide on one's contemporaries.

All four artists in the first generation studied at the Indochina Fine Arts College, which Victor Tardieu and Nam Sơn had established in 1925. The second generation moved forward, adopting a modernism while delving into tradition for a specifically Vietnamese vision. Those artists sought to free themselves from the Indochina Fine Arts College and to distance themselves from rigid socialist realism by charting their own course. For a long time, they were misunderstood and not allowed to show their work. Then, in 1984, on the eve of *Đổi Mới* (Renovation or Renewal), private exhibitions began to occur, largely through efforts of a group led by Đặng Thị Khuê (1946–), general secretary of the Việt Nam Association for the Plastic Arts. Later, three of those artists (Nguyễn Tư Nghiêm, Nguyễn Sáng, and Bùi Xuân Phái) received Hồ Chí Minh Awards, the country's highest commemoration.

Nguyễn Tư Nghiêm, the one remaining artist of the second generation, is more Vietnamese than his colleagues in that he successfully blends tradition (xylography, aerial perspective, and local colors) with modernity (expressionism and cubism). He has explored almost every ancient pagoda and temple in Việt Nam and has never ceased to expand his knowledge of his nation's history. It is not unusual for him to return to the same subject again and again, as is the case with his *Ancient Dance* (Điệu Múa Cổ). His best known works are based on traditional or historical themes, such as Gióng (the legendary boy genie who saved the country from Ân invaders coming from the North, that is, China), dragons, and scenes from *The Tale of Kiều* (Truyện Kiều).

Dương Bích Liên was more faithful to the spirit of the Indochina Fine Arts College and less innovative than the other three pillars of his generation, for he never departed from the preceding group's romanticism. Disenchanted by his convictions and his love life, he attempted suicide. Having failed, he took to drinking. His works are haunted by the regret of an artist who never fully realized his talent.

Nguyễn Sáng is perhaps the most politically engaged of these artists, judging from the number of works he dedicated to the August 1945 Revolution and the subsequent resistance, in which he participated from the beginning. Examples of his work include *The Enemy Torches My Village* (Giặc Đốt Làng Tôi, 1954, oil), *Study-Practice Hour* (Giờ Học Tập, 1960, lacquer), and *Joining the Communist Party at Điện Biên Phủ* (Kết Nạp Đảng ở Điện Biên Phủ, 1963, lacquer). Nguyễn Sáng is also appreciated for his portraits, his lyricism, and his work in lacquer. His art is simple in composition, vigorous in form, and bold in color. It reflects the open, frank, and exuberant temperament of southern Việt Nam. No wonder his memory is so treasured there, as I witnessed during a trip to his native province of Mỹ Tho (now Tiền Giang) not long ago.

Bùi Xuân Phái is the painter of old Hà Nội, which he revived through his depiction of deserted street corners, moss-covered walls, secular banyan trees, and houses with time-worn roofs. A favorite subject was *chèo* (traditional opera), whose glamorous singers he mischievously depicted. A passionate artist, Phái worked tirelessly, painting and drawing everywhere on any material and about any subject, renovating and changing wherever he went.

Vietnamese Landscape and
the Vietnamese Spirit

Cao Bằng: Home of the Tày

Cao Bằng, a province bordering China, is home to the Tày, Việt Nam's largest ethnic minority, with about 1.7 million people or 1.9 percent of Việt Nam's population. A large number of Tày live in Cao Bằng Province, mostly in its low valleys, where they mingle with the Nùng ethnic group. The Tày and Nùng belong to the Ka Đai – Thai ethno-linguistic family, which also includes the Thái, Lào, and the Zhuang in China. The Tày raise livestock and grow rice, fruit trees, anise, and cinnamon. Unlike the Thái ethnic minority, the Tày have added to their traditional religions the Việt religious practices of Taoism and Buddhism and the ethical way of Confucianism. The Tày have a rich heritage of folklore and literature written in a combination of Vietnamese and Tày ideograms.

At the dawn of our national history, several Tày settlements were established in present-day Cao Bằng and in China's modern-day Guangzi Province. Since the second century BCE, the destiny of the Tày has been bound to that of Việt Nam. In fact, the Tày chieftain Thục Phán (Dương Vương) annexed the Hùng kings' Văn Lang Kingdom to create the first Vietnamese state. He called himself King An Dương Vương and named his country Âu Lạc following merger of the Lạc Việt and Tày Âu (Tày, Nùng, Chuang, etc.) tribes. King An Dương Vương launched a victorious resistance against the Chinese Qing emperor's army. However, in 179 BCE, a Chinese warlord invaded and occupied Việt Nam, which became a Chinese colony for more than a thousand years.

Cao Bằng has a rich revolutionary and cultural history. During the 1000s, Nùng Trí Cao (1025–1055), a Tày hero, led a resistance movement against the Chinese aggressors. Under the Mạc Dynasty (1527–1677), Việt Nam experienced a remarkable cultural blossoming in architecture, sculpture, and ceramics. The Lê drove the Mạc from the Red River Delta in 1592; the Mạc took refuge in

Cao Bằng and ruled Cao Bằng and its environs until 1677, with support from the Qing (Chinese) Dynasty.

During colonialism, the French turned Cao Bằng Province into a military territory. Nevertheless, in 1941, Hồ Chí Minh set up his revolutionary headquarters in the mountains at Pác Bó in Cao Bằng, close to the Chinese border. The province was a secret operational base for the League for the Independence of Việt Nam (**Việt** Nam Độc Lập Đồng **Minh** Hội or Việt Minh) from May 1941 until August 1945. The victorious 1950 Border Campaign destroyed the French bases along the Vietnamese-Chinese frontier and liberated National Route 4, which stretches from Cao Bằng Provincial Capital in Việt Nam's far north to Lạng Sơn Provincial Capital and on to the East Sea (called by some the South China Sea). This victory allowed easy access to military materiel from China and the former Soviet Union, paving the way for the Winter-Spring 1953–1954 Campaign and the Vietnamese victory over the French in the Battle of Điện Biên Phủ on May 7, 1954.

From the Bronze Age to Medieval Doctors of Humanities

Nguyệt Áng is a rather poor village in Thanh Trì, an outlying district of modern-day Hà Nội. Although the villagers are rice farmers, they hold two claims to glory: the preservation of Bronze-Age artifacts and the number of villagers who earned doctorates of humanities from the triennial mandarin examinations.

In December 1993, archeologists excavating near the pond of the Nguyệt Áng Communal House discovered a boat-shaped tomb containing a broken coffin with bone fragments and bronze weapons (spears and axes). They determined that the artifacts date back to the fourth century BCE and the time of the tutelary god, His Highness the Third Brother of King Hùng (Ông Ba Đại Vương), whom villagers worship at their communal house. Villagers say that a mound some five hundred meters from the communal house is the prince's burial site. Twice a year, on the Twelfth Day of the Second Lunar Month and the Fifteenth Day of the Fifth Lunar Month, the villagers perform ceremonial rites to honor the god. The artifacts uncovered in Nguyệt Áng Village confirm that Hà Nội and its environs were sites of the Đông Sơn Bronze Culture from the second millennium BCE to the beginning of the Common Era.

Hà Nội lies in the heartland of the Red River (Sông Hồng) Delta. Tens of millions of years ago, the Red River Delta was a deep gulf, which gradually filled with alluvium from the surrounding mountains and foothills until it became an immense lagoon. During several thousand more years, the lagoon became a swamp with numerous rivers, lakes, and ponds filled with crocodiles and turtles. Men and women subsequently reshaped this area into the Red River Delta. The Việt people won their independence following a period of Chinese domination lasting more than a thousand years (179 BCE to 938 CE). In 1010, they established their capital at Thăng Long (present-day Hà Nội). A string of royal dynasties, which were subjected to strong Chinese influence, preserved the substratum of the Bronze-Age Việt Culture while enriching it with elements of Chinese culture. The archeological dig at Nguyệt Áng supplies convincing evidence of this history.

This small Bronze-Age village is also famous for its many laureates in the triennial mandarin examinations, a Chinese influence. Two square-shaped stone steles, erected in 1667 and 1876, stand on the esplanade devoted to the worship of Confucius. The steles display the names of ten villagers honored with the title of doctor of humanities. One was a first doctor (*trạng nguyên*), the top laureate, who was selected by the king.

A few figures from the regional competition held in Hà Nội in 1876 and 1879 illustrate the rigor of the triennial examinations, which were the entrance gate to the mandarinate. Seventy-five laureates (twenty-five licentiates and fifty bachelors) emerged from six thousand candidates. But that was only one out of several regional examinations. The licentiates were eligible to present themselves at the national-level doctoral competition held in the capital, where the selection became ever more rigorous. The title of first doctor, which was not always granted, was abolished in the 1800s.

The North Country (Ancient Kinh Bắc)

In earlier times, the Việt described Thăng Long (now Hà Nội) as surrounded by four regions. The North Region (Kinh Bắc), which covers present-day Bắc Ninh and Bắc Giang Provinces, is the heart of the rice-growing Red River Delta north of the capital, hence its name Kinh (capital) Bắc (north). The rich traditions of Kinh Bắc testify to a political, economic, religious, and intellectual center of ancient Việt Nam. Legendary King An Dương of Âu Lạc established his capital, Cổ Loa, in Kinh Bắc during the second century BCE. Later, Chinese governors organized their administrative headquarters at Luy Lâu and then at Long Biên. King Lý Thái Tổ (life: 974–1028; reign: 1009–1028), a native of Kinh Bắc, founded a brilliant dynasty, which lasted two hundred years. He moved the capital to Hà Nội in 1010.

Other illustrious people of Kinh Bắc include mythical heroes, such as King An Dương and his son, Dragon Lord Lạc Long Quân, as well as Gióng (savior of the Homeland); heroes of legends and tales, such as Tấm (the Vietnamese Cinderella), Trương Chi (the fisherman who died of love sickness), and Từ Thức (the scholar who strayed into the Land of the Spirits); great historical personages, such as King Lý Thái Tổ, Vạn Hạnh (938–1025, a Buddhist monk, poet, and mentor to King Lý Thái Tổ), Lê Văn Thịnh (?–?, the first doctor of humanities), Queen Lê Thị Ỷ Lan (1044–1117, poet, queen mother, stateswoman, and educator); and poets, such as Nguyễn Gia Thiều (1741–1798), Phạm Thái (1777–1813), and Cao Bá Quát (1809–1853).

Kinh Bắc is known for the Lim Festival on the Thirteenth Day of the First Lunar Month, when villagers gather to sing *quan họ* love songs between groups of young men and women. UNESCO (United Nations Educational, Scientific, and Cultural

Organization) has added *quan họ* to its Representative List of the Intangible Cultural Heritage of Humanity. The Gióng Festival on the Ninth Day of the Fourth Lunar Month, which is held at Phù Đổng Village east of the center of Hà Nội and across both the Red and Đuống Rivers, retraces the life of the legendary hero who drove away the Ân aggressors from the North (China). The Dâu Festival (Eighth Day of the Fourth Lunar Month) is celebrated by twelve villages, which pay tribute to the four goddesses of fertility adopted by Buddhism. The Đồng Kỵ Festival (Fourth Day of the First Lunar Month) is marked by a procession featuring enormous firecrackers. All these festivals include ritual ceremonies and popular games, such as cock-fighting, chess with human players, and traditional wrestling. Ceremonies and games are held both inside and outside the village communal house, temple, or pagoda.

Spiritual and religious sites in Kinh Bắc include Bút Tháp (Writing-Brush) Pagoda, which boasts a three-meter-tall statue of Bodhisattva Avalokitesvara (Quan Âm), the bodhisattva with a thousand arms and a thousand eyes. Dâu Pagoda, originally erected in the second century CE, is the first center of Buddhism in Việt Nam. Phật Tích Pagoda has a mixture of Vietnamese, Chăm, Hindu, and Chinese art. The Temple to Eight Kings of the Lý Dynasty (1009–1225) stands near Đình Bảng's imposing communal house.

Many villages are famous for a particular craft. Thus, Đông Hồ is known for Tết woodblock prints, Thổ Hà for ceramics, Đông Xuất for plows and harrows, Đại Bái for brass sculptures, Đa Sĩ for iron tools, Phong Khê for paper, Tiên Sơn for wooden sculptures, and Đồng Kỵ for firecrackers. Local people use their communal houses or temples to worship the patron saints who introduced these lucrative crafts to their villages.

During the second century CE, while under the Chinese administration of Shi Xie (a.k.a. Sĩ Nhiếp 137–226), Kinh Bắc became a center for Vietnamese acculturation of Chinese and Indian customs and beliefs. Acculturation over several centuries included the imported religions of Buddhism and Taoism as well as the ethical system of Confucianism. Chinese ideograms and classical

Chinese culture were introduced into Luy Lâu along with Tao-ism and particularly Buddhism. In the sixth century, Dâu Pagoda welcomed the first Indian Buddhist monks, including Vinitaruci (?–594 CE), a founder of the Dhyanist (Zen) Buddhist Sect in Việt Nam. While Confucianism was the prerogative of upper classes, Buddhism remained the religion of the masses and contributed to the preservation of indigenous values and resistance against Chinese assimilation. Many Buddhist monks were teachers and advisors to kings during the Lý Dynasty (1009–1225).

Kinh Bắc, the shield for the capital city, was often the site of bitter battles to check invasions coming from the North (China), while Yên Thế was the site of the famous insurrection that Đề Thám (a.k.a. Hoàng Hoa Thám, 1908–1913) led against the French colonizers and the fiefdom the French conceded to him, thereby inadvertently galvanizing other hopeful revolutionaries.

Hà Nội: City of the Soaring Dragon

In 2010, Hà Nội celebrated its millennium. In 1010, King Lý Thái Tổ (life: 974–1028; reign: 1009–1028), the founder of the first long-lasting national dynasty (the Lý, 1009–1225), decided to transfer his capital to Thăng Long, present-day Hà Nội. Before the transfer, he issued his "Royal Proclamation on Moving the Capital" (Thiên Đô Chiếu):

> In ancient times, the Thương Dynasty before the reign of Bàn Canh changed its capital five times, and the Chu Dynasty before the reign of Thành Vương changed three times. Could it be that those kings of the Three Dynasties, when moving their capital in this way, obeyed an unjustifiable whim? No, they simply wanted to choose a center favorable to the edification of an immense undertaking for ten thousand generations. Bowing to the Will of Heaven and meeting the aspiration of the people, they moved their capital whenever they deemed it necessary, thus ensuring the country's destiny, wealth, and prosperity. However, the

two dynasties of the Đinh and the Lê chose to ignore the Will of Heaven and did not follow the example set by the Chu. They stayed obstinately in place. Their dynasties were short lived and their fates, precarious. The common people were ruined, while untold resources remained unused.

And then there is Đại La, the former capital of His Highness Cao, located in the heartland of our country. Its location evokes the image of a coiled dragon or a crouching tiger. It is situated in the very heart of our country and corresponds to a favorable orientation of our mountains and rivers. Đại La is sufficiently vast and level, while the land is raised and well exposed to sunlight. The population is protected against floods and typhoons, so that its economy is well developed and prosperous. This is the most beautiful site in all of the country of the Việt. There, men and resources assemble from the four points of the compass. This site will also make an excellent capital for a Royal Dynasty lasting more than ten thousand generations.

Therefore, I wish to benefit from this favorable location by moving our capital to this site. What do you, members of my Royal Court, think of that decision?

This text in Chinese ideograms (*Hán*) is perhaps the third oldest Vietnamese document, after poems by two Buddhist monks in the tenth and eleventh centuries. For context, we should remember that Việt Nam's identity formed with its Bronze-Age culture in the first millennium BCE. The first Vietnamese state established its capital in the Red River Delta, between the hilly uplands and the swampy lowlands, which were not yet fit for cultivation. The second state moved the capital to Cổ Loa on a plain eighteen kilometers north of Hà Nội's present city center. A thousand years of Chinese rule followed. Imperial Chinese proconsuls established their administrative seat north of present-day Hà Nội until the ninth centure CE, when they built the Đại La Citadel on the site of Hà Nội. The leaders of insurrections against the Chinese held power for only brief periods. Since they were rebels, they established their

headquarters in their native regions, with the exception of Lý Nam
Đế (life: 503–548; reign: 544–548), who made Hà Nội (then called
Long Biên) the capital of his short-lived kingdom.

Ngô Quyền (life: 897–944; reign: 939–944) broke the Chinese
yoke in 938. The Ngô Dynasty established its capital at Cổ Loa.
King Đinh Tiên Hoàng (life: 924–979; reign: 968–979) restored
order and, for the sake of better defense, moved the capital to Hoa
Lư in a hilly region about a hundred kilometers south of Hà Nội
in modern-day Ninh Bình Province. The capital remained at Hoa
Lư until King Lý Thái Tổ (life: 974–1028; reign: 1009–1028) moved
it to Hà Nội. Geopolitical considerations surely dictated Lý Thái
Tổ's choice. By the time he took power, Việt Nam had established
its independence and needed to create the economic and cultural
conditions required for a prosperous and powerful kingdom. A
glance at the map shows that mountains protected the site from
invasion on its northern flank. All the waterways converge like the
fingers of one hand at Hà Nội and then continue on to the sea.
Both river and land routes made Hà Nội a favorable center for easy
communication by sea with Việt Nam's coastal settlements and
with overseas cultures, thereby creating a favorable site for trade.

Of course, in the time of Lý Thái Tổ, geopolitical reasons vindi-
cating Hà Nội as the choice for a capital were felt rather than analyzed. The king was obeying two imperative cultural commands:
the Confucian notion of Heavenly Mandate (*Thiên Mệnh*) and the
principles of geomancy. Following the rules of geomancy, the position of the capital would evoke "a coiled dragon, a crouching tiger"
and would be "situated at the very heart of our country . . . [and]
also make an excellent capital for a royal dynasty lasting more than
ten thousand generations."

King Lý Thái Tổ's text reflects the ambivalent relations between Việt Nam and China. On the one hand, the Vietnamese rejected everything emanating from the historical invader; on the
other, they were attracted to their neighbors' richer culture, which
often served as a model. Thus, Lý Thái Tổ cited examples set by
Chinese dynasties to justify his decision. Yet at the same time, he
called his capital Thăng Long (Soaring Dragon), showing that he

had reclaimed the traditions of the Việt, who believed they were descendants from the union of a dragon and a fairy. The dragon, which was thought to bring rain to the rice fields, also represented royalty and nobility. Thăng Long or Long Thành (Dragon City) has been called Hà Nội (Inside the River) since 1831, when the Nguyễn Dynasty (1802–1945) moved its capital to Huế. Hà Nội resumed the status of capital after the August 1945 Revolution.

Old Hà Nội

Ngõ Phất Lộc is the only lane of its sort in Hà Nội. Located in the heart of the Thirty-Six Streets and Guilds close to the Red River Dike, this lane is narrow and short (about one hundred meters) and opens into two streets—Phố Hàng Mắm (Salted-Fish Market Street) and Phố Hàng Chĩnh (Ceramics Market Street). Early in the 1700s, Phất Lộc Street still ran quite close to the bank of the Red River. A student from the School for the Sons of the Nation, which had been established by the Bùi clan of Phất Lộc Village in Đông Quan District, Thái Bình Province, settled with his family on that spot.

Soon, other families from the same village arrived, and a new village formed as the nucleus of the future Phất Lộc Lane. The house at 30 Phố Phất Lộc became the Bùi family's shrine. Over time, the amalgamation of other villages like Phất Lộc gradually formed old Hà Nội. These villages belonged to several types—a long-term local village, a village formed by people migrating from a village in another region, and a village of people engaged in the same craft or trade (e.g., Hemp Market Street and Silk Market Street).

Since each street was originally a village, it had its own communal house devoted to the worship of its particular tutelary god. Inhabitants of streets formed by migrants from distant villages like Phất Lộc practiced worship-from-afar of their home-village tutelary god. At one time, only members of the Bùi clan occupied Phất Lộc Lane. Later, several families from the Ngô clan arrived. Today, only a few direct descendants from Phất Lộc Village live on Phất Lộc Lane.

The Bùi clan's family altar as well as altars for the Tiger Lord, the mother goddesses, and Buddha occupy the first floor of the communal house at 30 Phố Phất Lộc. When I visited some years ago, the owner was Mr. Bùi Huy Tuyên, a barber then age sixty-seven and head of the Bùi clan. He lived there with his wife, a hairdresser, and the families of four of their seven children. Their modest revenues did not allow them to modernize the house.

The traditional tube houses on the narrow Thirty-Six Streets and Guilds in Hà Nội's Old Quarter are long (from seventy to a hundred meters) and narrow (from three to six meters), often spanning a block and opening onto two streets. In olden times, the front of the house was a shop with a truncated second floor, which served as a storeroom or bedroom. This story had a window looking onto the street. Traditionally, occupants divided their houses into several sections separated by small, unroofed inner courtyards, which were too small for productive gardens. The owners decorated these open spaces with potted plants and tiny ponds, which had miniature islands with mountains. The last courtyard was next to the kitchen.

In the early 1900s, sugar-refiners, families selling textiles, and coopers making small wooden casks for fish sauce (*nước mắm*) lived on Phất Lộc Lane. By the 1920s and 1930s, the Red River wharves had become the venue for pickpockets, prostitutes, opium addicts, and poor peddlers selling tea, rice gruel, and steamed glutinous rice. During the two months (from December 19, 1946 to February 17, 1947) that the French besieged Hà Nội early in our Resistance War Against France (1945–1954), Phất Lộc Lane served as a secret entry point for supplies from revolutionary fighters outside the city and as an exit for civilians escaping across the Red River to Việt Bắc, the Northern Liberated Area.

At the Palace of the Trịnh Lords

Lê Hữu Trác (1720–1791), a father of Vietnamese traditional medicine, used the pseudonym Lãn Ông (The Idler). In addition to medical treatises, his extant writings include *A Visit to the Capital*

(Thượng Kinh Ký Sự), in which he describes what he saw in Thăng Long (ancient Hà Nội) while providing medical care to the Trịnh lord's heir. *A Visit to the Capital* is rich with characters, dialogue, ailments, and remedies as well as with Lê Hữu Trác's extensive descriptions of living with staff at the Royal Palace. The following passage describes the aristocracy's idle, luxurious life in the sumptuous palace of which no trace remains today. Here, "Southern" refers to Việt Nam, while "Northern" refers to China.

Diagnosing the Crown Prince
(Chẩn Bệnh Thế Tử, Excerpts)

When we arrived at the rear entrance to the Palace, the accompanying mandarin led me through two additional gates and then down an alley to the left. I raised my head and looked around. All about me was luxuriant foliage with singing birds and flowers, their fragrances wafting on the breeze. Messengers shuttled back and forth along the passages and corridors. Every person passing through each gate stated his business and presented his tablets guaranteeing access.

I thought to myself: "I am the scion of a family of ranking officials. I was born and raised in the capital, but this is my first time in the Forbidden City. Only now can I understand this City with my own heart. Before, I had access only to hearsay. Only now can I be truly cognizant of the wealth and honors that are the preserve of the King and his high-ranking lords." I cannot help but compose a poem to express my feelings:

> We pass the guards with gold axes,
> This most venerated Palace under Southern skies,
> As stunning as pavilions along majestic rivers,
> Curtains with gems shimmer in the sunlight.
> The Palace flowers exude their sweet perfume,
> The Imperial parks resound with parrots calling,
> A rustic flavor to this fluttering music,
> I'm lost, as if arriving in Fairyland.

The Vietnamese Landscape and the Vietnamese Spirit 211

After walking a few hundred steps and passing the women's apartments, we reached the Headquarters of the Rearguard Footmen. That post stands at the edge of a lake lined with odd-shaped rocks and rare species of trees. This is where the Great Chancellor rests after returning from the Royal Court. . . .

After traversing many westward passages, we came to a large building—tall and wide. On each side were red-and-gold royal palanquins and accompanying royal equipage. In the middle of this palace was a platform with a gilded royal bed, which had a pink canopy. In front of the platform and on both sides were small tables with enticements one does not usually get to see. I took only a cursory glance, shyly looked away, and kept walking.

We passed through another door and arrived at a large, tall building with corner beams and pillars lacquered red and gold from top to bottom. When I asked, the mandarin said, "The building we just passed through is called the Prince's Palace and is reserved for the crown prince. We also call it the Tea Room. We call his medicine 'tea,' but in fact, it is medicine."

At that moment, there were eight or nine people in the Tea Room. I could see the great chancellor approaching. Everyone stood up.

. . .

After we had finished our meal, a high-level mandarin assistant went running to take orders from the great chancellor. I followed the eunuch until we reached the Tea Room. Since the eunuch worried I might lose my way, he ordered me to stay close to him. Suddenly he pulled aside brocade hangings, and we entered a room so dark that I could not discern any other opening. As we progressed, hangings succeeded hangings, with each hanging lit by a candle, which allowed us to see our way. After crossing four or five sets of tapestries, we came to a spacious room with a bed inlaid with gold.

On the bed sat the little prince, a child of five or six clad in red silk. Several people stood in the background. A large candle on a bronze stand gave some light. Close to the bed was a dragon-sculpted royal armchair with ornamentation of lacquered red and gold and a brocade cushion. Maids huddled behind a silk hanging. I could barely see their painted faces and pink garments. The room smelled of flowers and incense. I surmised that his Highness had just left the royal armchair and was about to retire behind a tapestry so that he could feel at ease when I was taking his pulse.

The Cultivated Manners of Tràng An (Hà Nội)

Without perfume, it is still jasmine
Without polish, he is still from Tràng An.

*Chẳng thơm cũng thể hoa nhài
Dẫu không thanh lịch cũng người Tràng An.*

These folk lines in six-eight meter (a six-word line followed by an eight-word line) laud the cultural refinement of people from old Hà Nội. The phrase "*Tràng An*," which means "long-lasting tranquility" or "peace," was used in ancient Việt Nam and China to designate the capital. According to a classical poem, sacred breath from Lô River and Mount Tản shaped the men of Tràng An in a capital blessed by exceptional geomancy. Men born in Tràng An were reputed to be industrious, energetic, lovers of letters and flowers, generous with a touch of fancy, simple and courteous, wise about living well with others, and careful to avoid coarseness and the ridiculous. Neighbors on the streets and villages of Tràng An were on friendly terms. A man absent from his home could entrust its care to his neighbors. In summer, a household would place by its front door a terra cotta jar of refreshing eugenia tea together with several bowls so that passing travelers from the countryside could quench their thirst.

The Tràng An residents' spoken language set the country's standard. Speakers chose their words carefully to avoid obscurity and rudeness. Pronunciation was exemplary. Communication was simple and direct, with courtesy the rule. When offering food to someone deemed to be a superior (either because of age or social position), a man used "*xơi*" instead of the more common "*ăn*" for "eat." An employer asking his employee for a service or an object would say, "*Tôi xin*" (I ask you, please). "*Cho*" was commonly used for "give," but a speaker giving something to someone he respected would use "*biếu*" and reserve "*tặng*" for equals or inferiors.

When a host handed a visitor a book or a cup of tea, he did so respectfully with both hands. Everyone was attentive to detail. A schoolmaster returning from a visit where his host had given him a betel quid would place the quid on a plate before presenting the gift to his wife. One's behavior with a visitor had to be correct, neither humble nor arrogant. To welcome a visitor, the host donned a long gown and turban. He ordered tea to be prepared, or better still, he prepared it himself by rinsing the cups with boiling water and filling a cup with water for his guest to rinse his mouth before tasting the tea. The tea had to be neither too strong nor too weak. The host first poured the tea into a big cup and left it to decant before serving his guest a tiny cup of refreshment.

Everyone observed correctness in dress, especially on the street. Only men doing back-breaking labor could strip to the waist. One could wear patched but not torn clothes. Anyone wearing brocade, satin, or some other expensive fabric covered his gown with a robe of ordinary gauze. Only the elderly wore colored robes. Maidens did not fasten the top button of their gowns, leaving visible a hint of their undergarments.

From generation to generation, one strove to preserve the good manners of Tràng An. Villagers migrating to the capital adopted these manners. People in the provinces looked on visitors from Tràng An as extraordinary, murmuring among themselves, "He is from the capital."

Tết in Old Hà Nội and Tết Couplets

When I was a boy growing up in Hà Nội's Old Quarter, begining about a fortnight before Tết (the Lunar New Year), calligraphers would sit on mats spread at a street corner or in a market. There, they would trace on crimson paper beautiful characters in classical Chinese script (*Hán*) or ideographic Vietnamese script (*Nôm*). Dipping their large brushes onto slabs filled with India ink, they would write ideograms for "Happiness," "Longevity," or "Talent" on squares of crimson paper. Or they would write wishes for prosperity on two long rectangles of crimson paper.

An old folk saying summarizes these essential features of Tết:

> Fatty pork, pickled shallots, couplets in crimson,
> Tết pole, firecracker strings, green *bánh chưng*.[1]

> *Thịt mỡ, dưa hành, câu đối đỏ,*
> *Cây nêu, tràng pháo, bánh chưng xanh.*

During traditional Tết, each family would have a couplet written on crimson paper, since red is the color of happiness and good fortune. They usually hung these banners on each side of the main door or on each side of the ancestors' altar. The couplet expressed wishes for a better life in the New Year.

An example is this ironical composition by the scholar Nguyễn Công Trứ (1778–1858), where the "Thirtieth" is the Last Day of the Old Year, and the "First" is the First Day of the New Year.

> On the Thirtieth afternoon, as your creditors flock, bend
> your legs to eject Poverty,
> On the First morning, tipsy from rice whisky, open your
> arms to welcome Wealth.

---

1 *Bánh chưng* is a non-sweet cake about 15 x 15 x 4 centimeters and made from glutinous rice, green beans, and pork. The cakes are wrapped in *dong* leaves and boiled for about twelve hours; the *dong* leaves turn the glutinous rice a delicate green.

Chiều ba mươi, nợ hỏi tít mù, co cẳng đạp thằng Bần ra cửa,
Sáng mùng một, rượu say túy lúy, giơ tay bồng ông Phúc
vào nhà.

This is an example of parallel sentences, a famous Vietnamese literary form. Note the parallel structure in the two lines. Each line has the same number of words, while comparable phrases contrast in meaning and tone.

In the old days, if the household's courtyard had enough space, the family set up a bamboo Tết pole five or six meters tall. On top, they hung a bamboo circle from which they suspended little clay gongs, a carp made of paper, and gold ingots also made from paper. On the ground, the family traced with slaked lime a hunting bow and arrows to frighten away evil spirits. This custom can still be found in the countryside.

In contrast to the Tết pole, all families still hold to the custom of first visitor. On the First Day of Tết (the First Day of the First Lunar Month of the New Year), the family waits for the first visitor of the year in hopes that he will bring a propitious future. Many families arrange in advance for this visitor to be a man whom fate has favored with wealth, honors, a long life, and numerous descendants. Meanwhile, family members awaiting the New Year's first guest exchange best wishes among themselves.

Throughout the Tết season, hosts and visitors exchange good wishes for the New Year. To a newlywed couple, visitors might say, "May you have a son early in the year and a daughter toward year's end." Often visitors will stay only a few minutes, exchange wishes with the host (or his wife), drink a cup of lotus-scented tea, and taste some candied fruit or perhaps a bit of *bánh chưng*. Women go to temples and pagodas to consult the oracular paper (*xin lá số*). Kneeling before the altar, each woman shakes a holder filled with bamboo sticks until a stick jumps out. Each stick has a number determining the oracular paper, which the soothsayer will interpret.

Hoàng Đạo Thúy (1900–1994), the father of the Boy Scout Movement in Việt Nam and founder of the Signal Corps for the

Việt Nam People's Army, died at age ninety-seven. In the excerpts below, he evokes Tết in Hà Nội during the early 1900s, when the newly established colonial administration had only blurred the festival's traditions. In Vietnamese, "*tết*" means "festival" and is applied to many occasions. Hoàng Đạo Thúy uses the title "Grand Tết" (Tết Lớn) in this edited excerpt to describe the major *tết* festival, which is the Lunar New Year and Việt Nam's major holiday:

> Everyone anticipates Tết. Peasants have finished harvesting and savor the days when a spring drizzle falls. Children have a vacation, wear new clothes, and eat *bánh chưng* cakes made with glutinous rice, green beans, and pork. They light firecrackers; their elders will "open the market" with presents. Yet most adults worry, for families must repay their debts before the Old Year ends. If they don't, their creditors' thugs will burst into the house, seize the sacred urn from the family's ancestral altar, and urinate into it.
>
> At midnight on Tết Eve, Father lights incense, and the boys set off firecrackers to welcome the ancestors' returning spirits; in the courtyard, Mother presents Tết dishes to Earth and Heaven. On the First Day, the family visits Grandfather, who spreads red paper and writes ideograms: "Piety" (*Hiếu*), "Submission" (*Đễ*), "Loyalty" (*Trung*), and "Faithfulness" (*Tín*). He instructs everyone, "Show filial piety to parents, submission to older siblings, loyalty to country, and faithfulness to friends."
>
> Grandmother gives each grandchild two new pennies. Grandfather lights incense, and all members of the family prostrate themselves before the ancestral altar. Back home, Father composes a poem in classical ideograms. Each schoolboy writes characters for the ritual, "New Year Writing." Guests praise Father's narcissus as a "cup of gold in a world of jade." Everyone avoids any unseemly behavior.

A saying describes Tết customs during subsequent days:

On the Second, greet guests from distant villages.
On the Third, burn ritual money for the departing
ancestors.

The Fourth Day of Tết brings the ritual, "Opening Shops."
Boys return to school to find their master has posted four ideograms: *"Năm Mới, Đức Mới"* (New Year, New Virtue).

The East Country (Xứ Đông)

The East Country, or Xứ Đông in reference to Thăng Long (Hà
Nội), comprised Hải Phòng City as well as Hưng Yên and Hải
Dương Provinces and part of Quảng Ninh Province. Hải Dương
and Hưng Yên Provinces in the Red River Delta traditionally produced rice, jute, and peanuts. Farther to the east and spreading
to the sea are hills and hollows with estuaries of brackish water.
There, in the past, the impoverished population waged a constant
battle against nature to stave off the sea.

The East Country is the site of brilliant victories against invaders arriving by sea and overland from the North (China). During
the sixth century, General Triệu Quang Phục, who later became
King Triệu Việt Vương (life: ?–571; reign: 548–571), retreated to
Dạ Trạch (Nightly Pond) Swamp in Hưng Yên, where he waged
an effective war of attrition against the Chinese invaders until his
death. During the 1200s, the East Country fought decisive battles
against the Sino-Mongols. General Trần Hưng Đạo (1228–1300)
set up his headquarters at Vạn Kiếp in Hải Dương.

Many famous commanders under Trần Hưng Đạo came from
the East Country. Oral history has it that Yết Kiêu (1242–1301),
a young peasant from the area, dove into the river and remained
under water long enough to drill holes in the hulls of the enemy's
war ships. Tradition says that Phạm Ngũ Lão (1255–1320), a Vietnamese general who was victorious over the Mongols, was a teenager
weaving a basket along the roadside and so absorbed in thoughts
about resisting the Chinese aggressors that he did not hear the king's

recruiters arrive until they had poked his thigh with their lances. The East Country was also a base for the Duke of He (Quận He), the title given to Nguyễn Hữu Cầu (?–1751), who, from 1741 until 1751, led hundreds of thousands of insurgent peasants against the royal Lê and their Trịnh lord regent. Patriotic scholar Nguyễn Thiện Thuật (1844–1926) waged guerrilla war for seven years (1885–1892) against the French by hiding out in Bãi Sậy and Dạ Trạch Swamps.

Many illustrious men of letters were born in the East Country, including: Mạc Đĩnh Chi (1280–1346), an ancestor of the Mạc Dynasty; Nguyễn Dữ (1500s), author of *Vast Collection of Legends of the Supernatural* (Truyền Kỳ Mạn Lục); Nguyễn Bỉnh Khiêm (1491–1585), a philosopher and poet; and the founders of Vietnamese traditional medicine, Tuệ Tĩnh (1330–?) and Lê Hữu Trác (1720–1791). Mộ Trạch Village (Hải Dương Province) holds the national record for the greatest number of doctors of humanities (thirty-two from the 1300s to the 1700s), with one first laureate. With her father's assistance, Nguyễn Thị Duệ (c. 1574 – c. 1654) from Kiệt Đặc Village in Chí Linh District, Hải Dương Province disguised herself as a man to take the triennial mandarin examination, which excluded women. She placed first. King Mạc Mậu Hợp (life: 1560–1592; reign: 1562–1592) allowed Nguyễn Thị Duệ to teach, even though the punishment for attempting to deceive the king was decapitation.

The East Country has been considered an ideal place for spiritual retirement. During the 1200s, Trần Dynasty kings often visited Côn Sơn Pagoda, a site of Việt Nam's Bamboo Forest Zen Buddhist sect (Trúc Lâm Thiền) in Chí Linh District, Hải Dương Province. After his victory over the Mongols, Trần Hưng Đạo retired to Vạn Kiếp, where he raised medicinal plants. Chu Văn An (1292–1370), a teacher renowned for his erudition and integrity, chose Phượng Hoàng (Phoenix Mountain) as his asylum in Chí Linh District. Minister Regent Trần Nguyên Đán (c. 1325–1390) and his grandson, the great humanist and strategist Nguyễn Trãi (1380–1442), chose Côn Sơn in Chí Linh District as a retreat.

Quỳnh Lâm Pagoda, built in the 1000s by the Buddhist monk Không Lộ (1016–1094) at Đông Triều, was an important site for training Zen (Thiền) bonzes. Quảng Ninh Province's Mount Yên Tử (elevation: 1,068 meters), which is shrouded all year by clouds, has eleven pagodas for Zen ascetics. Đa Hòa Temple in Châu Giang District, Hưng Yên Province is dedicated to legendary Chử Đồng Tử from the birth of our nation. Chử Đồng Tử was so poor that he and his father had only one loincloth between them. One day, when his father was wearing the loincloth, Chử Đồng Tử went to fish from the river bank. The princess was out on the river for an excursion. When Chử Đồng Tử saw the princess stopping on the bank to bathe, he hastily buried himself, hiding under the sand. However, the princess's bath water exposed him. The shock for the princess at seeing a naked man led her to marry the poor fisherman. They subsequently made their living from the river.

The West Country (Xứ Đoài)

According to the principles of geomancy, the sacred vital breaths (khí) of the universe confer special traits and a distinctive soul and sensibility on a region. These traits crystallize into a region's topography. Two such attributes of the West Country (Xứ Đoài west of Hà Nội) are the Đà (Black) River and Ba Vì (Three Peaks) Mountain, which has an elevation of 1,228 meters and three peaks, as its name indicates. Ba Vì stands at the confluence of the Black and Red Rivers and is the northern point where the Red River Delta begins. However, according to another popular interpretation, "Ba Vì" comes from "Tam Vị" (Three Gods). The royal certificate at the temple on the central peak refers to the three senior gods of Tản Viên Mountain. "Tản Viên" means "round like a parasol," but it also refers to the Mountain God who, according to legend, protects the population from floods caused by the Water God. It is said that each year the Water God unleashes the Red River's floods in revenge against the Mountain God for securing the hand of the princess whom the Water God had intended to marry.

With the exception of flood season, the West Country is an arid region famous for its laterite, which villagers use to build walls, giving their houses a characteristically rough, reddish look. West

Country people have a reputation for poverty, diligence, stubbornness, and toughness. Some people deride West Country women for their plain appearance. An oral folk poem (*ca dao*) mocks the women's bowlegs, bodices with holes like roughly woven baskets, and teeth lacquered as black as cherry stones. Another oral poem notes the residents' poverty:

> Whose voice is that? Someone from the West Country,
> Where people exist on sweet potatoes rather than rice.

West Country residents' accents are considered harsh like those of people from the center of Việt Nam; some say the water that West Country people drink is the cause. Many local words differ from vocabulary used elsewhere in Việt Nam. For example, an elderly man is a "*mọ*" or "*bố*" but not a "*cụ*," while an elderly woman is a "*bủ*" but not a "*bà già*." A sweet potato is "*khoai dẻo*" not "*khoai lang*." Many other words for foods, household objects, and tools are special to the region.

All this has not prevented West Country young people from showing a great love of learning or from obtaining brilliant results at the triennial examinations. The West Country has produced heroic figures, such as Phùng Hưng (or Bố Cái Đại Vương, life: ?–791; reign: 766–791); Ngô Quyền (life: 897–944; reign: 939–944), who ended centuries of Chinese domination in 938; eminent Buddhist priests, such as Từ Đạo Hạnh (1072–1116); prominent scholars, such as Nguyễn Trực (1417–1474), who was honored with the title of doctor of humanities in both Việt Nam and China; poet-mandarin Phùng Khắc Khoan (1528–1613); Phan clan historians Phan Huy Chú (1782–1840) and Phan Huy Ích (1751–1822); poet Tản Đà (1889–1939); and poet Quang Dũng (1921–1988), a fighter in the Resistance War Against France.

The South Country (Sơn Nam)

The region to the south of Hà Nội, Sơn Nam (South Country), covered the current provinces of Hà Nam, Nam Định, and parts of some other provinces. In ancient times, this lowland in the delta created by the Red and Thái Bình Rivers produced food (rice, maize, potatoes, and peanuts) and industrial crops (sedge reeds for mats, sugar cane, jute, mulberry, and ramie from the nettle family for weaving cloth).

Tức Mặc Village in Mỹ Lộc District, Nam Định Province is the homeland of the Trần victors over the Mongol aggressors during the 1200s. The Trần Dynasty (1225–1400) built numerous palaces and temples in the ancient prefecture they called Thiên Trường. These include Tower Pagoda (Chùa Tháp or Phổ Minh), which they built to hold the relics of King Trần Nhân Tông, (life: 1258–1308; reign: 1278–1293), founder of the Vietnamese Bamboo Forest Zen Buddhist sect (Trúc Lâm Thiền).

The people of the South Country are reputed to be hardworking and to love learning. Two scholars made original contributions to classical literature. Yên Đổ (1835–1909, given name: Nguyễn Khuyến) left many satirical works and pastoral poems, while Tú Xương (1870–1907), also a satirical poet, lambasted profiteers during the French occupation. Scholar Phạm Văn Nghị (1805–1884) trained brilliant disciples and conducted an armed struggle against the French invaders. Finally, many villages of Sơn Nam are known for handicrafts: Vân Chàng (blacksmiths), Tống Xá and Cộng Lực (bronze casting), La Xuyên (wood sculptures), and Cát Đằng (lacquered wood).

Nam Định's exquisitely small royal bananas, which are the size of a fat finger and very sweet, are famous throughout Việt Nam. However, Nam Định is best known for Nam Định Provincial Capital, which is eighty-seven kilometers south-southeast of Hà Nội. An industrial, commercial, and intellectual center, Nam Định City is the third largest urban area in northern Việt Nam after Hà Nội and Hải Phòng; it has the second largest northern river port. Unfortunately, Nam Định has lost its economic importance, since its textile industry has declined and the city is far from new communication hubs.

Đọi Tam: The Village of Drums

Đọi Tam Village (Đọi Sơn Commune, Duy Tiên District, Hà Nam Province) is about fifty-seven kilometers south of Hà Nội. It lies at the foot of a beautiful mountain. Đọi Sơn Pagoda, which is hidden in a forest, is a peaceful haven for meditation. The pagoda was built in the 1100s, but the Chinese army almost completely demolished it in the 1400s. Successive wars destroyed attempts at reconstruction. There remain six stone statues of the Buddhist Guardian Spirits (Kim Cương), a bronze statue of the Buddha Maitreya (Di Lặc), decorative terra cotta pieces, and a stone stele, Sùng Thiện Diên Linh (dated 1121), in tribute to King Lý Nhân Tông (life: 1066–1128; reign: 1072–1128).

Đọi Sơn also houses another temple of relatively recent origin. This is in fact a modest funeral monument dedicated to a semi-historic personage, Nguyễn Tiến Năng, also called Trạng Sấm (Thunder Doctorate). After helping Lê Lợi (life: 1385–1433; reign: 1428–1433) drive away the Ming Chinese invaders, this valiant warrior reportedly settled in the region and taught the local people the art of drum-making, which he had brought from his native province of Thanh Hóa.

Since the end of the American War and especially since *Đổi Mới* (Renovation or Renewal, which began in late 1986), our country has established a movement to restore cultural and religious traditions. Communal houses, temples, pagodas, village festivals, ceremonies, and processions require drums of all sizes and shapes. Drums mark Vietnamese life—its joys and sorrows, its celebrations and funerals, and the profane and the sacred. Of all musical instruments, the drum is the most popular in Việt Nam. Its sounds—whether light or deafening, slow or pressing, calm or impetuous—permeate our legends and myths, our history and daily occupations, our past and our present.

Tày Hamlet in Bắc Sơn District

People of my generation all recognize these lines from "Bắc Sơn," a revolutionary song by Văn Cao (1923–1995):

> Anyone here long ago remembers the blood-stained forest

. . .

The Revolution that ebullient autumn:
Stars highlighted our flag over our Resistance Base
　. . .

Bắc Sơn! Here, that battlefield of old,
Bắc Sơn! Here, our mountainous Resistance Base!

We should go back to 1940 to understand the role that Bắc Sơn
District, Lạng Sơn Province and its population of ethnic minorities played in Việt Nam's August 1945 Revolution. In June 1940,
the Germans occupied half of France. In September 1940, the Japanese army issued a surrender ultimatum to the Vichy French colonial forces occupying Indochina (modern-day Việt Nam, Laos,
and Cambodia) and attacked a French garrison in Lạng Sơn Province, which borders China. The French forces and their indigenous
Vietnamese troops fled toward Hà Nội by way of Bắc Sơn District, also in Lạng Sơn Province. However, the embryonic ethnic-
minority Bắc Sơn revolutionary guerrillas and the population
routed the fleeing troops and disarmed them. The guerrillas then
seized the French military post at Mỏ Nhài, Quỳnh Sơn Commune
in Bắc Sơn District on September 27, 1940. These events became
known as the Bắc Sơn Uprising. Many indigenous Vietnamese soldiers, who had been serving the French at Mỏ Nhài, joined the
revolutionaries.

Soon, however, the Japanese worked with the French Vichy
administration, which was allied with the Nazis, to repress the Bắc
Sơn Uprising and the Revolution. Following a Communist Party
directive, the Bắc Sơn guerrillas under Chu Văn Tấn (1909–1984,
a Nùng ethnic-minority guerrilla, who later became an army general) formed themselves into the first squads of the National Salvation Army (Cứu Quốc Quân), which was based in the mountains
along the Chinese border. In May 1941, under Hồ Chí Minh's leadership, the Communist Party widened its revolutionary movement
to create the League for the Independence of Việt Nam (**Việt** Nam
Độc Lập Đồng **Minh** Hội or Việt Minh), which included patriots
who were not communists.

In 1943, the Bắc Sơn guerrillas joined with operations of armed public education under Việt Minh command and helped build the Revolution's first bases. On December 22, 1944, on orders from Hồ Chí Minh, Võ Nguyên Giáp set up the first unit of the Việt Nam Public Education and Liberation Army, which became modern Việt Nam's first main-force army. On May 15, 1945, the Việt Nam Public Education and Liberation Army merged with the National Salvation Army to form the Việt Nam People's Liberation Army, which the Americans would later call the North Vietnamese Army or NVA. The placement of "Public Education" first in the army's original name emphasized the Vietnamese tradition of people first, weapons later.

The Bắc Sơn Uprising illustrates the traditional solidarity between the Việt ethnic majority and ethnic minorities. From earliest recorded history and even from legendary times, Việt Nam's lowland peoples (who needed forest products) and the nation's highland peoples (who needed salt and metal tools) joined in economic solidarity. Political solidarity grew during wars against foreign invaders—the Mongols in the 1200s, the Ming in the 1400s, the French in the 1800s, and the French and Americans in the mid-1900s. The French and American policy of divide-and-rule was largely ineffective in northern Việt Nam.

Thái Nguyên was the first provincial town liberated after formation of the Việt Nam Public Education and Liberation Army. During the Resistance War Against France (1945–1954), Thái Nguyên Province was also the stronghold sheltering the secret headquarters of the newly formed Democratic Republic of Việt Nam (DRVN). The border area between Thái Nguyên, Bắc Cạn, and Tuyên Quang Provinces in the northern highlands was known as ATK (An Toàn Khu, the Secure Zone) in Việt Bắc (the Northern Liberated Area). To ensure security, ATK spread over a wide area. During the Resistance War Against the United States, American bombing razed Thái Nguyên Provincial Capital, which has since been rebuilt.

I was fortunate to visit Tày Village in Thái Nguyên Province's historic Bắc Sơn District, where we were invited to a *then* ritual in a private home. The word *"then"* designates supernatural forces and also a shaman (usually a woman). The ritual we watched that evening was an exorcism to ward off the evil spirits that could harm the master of the house, who was turning fifty-three, an age believed to be a possible cause of misfortune. The shaman, who was about sixty years old, wore an indigo costume and surrounded herself with offerings—specialty dishes, paper votive objects, candles, and incense. She sang a long poem to the accompaniment of a string instrument with a small, round body and a long neck. She also performed sacred dances. This traditional ceremony lasted into the wee hours in the morning.

Quảng Bình Province

Quảng Bình is a relatively small province in central Việt Nam, but it has a distinctive character. Although its coastline is a hundred and fifty kilometers long, the province is only fifty kilometers wide in some places. The fertile soil in its narrow coastal plain is very limited because sand dunes, which can reach ten meters in height, consume much of the area. The rest of the province is mountains and laterite hills. The climate is harsh. In summer, the heat is torrid with a burning, hot wind from Laos. Autumn brings torrential rains. Streams flowing from the Trường Sơn Range swell suddenly into devastating flash floods. Typhoons (storms with very high winds) besiege Quảng Bình in November. These natural calamities create chronic food shortages for the population, which lives largely on subsistence rice farming and fishing.

Quảng Bình's history crystallizes around two sites: Transverse Pass (Đèo Ngang) and Gianh River. In ancient times, Transverse Pass, the border between modern-day Hà Tĩnh and Quảng Bình Provinces, separated the Việt and Chăm peoples, yet by the beginning of the Christian era, the Chinese dominated both north and south of the pass. Then, during the second century CE, Chăm Chieftain Sri Mara (Khu Liên) secured a fief, which he called Chăm Pa (Lin Yi Kingdom or Lâm Ấp). It stretched from modern-day

Thừa-Thiên Huế Province south through Quảng Nam Province in central Việt Nam. In the fourth century CE, Chăm Pa expanded north and conquered modern-day Quảng Bình.

During the tenth century, the Việts regained their independence from China; then, in the 1000s, the Lý kings launched many expeditions against Chăm Pa. The victorious expedition under King Lý Thánh Tông (life: 1023–1072; reign: 1054–1072) and General Lý Thường Kiệt (1019–1105) captured the Chăm king, Rudravarman III (Chế Củ, life: ?–?; reign: 1061–1074), who offered King Lý Thánh Tông the province of Quảng Bình in exchange for his freedom. Soon afterwards, General Lý Thường Kiệt sent impoverished Vietnamese peasants on a march to the South to serve as soldiers in newly occupied Chăm Pa and to till its land. The second stage of occupation proceeded peacefully in 1301 through the marriage of Vietnamese Princess Huyền Trân, daughter of King Trần Nhân Tông (life: 1258–1308; reign: 1279–1293), and the Chăm king, Simhavarman III (Chế Mân, life: ?–?; reign: 1288–1307). The Chăm king offered a dowry of Châu Ô and Châu Rí (or Lý), which were to become the Vietnamese province of Thuận Hóa (an ancient name for the region comprising modern-day Quảng Bình, Quảng Trị, and Thừa Thiên-Huế Provinces).

Whereas Transverse Pass is emblematic of the struggle between the Việt and the Chăm, Gianh River to the south embodies the feudal Trịnh-Nguyễn lords' conflict, which lasted more than two centuries (1570–1786). The Trịnh lords launched six offensives against the South, while the Nguyễn lords conducted one offensive against the North. (For the changing definition of "North" and "South" during Việt Nam's history, see p. 9.) Although the Trịnh entrenched themselves on Transverse Pass, the actual North-South line was the Gianh River farther south. Ba Đồn (Three Military Posts) on the Gianh River's northern bank was the regrouping area for the Trịnh army, which had a hundred thousand soldiers, five hundred elephants, and five hundred ships equipped with old-style guns. The Nguyễn had a smaller army, but their troops were better trained and had two solid, fortified defensive lines designed by scholar Đào Duy Từ (1572–1634). The Trường Dục Wall was ten kilometers long, while the Lũy Thầy (Master Wall) was eighteen kilometers. The latter was also called Đông Hải (East Sea, called by some the South China Sea), mispronounced as "Đồng Hới" by the French and now the name of the provincial capital of Quảng Bình Province. The Trịnh and Nguyễn lords finally made peace. The Gianh River served as the border between the two states for a century, until the Tây Sơn Uprising re-unified the country in 1789.

In 1885, King Hàm Nghi (life: 1871–1943; reign: 1884–1885), advised by Regent Tôn Thất Thuyết (1839–1913), took refuge for three years in the Quảng Bình highlands during the scholars' Save-the-King (Cần Vương) Movement. The French captured Hàm Nghi in 1888 and exiled him to Algeria. At the beginning of the Resistance War Against France, Cần Vương Village at the foot of Transverse Pass distinguished itself by building a system of underground tunnels, which enabled guerrillas to foil French attacks.

During the American War, US bombers razed Đồng Hới Provincial Capital. Quảng Bình Province is said to have resisted four tons of bombs and shells for every inhabitant by downing hundreds of American aircraft. Tempered by trials of nature and history, the people of Quảng Bình have acquired remarkable qualities, including sobriety and courage. Among the province's distinguished scholars and warriors is Nguyễn Hữu Cảnh (1650–1700), a great captain and founder of Mekong Delta Provinces, particularly the port city of Sài Gòn over three hundred years ago. A famous modern-day Quảng Bình military commander is Võ Nguyên Giáp (1911–2013), the victorious general over the French at Điện Biên Phủ (1954) and in the Hồ Chí Minh Campaign to Liberate Sài Gòn (1975) at the end of the American War.

Nghệ An and Hà Tĩnh

Vietnamese often call Nghệ An and Hà Tĩnh Provinces in central Việt Nam by the combined name of Nghệ Tĩnh. People of ancient Việt Nam regarded Nghệ Tĩnh as a far-away land with savage and mysterious beauty. A folk couplet (*ca dao*) notes:

The way to Nghệ country presents twists and turns,
Green mountains and blue waters—a true painting!

Hồng Lĩnh Mountain and Lam River are the area's most famous landmarks. A large part of the land is forests, while the narrow coastal strip devoted to rice growing is far from fertile. Agriculture is subject to the whims of a harsh climate caused by a scorching wind, which carries dry heat from neighboring Laos to the west, causing agricultural plants to wither.

In ancient times, Việt Nam and Chăm Pa fought over this area. The first Vietnamese settlers in Nghệ Tĩnh were soldiers, exiles, and adventurers. The constant population movements and repeated struggle against a harsh climate and hostile neighbors gave the people distinctive traits: resilience, toughness, courage, industry, intelligence, but also stinginess. A story notes that a man from Nghệ Tĩnh was so tight-fisted that he would accept nothing to accompany his rice at a local inn. The traveler removed a wooden fish from his basket, dipped the wooden fish in a little fish sauce, and licked it. Hence, people have given Nghệ Tĩnh residents a nickname: Wooden Fish (*Cá Gỗ*).

King An Dương Vương, who founded the second Việt state (Âu Lạc) in the third century BCE, is venerated at a temple in Diễn Châu, a district in modern-day Nghệ An. Mai Hắc Đế (?–722), the leader of a revolt against the Chinese, is worshipped at Nam Đàn, another district in Nghệ An, where he established a resistance base. In 1788, Nguyễn Huệ, who later mounted the throne as King Quang Trung (life: 1753–1792; reign: 1788–1792), arrived from the south with an army of peasant insurgents. Ninety thousand men joined him in Nghệ Tĩnh for the offensive against the Chinese Qing army then occupying Thăng Long (Hà Nội).

In more contemporary history, Nghệ Tĩnh hosted many famous episodes in the patriotic struggle for national liberation. These included the Save-the-King (Cần Vương) Scholars' Movement led by Phan Đình Phùng (1847–1896); the Nghệ Tĩnh Uprising (1930, with its soviet administrative councils earning the name Soviet – Nghệ Tĩnh); and the Đô Lương Mutiny (1944). The

French colonial administration savagely repressed all these resistance movements. During the American War, the United States dropped three thousand tons of bombs on the region and razed Vinh, the Nghệ An provincial capital.

Nghệ Tĩnh scholars are famous for their love of study. During the triennial examinations, Quỳnh Đôi Village alone accounted for ninety-four doctors of humanities and 152 licentiates of humanities, a record. Last but not least, Nghệ Tĩnh is the home of some of the nation's most illustrious leaders: poet Nguyễn Du (1766–1820), author of the immortal national epic, *The Tale of Kiều*; sensual poet Mme. Hồ Xuân Hương (1772–1822); scholar-poet Nguyễn Công Trứ (1778–1858); historian Sử Hy Nhan (?–1421); physician Lê Hữu Trác (a.k.a. The Idler, 1720–1791); philosopher Nguyễn Thiếp (a.k.a. La Sơn Phu Tử, 1723–1804); scholar-patriot Phan Đình Phùng; and revolutionary Hồ Chí Minh (1890–1969).

A Quick Visit to Cochin China

Some years ago, I made a short visit to several Mekong Delta provinces, which were part of Cochin China (the Southern Region, Nam Kỳ) during French colonial times. Below are excerpts from my travel notes:

Because the Mekong Delta is land reclaimed from marshes relatively recently compared with the marshes of the Red River Delta, it has fewer temples, pagodas, and other ancient cultural vestiges. One of the oldest structures is the Chinese Guangzhou Assembly Hall in Cần Thơ City. The hall was built between 1894 and 1896 and dedicated to the singular and intrepid Chinese warrior, Guan Yu (Kuan Yu, Quan Vũ, or Quan Công, 160–219). The Munirangsyaram Pagoda in Cần Thơ is a magnificent example of Khmer Theravada Buddhist pagodas.

Yet another interesting building is the Funeral Monument for the Royal Family (Lăng Hoàng Gia), called this because it includes the Phạm family's temple and tombs. Especially important is the tomb of Phạm Đăng Hưng (c. 1765–1825), who was a loyal mandarin serving Emperor Gia Long (a.k.a. Nguyễn Ánh, life: 1762–1829; reign: 1802–1820). The story of the stele that King Tự Đức (life: 1829–1883; reign: 1846–1883) made for Phạm Đăng Hưng (c. 1765–1825) is an example of historic reversals. During early phases of the French colonial conquest, workers were moving Phạm Đăng Hưng's stele south from a quarry in Đà Nẵng when French troops absconded with it. The French used the stele for the tomb of a French officer, whom Vietnamese guerrillas had killed. The French altered the text commemorating Phạm Đăng Hưng to read: "Nicholas Michel Auguste Barbé, captain in the Marine infantry, 1860." Many years later, the tribute on the stele was restored to honor Phạm Đăng Hưng.

Two local sites in the Mekong Delta—Tầm Vu (Cần Thơ Province) and Ấp Bắc (modern-day Tiền Giang Province, formerly Mỹ Tho Province)—commemorate strategic victories from our two recent resistance wars for national liberation. In February 1954, toward the end of the Resistance War Against France, Vietnamese resistance forces at Tầm Vu coordinated their regular troops and local guerrillas to defeat the entire French-affiliated 502nd Vietnamese Battalion and the French 14th Company. The Vietnamese seized a large quantity of weapons and military equipment, including an American-made French 105-mm howitzer. That daring victory in broad daylight on open, delta terrain had huge repercussions, particularly in the way it frightened the enemy.

Revolutionary Vietnamese troops at Ấp Bắc on January 1, 1963 during the American War proved they could confront and defeat US tanks and helicopters by using only light arms. Their strategy and tactics were vital, since they had far fewer men and armaments than the enemy. The National Liberation Front forces waited for the helicopters to land and the US-backed soldiers to disembark and disperse before they struck. Both Tầm Vu and Ấp Bắc Hamlets lacked fortifications and natural shelters, making the Vietnamese farmers' courage in confronting formidable modern weapons all the more astonishing. The majority of Tầm Vu guerrillas carried only pointed bamboo sticks—later known as "Tầm Vu stakes."

Of course, the Mekong Delta also has many noteworthy sites reflecting the region's history in more peaceful years. The house of District Governor (Đốc Phủ Sứ) Hải in Gò Công District Town, Gò Công District in present-day Tiền Giang Province is a typical residence of the propertied class and a perfect example of Asian-European architecture. Craftsmen made successive renovations on the house between 1860 and 1890, when the French colonizers had just arrived and Western acculturation was beginning. The juxtaposition of indigenous Vietnamese, Chinese, and French elements is apparent. The basic building—a traditional Vietnamese construction with three compartments, thirty-six columns, and a lean-to on each side—has sculptures of traditional Gò Công wood inlaid with mother-of-pearl. The Chinese elements are the panels with ideograms and classical decorative motifs, such as the four sacred animals (azure dragon in the east, white tiger in the west, vermillion bird in the south, and black tortoise in the north) and the four noble plants (orchid, bamboo, chrysanthemum, and plum). The French influence is apparent in the square Gallic columns and the masonry decorated with grapevines and grapes.

Ms. Khuê, a painter, has noted that people in northern Việt Nam are more concerned with appearances and pointed out that Đổi Mới (Renovation or Renewal, which began in late 1986) has brought everyone a better living. Northern peasants, she added, build their new houses according to their own wishes, copying styles from the urban nouveau riche. Yet these buildings have destroyed traditional village landscapes. However, traditional social conventions have had less effect in southern Việt Nam. Even though building materials have changed, the landscape has remained the same, with houses and gardens amidst coconut trees along small canals.

Floating markets, a unique charm of the marshlands in southern Việt Nam, are held very early in the morning along the Mekong Delta's network of small canals. Boats brim with produce: eggplants, potatoes, maize, coconuts, longans, bananas, avocados, sapodillas, mangoes, jackfruits, oranges, and mandarin oranges. It is great fun to glide along in a small boat and listen to vendors bargaining and chatting in high spirits.

People in southern Việt Nam prefer hot, spicy dishes. A practitioner of traditional medicine explains, "If we introduce hot foods (yang) to the human body, the organism will react by creating coolness (yin). Therefore, in the summer months, it is better to drink hot tea than iced drinks." Southern dishes are also quite sweet due to the influence of cuisine from Guangdong, a Chinese province near Hong Kong. Even the sacrosanct Vietnamese noodle soup, *phở*, is slightly sweetened, while the traditional southern sour soup made with fish is prized for hot days. Cooks often serve a mixture of leaves and buds, including young mango leaves, pumpkin flowers, and budding bananas, as condiments for *phở* and for choice cuts of meat and fish.

Caodaism and Its Beginnings
in Tây Ninh Province

The grey soil in southern Việt Nam's Tây Ninh Province, which borders Cambodia, lends itself to planting rubber trees, orchards, rice, and secondary food crops, while the red soil is suitable for cultivating industrial crops, such as coffee, tea, and sugar cane. Yet farmers in Tây Ninh can barely make a living because of poor irrigation. Tây Ninh Province served as a resistance base during the wars with France (1945–1954) and the United States (1954–1975). The province has many Khmer and Chăm ethnic-minority villages; its most famous natural landmark is Bà Đen (Lady Black) Mountain, the highest peak (elevation: 986 meters) in southern Việt Nam. However, Tây Ninh is most famous as the site of the Holy See of Caodaism.

The Cao Đài Holy See, which was built in 1941, evokes comparison with both Catholic cathedrals and Buddhist pagodas. A giant eye beams down from atop the facade. The amalgamation of Eastern and Western cultures is evident. A gaily colored fresco at the entrance features guiding spirits: Nguyễn Bỉnh Khiêm (1491–1585, a Vietnamese poet-scholar from Hải Phòng in northern Việt Nam); Nguyễn Du (1766–1820, author of Việt Nam's national epic, *The Tale of Kiều*); Victor Hugo (1802–1885, a French poet, novelist, and playwright); and Chinese revolutionary Sun Yat-sen (1866–1925). The inscriptions in French and Chinese ideograms (*Hán*) say, "God and Humanity" and "Love and Justice."

At the other end of the great hall are portraits of three saints: Lao-tzu (604–531 BCE), Buddha (c. 563 – c. 483 BCE), and Confucius (551–479 BCE). The second rank includes Buddhist Bodhisattva Avalokitesvara (Quan Âm), Chinese warrior Guan Yu (Kuan Yu, Quan Vũ, or Quan Công, 160–219, who represents loyalty), and a minor Chinese poet, Li Tai Pei (whom Cao Đài leader Lê Văn Trung claimed he had seen in 1925 in the dream where he received his appointment as interim Cao Đài pope). The third rank includes Jesus, Jiang Ziya (a Chinese sage from the 1000s), and Lã Vọng (a Chinese general and king from about the 1100s BCE).

The building's interior is reminiscent of a Catholic church, but its decorative motifs—dragons coiling around tall columns, unicorns, phoenixes, tortoises, and lotus blooms—evoke the East. Hundreds of believers in white and yellow robes attend noon masses, with men on the left and women on the right. They burn incense, pray, and sing hymns praising God and the three saints.

What is Caodaism?

"*Cao Đài*" (literally, Supreme Palace) is a Taoist and Buddhist term for "*Đức Chí Tôn*" (God or the Supreme Being), symbolized by the Divine Eye (Thiên Nhãn) that sees all and knows all. According to the Holy See's guidebook, Caodaism is a syncretism of Buddhism, Taoism, and Confucianism with Buddhist and Taoist rites and a hierarchy based on that of the Catholic Church.

The official name is Great Religion of the Third Divine Revelation for Universal Salvation (Đại Đạo Tam Kỳ Phổ Độ). The First Revelation involved Brahma (the Hindu god of creation), Shiva (a Hindu god), Vishnu (a Hindu god), Fu Xi (first of the three sovereigns of ancient China, around the twenty-ninth century BCE), Shennong (one of the three sovereigns of ancient China), Huangdi (one of the legendary ancient sovereigns), Moses (1391–1271 BCE), and Abraham (?–?). The Second Revelation came from Lao-tze (c. 604 – c. 531 BCE), Gautama Buddha, Confucius, Jesus, and Mohammed.

How could Caodaism rally hundreds of thousands of adherents by 1930, only five years after it began and, now, have between two and three million followers?

A socio-political perspective would say that Caodaism emerged from within a colonial context and unfolded in the Southern Region (Cochin China, Nam Kỳ) at the same time as other peasant movements, including the revolutionary Hòa Hảo. New religious sects could develop only in the Southern Region, a relatively recently settled land compared with Việt Nam's Northern Region (Tonkin or Bắc Kỳ), which was more attached to Confucian traditions. Further, during French colonialism, the Southern Region, as a colony, had greater freedoms than the two protectorates—the Northern and Central Regions.

Caodaism emerged during the political, economic, and social conditions of Việt Nam's Southern Region in the 1920s and 1930s. Big landowners had bought up the rice fields and were shifting the traditional, subsistence-based agricultural economy into a profit-oriented export economy. Colonial exploitation exacerbated the economic crisis, affecting even well-off Vietnamese. They and the illiterate, impoverished peasants who had been left without resources aspired to a new belief enabling them to overcome the crisis.

Caodaism was a response of Việt Nam's faltering traditional culture to the invasion of Western (French) culture—a defensive reaction accompanied by compromise through acculturation. Socio-economic pressures provided an excellent opportunity for the Cao Đài founders, who were landowners, intellectuals, politicians, and functionaries from the medium and upper levels in the colonial economy. Although they belonged to the upper classes, they also felt like second-class citizens. Like their following of poor peasants, they lived in a period of local political upheaval and nationwide patriotic movements, including armed revolts led by Phan Bội Châu (1867–1940) and Nguyễn Thái Học (1902–1930); bourgeois reforms advocated by scholars, such as Phan Châu (Chu) Trinh (1872–1926) and Bùi Quang Chiêu (1872–1945); and communism, which had begun to spread throughout Việt Nam during the late 1920s.

On the one hand, Caodaists advocated a traditional monarchy represented by Prince Cường Để (1882–1951), the nationalist senior-line descendent of Emperor Gia Long (life: 1762–1820; reign: 1802–1820). Prince Cường Để had taken refuge in Japan. On the other hand, they wished to renovate the traditional and popular values of Buddhism, Confucianism, animism, the mother goddesses, and shamanistic practices. They also imported foreign humanist elements, mostly from the West. These included the teachings of Jesus, Victor Hugo, and Sun Yat-sen; the lessons of the 1789 French Revolution; and occult sciences and spiritualism. Caodaism's surprising success lay in its clergy and senior leaders' nationalist, moral, and spiritual desires as well as in the material benefits the leaders brought to poor peasants, including distribution of rice fields, health care, and education. Further, Caodaism offered a sanctuary during war.

Ngô Văn Chiêu (1878–1932), the Tây Ninh provincial governor and a passionate follower of spiritualism, helped create the religious sect, while Lê Văn Trung (1876–1934), a former government secretary and businessman, organized the Cao Đài Movement. Phạm Công Tắc (1890–1959), a former customs director, assisted Lê Văn Trung. Upon Trung's death, Phạm Công Tắc became the Superior (Hộ Pháp) of the Cao Đài Church. He applied his determination and opportunism to the Cao Đài Movement.

For some time, Caodaism was politicized and militarized. The colonial administration repressed the movement, exiling Phạm Công Tắc from 1941 until 1946 because of his pro-Japanese leanings. They sent him to Comoros, an island northwest of Madagascar. During the French War (1945–1954), the Cao Đài served the French and opposed the Democratic Republic of Việt Nam (DRVN) by creating a de facto state within the official state. However, Ngô Đình Diệm (1901–1963), whom the Americans had brought from the United States before the signing of the Geneva Agreements in 1954 to serve as prime minister of South Việt Nam, dismantled the Cao Đài state. Phạm Công Tắc took refuge in Phnom Penh in 1956, where he died three years later. Since the end of the American War in 1975, Caodaism has spread and is present across Việt

Nam. The Cao Đài Holy See in Tây Ninh no longer functions as its own state but as the Holy See for a flourishing religion supported by a strong, recognized organization.

Poulo Condor (Côn Đảo)

Poulo Condor (also known as Côn Lôn, Côn Đảo, or Côn Sơn) is the island where the French and the American – Sài Gòn regimes held political prisoners. It lies two hundred and thirty kilometers south of Hồ Chí Minh City – Sài Gòn. For me, its name evokes a man and a poem. The man is my late cousin, Nguyễn Đức Thụy, who was freed from Côn Đảo along with several other patriotic militants in 1936 thanks to the intervention of activists in the French Popular Front.

My cousin had left Hà Nội in the 1920s for China, where he worked with several clandestine Vietnamese revolutionary organizations. He was not yet twenty years old. The French police arrested Thụy after his return to Việt Nam in 1929 and sent him to Côn Đảo Prison on the Côn Đảo Archipelago. What struck me most about Thụy upon his return from Côn Đảo was the vast knowledge he had acquired while in prison. During incarceration, he studied along with a generation of valiant, young and older militants, whose devotion to national liberation had led to their clashes with the all-powerful colonial authorities. Some of the prisoners were among our most famous scholars and teachers, yet while in prison, every revolutionary became a student as well as a teacher.

The poem that comes to light when I think of Côn Đảo was written by Phan Châu (Chu) Trinh (1872–1926), who came from the generation of modernizing Confucian scholars. (For an essay on Phan Châu Trinh, see p. 73.) Here are the opening four lines of his "Smashing Rocks at Côn Lôn" (Đập Đá Côn Lôn), which he wrote in seven-word meter on a prison wall:

> As a man standing on Côn Lôn,
> He is couragous and proud, splitting mountains;

His hammer crushes piles, piles, more piles,
By hand, he splits hundreds of rocks.

Côn Đảo will forever remain a symbol of the Vietnamese people's thirst for independence in the face of the most cruel, colonial barbarism. Yet the island has the three *S*'s (sun, sea, sand), coral reefs, fishing boats floating in bays like mirrors, and towering mountains covered with primitive forests. The Côn Sơn (Côn Đảo, Côn Lôn) National Park has 882 plant species and 144 animal species. Its turn-of-the century French bungalows feature all the amenities of a tourist's paradise, including the fact that tourism has not yet exploited its natural beauty.

Côn Đảo and fifteen smaller islands form a district of Bà Rịa – Vũng Tàu Province. They are virtually cut off from the rest of the world yet linked by motor launches and small airplanes. With only several thousand inhabitants (not including the garrison), the island is free of physical and moral pollution. Visitors will not find prostitution or drugs; there is little commerce and slightly more than a few hundred cars.

The world is ignorant of Côn Đảo's utopian qualities and knows only about its horrific prison history. For 113 years, from 1862 to 1975, this prison founded by the French colonizers and then modernized by the US – Sài Gòn administration, worked to silence tens of thousands of political prisoners. Visitors can glimpse the horrors that took place there by visiting Prisons I, II, and III, the notorious tiger cages, and arches of the unfinished Ma Thiên Lãnh Bridge, the construction of which took the lives of 356 prisoners.

It is with great surprise that I read in the Côn Đảo Guest House (Côn Đảo Công Quán) the following words on a brass plaque: "In this house, the great composer Camille Saint-Saëns [1835–1921] lived from March 20 to April 19, 1895. It is here that he finished his opera *Brunehilda*." Certainly, Saint-Saëns found his inspiration in Poulo Condor's landscape, not in the island's prison, of which he was probably ignorant.

The island has a long recorded history compared with other sites in southern Việt Nam. During the ninth century CE, Arab merchant ships dropped anchor at Côn Đảo. Marco Polo (1254–1324) sought refuge on the island after a heavy storm in 1294, when he was returning from China. During the 1500s, a Spanish fleet visited the island after conquering the Philippines. During the 1600s and 1700s, two businesses—one French and one English—each set up a bank but soon abandoned those enterprises.

In 1784, after the Tây Sơn Brothers' victory during the Tây Sơn Uprising, Nguyễn Ánh (a.k.a. Gia Long, life: 1762–1820; reign: 1802–1820) took refuge on the Côn Đảo Archipelago with what little was left of his army. According to legend, he shut himself up in a grotto on Hòn Bà (Madame's) Island with one of his wives, Phi Yến. In 1787, Phi Yến refused to let French Bishop d'Adran (a.k.a. Pierre Joseph Georges Pigneau, 1741–1799) take her son, Prince Hội An (a.k.a. Nguyễn Phúc Cải, 1778 – c. 1787), with him to France to seek French assistance for Nguyễn Ánh. Prince Cải was thrown into the sea and replaced by Prince Nguyễn Phúc Cảnh (life: 1780–1801), the son of another wife, whom the bishop took to France. After Nguyễn Ánh's departure from Côn Đảo, Phi Yến remained on the island until her death. The local population worships her as a goddess.

In 1787, Bishop d'Adran, in the name of Lord Nguyễn Ánh, signed the Treaty of Versailles with the French Royal Court of Louis XVI (life: 1754–1793; reign: 1774–1791). This treaty promised French military aid to Nguyễn Ánh to fight the Tây Sơn in exchange for transfer of Poulo Condor and Tourane (Đà Nẵng) to France. However, the transfer of Poulo Condor did not take place until 1861, more than seventy years later but still early in the French military conquest of Việt Nam. That same year, the French began building their prison for political prisoners.

Võ Thị Sáu (1933–1952) receives the same honor of local worship as Phi Yến, although to a much greater extent. An unshakable communist, this young prisoner lost her life to a French firing squad after singing the national anthem and shouting, "Long live Hồ Chí Minh!"

Vietnamese Women
and Change

Teeth Lacquering and Chewing Betel Quids

In ancient Việt Nam, women (and also men) lacquered their teeth black. Many oral folk poems allude to the beauty of women with lacquered teeth. Here is one example:

> I love you first for the escaping curl that grazes your shoulder,
> Second, for your speech full of life and beguiling charm,
> Third, for your cheeks with dimples as round as coins,
> Fourth, for your teeth brighter than black pearls.

"Teeth Lacquered in Black: A Comparison between Vietnamese and Japanese Customs," a survey conducted by Phan Hải Linh in 1996 in a hamlet of Bạch Cốc Village (Hà Nam Province), shows that out of a population of 546 persons, only eleven people (ten women and one man, or about 2 percent) in the sixty-to-seventy age group had lacquered teeth. Yet according to Pierre Huard and François Bizot's article, "Anthropological-Biological Characteristics of the Indochinese" (Les Caractéristiques Anthropo-Biologiques des Indochinois), which they presented at the Congress of the Association of Tropical Medicine in the Far East in Hà Nội in 1938, about 80 percent of Vietnamese peasants still had lacquered teeth. Today, it can be said that no one in Việt Nam under the age of seventy-five has lacquered teeth.

In his famous treatise, *Customs and Habits of Việt Nam* (Việt Nam Phong Tục, 1915), scholar Phan Kế Bính (1875–1921) noted that lacquering the teeth was a long-standing custom: "For men to keep their teeth white, that's tolerable. But for women of good standing to leave their teeth white looks somewhat strange." Yet by the second decade of the 1900s, Westernization brought about particularly by French colonization had affected style. Many men had removed the lacquer from their teeth or no longer lacquered their teeth, while the majority of women remained loyal to tradition.

243

At one time, Vietnamese called white teeth "ghost teeth" (*răng cải mả*) and compared them to the teeth of the dead exhumed for definitive burial. Residents of northern Việt Nam still follow the custom, *thay áo* (literally, change the shirt). They exhume a coffin three years after the burial and perform special rites while washing the bones in perfumed water before re-burying them in a small terra cotta box. Following this definitive burial, the family will establish a permanent gravestone. This is the reason northern cemeteries have so many unmarked mounds. Those graves are not neglected. Rather, the grieving families are awaiting the propitious dates for the definitive burials three years after their loved ones' deaths.

But were burial customs and the Vietnamese stigma about white teeth the origin of teeth lacquering?

It is believed that the lacquering of teeth coincided with the chewing of betel. According to Japanese researcher Masao Hattori from the University of Toyama, chewing betel quids (which has been practiced for a long, long time in South Asia) gives the teeth a reddish-brown color. A betel quid is made by spreading a fine layer of lime on a betel leaf (*Piper betel*, a vine) and then wrapping the leaf around a sliver of a nut from an areca palm (*Areca catechu*). Only society's upper classes could indulge in betel chewing. Teeth color became a sign of social distinction, but the question of origin remains unanswered. In any case, this custom must have been rooted in many reasons: aesthetic concepts; social distinction (upper class); maintaining national identity (Vietnamese lacquered their teeth to distinguish themselves from the Chinese); and a hygienic measure to prevent tooth decay.

Women Conquer the World of Science

In traditional Việt Nam (a very Confucian society), a woman lived only within the confines of her house. Her roles were labor and procreation. Women did not have the right to study. During nine centuries of Sino-Vietnamese teaching, the only woman to enter a triennial competition was Nguyễn Thị Duệ (late 1500s – early 1600s), who lived during the Mạc Dynasty (1527–1677) in the northern province of Cao Bằng. She disguised herself as a man to pursue a university title and achieved her goal. However, her ruse was discovered. Attempting to deceive the king was a capital crime, but the king forgave her and employed Nguyễn Thị Duệ as a teacher for his harem.

Vietnamese girls finally had the chance to go to school at the beginning of the twentieth century, with the country's first modernization under the French colonial regime. But this applied to only a few girls, and even they didn't go far. A few earned primary-school diplomas. Rare were women holding baccalaureates, and extremely rare were those with masters and doctorates until the end of World War II. The first Vietnamese woman to earn a doctorate in science was Hoàng Thị Nga, who graduated from a French university in the 1930s.

One should note that science—as a field of knowledge acquired by study, observation, and experimentation—made its late appearance in Việt Nam only in the 1930s. Our Confucian scholars had until then despised science, confusing it with technical applications, which they deemed too materialistic and unworthy of the attention of Confucians. However, that spirit changed as the result of two major factors. First, a younger generation of Vietnamese began returning home after studying in France. Second, the French colonial administration established technical schools between 1940 and 1945 to address the isolation that accompanied the Japanese occupation.

The August 1945 Revolution, which ended French colonization and Japanese occupation, favored development of education and science. The number of Vietnamese women scientists began to grow. During the War of Resistance Against France (1945–1954), our schools of medicine, pharmacy, and agriculture educated a stellar contingent of women specialists, without mentioning those who went on to study in the Soviet Union, China, and other socialist countries. During the War of Resistance Against the United States (1954–1975), this strength increased with many women trained in South Việt Nam and in Western countries. After Việt

Nam was re-unified and after *Đổi Mới* (Renovation or Renewal in late 1986), the policy of openness brought an increase in the number of women in science, although the biggest handicap to their scientific research remained traditional family responsibilities.

To complete the picture, let me mention several important Vietnamese women in science.

Dương Quỳnh Hoa (1930–2006), a medical doctor who trained in France, is well known for her political work as minister of health for the Provisional Revolutionary Government of South Việt Nam (PRG or Việt Cộng) as well as for her contributions as a pediatrician and head of a post-war pediatric hospital. From several meetings I had with her in the company of our mutual friend, French poet Françoise Corrèze, I felt I was meeting a patriot who was energetic, good-hearted, and unyielding in her opinions.

Hoàng Xuân Sính (1933–) was the first Vietnamese woman to receive a doctorate in mathematics at the Sorbonne. She participated in anti-French activities in occupied Hà Nội. During the American bombing, she taught in the jungle while preparing her thesis. An independent-minded woman, she created the first non-State-run university in Việt Nam.

Võ Hồng Anh (1939–2009) earned her doctorate in physics and mathematics in the Soviet Union and received the first Vietnamese International Kovalevsky Prize for Women in Science. She is the daughter of General Võ Nguyên Giáp and militant revolutionary Nguyễn Thị Quang Thái, who died of typhus during her imprisonment at Hỏa Lò Prison, known to Americans as the Hà Nội Hilton.

Vũ Thị Phan (?–?) was born in a colonial prison to a revolutionary mother. Phan became a specialist in parasitology. As an army doctor, she spent forty years fighting the malaria that wreaked havoc among our soldiers on the Hồ Chí Minh Trail during the American War. Professor Vũ Thị Phan subsequently served as director of the Malaria Institute and is a recipient of the International Kovalevsky Prize for Women in Science.

During the American War, Nguyễn Thị Thiều Hoa (1959–) won a silver medal at the International Mathematics Competition for secondary school students in Vienna and later earned a doctorate from the Soviet Union.

Nguyễn Thị Lê (?–?), whose father fought in the French War, served as president of the Society of Vietnamese Parasitologists. She discovered a new species in the genus *taenia* (tapeworm). The name of the newly discovered species references her name.

Lê Hồng Vân (c. 1933–), a mathematician, was the first and only woman to win a prize from the Abdus Salam International Centre for Theoretical Physics in Italy.

Cao Thị Bảo Vân, Ph.D. (1962–), deputy-director of the Pasteur Institute in Hồ Chí Minh City, identified the A/H1N1 virus and worked on the Institute's vaccine. Her mother is Dr. Nguyễn Thị Ngọc Toản, while her father is General Cao Văn Khánh, with whom I taught many, many years ago, when I was a young man in Huế. (For an essay mentioning Cao Văn Khánh, see p. 122-23.)

Who Designed the Áo Dài?

For about two thousand years, Việt Nam lived under the influence of Confucianism, with a sense of community characterizing traditional culture. Women were a tool for procreation to perpetuate the family line and assure continuation for worship of the ancestors. Parents arranged their children's marriages. Since girls had no freedom to choose their partners, they cared less about clothes and ornaments than in the West, especially after marriage. Women of good standing traditionally wore clothes that hid their bodies. Those with more buxom figures compressed their breasts with cloth bands. Hearing the word "breast" (*vú*) reddened the cheeks of well-educated men and even common laborers.

The modern *áo dài* breaks those clothing taboos. Molded to the body, it does nothing to hide a Vietnamese woman's curves.

Some say the *áo dài* first appeared in Việt Nam's Southern Region (Cochin China, Nam Kỳ). Many newspaper articles printed in Sài Gòn in the 1930s testify to this fact. One even cites a Paris document from 1921 affirming that the *áo dài* existed at that time in France. However, the general public tends to think that painter Cát Tường (1912–1946), a graduate of the Indochina Fine Arts College, created the *áo dài*. As a result, it is often called the "Lemur tunic," which plays across words in both French and Vietnamese. "Lemur" was Cát Tường's pseudonym because "*Tường*" (his name) means "wall," which is "*le mur*" in French.

The *áo dài* was, in fact, a new version of the traditional women's tunic, the five-piece, multi-colored dress (*năm thân*) or the four-piece, multi-colored dress (*tứ thân*). Other changes accompanied the introduction—or re-introduction, as it were—of the *áo dài*. During the 1920s and 1930s, women stopped lacquering their teeth and began to wear trousers instead of skirts, although traditional skirts were popular for a long time in rural areas. These reforms appeared during French modernization and changed Vietnamese customs and habits.

The Vietnamese wives of French men launched this fashion, which female teachers, nurses, and students adopted. These modern women wore white trousers with their *áo dàis* and refused to lacquer their teeth. Women of good standing eventually picked up the style. The triumph of the *áo dài* in the towns was in 1934. With this change came Vietnamese women's self-affirmation. The *áo dài* demonstrated women's aspiration to make their own decisions, enjoy individual freedoms, join society's activities, cultivate their minds, and take control over their bodies.

The Life of Single Women

My friend Lê Thi (1926–), a researcher specializing in women and the family, offered me her book, *The Life of Single Women in Việt Nam* (English version, 2005; Cuộc Sống của Phụ Nữ Đơn Thân ở Việt Nam, 2002). She acknowledged her work's limitations: "Our knowledge about the life of single women is not great. It cannot reflect the situation in the whole country, particularly in the southern and central regions, even with regard to typical cases." Despite her reservations, Lê Thi's research has a burning character and is of evident social interest. The subject of single women remains curtailed and even taboo in our society, which Confucianism still influences despite deep upheavals caused by war, the Revolution, the policy of Đổi Mới (Renovation or Renewal, which began in late 1986), and globalization.

Lê Thi based her work on studies conducted by various organizations in Phú Thọ, Tuyên Quang, Thái Nguyên, and Hà Giang Provinces. The studies also included state farms in Hòa Bình Province, villages in Sóc Sơn (an outlying district of Hà Nội), and, in particular, at Lời Village in Nghệ An Province. Lời Village formed more than three decades ago in a deserted region. Single mothers gathered there to avoid the hostility they had faced in their own hamlets. But then, Lời Village's fame attracted so many journalists, writers, photographers, and researchers that many Lời inhabitants moved elsewhere.

The status of Vietnamese women appears enviable compared with some countries. Yet, in general, single Vietnamese women face material difficulties and moral suffering. Lê Thi's study supplied figures from the General Statistical Bureau in 1999. These numbers showed that among all single adults, the proportion of women (including widows, divorcees, and separated spouses) was much higher than the proportion of men: 84.27 percent compared to 15.73 percent. The percentage of widows was the highest (87 percent). That figure could be explained by the many men killed during war.

While the single life is a normal phenomenon for Western women, it is considered abnormal in Việt Nam, where traditional society dictates that an absurd feeling of sin must afflict the single woman's innermost conscience. Many factors influence this phenomenon, which can gravely affect these women's psychology and comportment. First, there is the lingering, although weakened, influence of Confucianism, especially in the countryside. In this world-view, a woman is considered an instrument of procreation to ensure the husband's lineage. Thus, society rejects a woman without a husband and children. However, some social practices are losing ground. Widows no longer remarry within the husband's family in order to continue devoting themselves to their in-laws. Many widows do not want to remarry and prefer to concentrate on their children. Some divorcees fear an unhappy remarriage, for acts of domestic violence are not rare.

Many women also fear the disdain held for spinsters—single women above age twenty-six or twenty-seven in the countryside and above thirty in the towns. The women of these ages who are still without a suitor are considered left on the shelf. Society has also traditionally held single, unmarried women in disregard. The many women who worked during the war in the Volunteer Youth Program on the Hồ Chí Minh Trail and at state farms and forests have brought about some changes. Like the soldiers, they served for the war's duration, spending their marriageable years at the front. These women returned home to a dearth of marriageable men, because so many had been killed. Sympathy for them and the appearance of liberal tendencies brought to Việt Nam by Western feminists have caused some change in traditional values, especially in urban centers.

Occasionally, though, the passive mentality of single women sustains backward ways of thinking. Many single women think their existence is due to fate. Some village officials explain the occurrence of single women in the countryside by highlighting their extremely reserved attitudes and their limited chances to associate with men. In addition, authoritative parents prevent many village girls from marrying as they wish.

Lê Thi concluded her study, saying, "The few women (in towns) who choose to be single have stable jobs and are financially independent. They are doctors, engineers, journalists, company directors.... They live as they wish, attached to their professions. But these conditions are not available to the majority of single Vietnamese women, who are held captive by multiple worries—no electricity, the need for daily rice, and dilapidated, leaking roofs. For them, remaining single is not voluntary but, rather, is imposed. They wish their extended families (parents and relatives) and their communities would extend assistance."

A difficult ideological shift must take place so that society and single women can end discriminatory Confucian prejudices; this must occur alongside effective administrative measures.

Single Parenting

Single parenting, although still a new notion in Việt Nam, is gaining acceptance. But unlike in the West, where middle-class career building and the disintegration of the nuclear family are the main causes, the new phenomenon of single parenting in Việt Nam is another consequence of war. Many women spent their best years fighting and thus missed their chance for marriage. Lonely, they desperately wanted to have children. "*Xin con*" (ask for a child) gained currency in many places. Ms. Lê Thị Nhâm Tuyết (1927–2012), a sociologist, surveyed An Thiệp Village in Thái Bình Province, where she found that of the eighty-five single, middle-aged women interviewed, twenty-one had actively chosen single parenthood.

Phạm Thị Bùi, age forty, is a determined advocate of single parenthood. She began by asking to be relieved of her duties on the executive committee of the local Women's Union so she could have a child. When her request was denied, Ms. Bùi nevertheless continued with her quest and used a more direct approach. She invited to tea the father of four daughters and told him her wish. The man asked her to become his concubine. That way, he reasoned, she could give him a male heir.

"No," Bùi said, adamant. "I asked you only to 'give' me a child. If you say 'No,' I'll find another man."

Finally, the two reached an agreement. Bùi later gave birth to a boy, who was well received by her family.

Ms. Nhâm Tuyết's survey also showed that public opinion approved of the unmarried mothers and the children they had borne. The initiative usually came from the women, with older villagers acting as go-betweens. A commonly used message cannot be plainer: "I want a child, and I'll give a hundred kilograms of un-husked rice for a daughter and two hundred kilograms for a son." Of course, all such arrangements are strictly confidential.

The case study in An Thiệp Village led to the following conclusions:

- Unmarried women in this village and perhaps in many other places want to have at least one child, not through adoption but from procreation.

- The extended families and the community supported these single women and the children they bore.

- Single parenting has dealt Confucian tradition a heavy blow yet has also strengthened it by continuing to attach greater importance to male offspring.

This new trend marks a great leap forward from traditional thinking. In the old days, a woman with an illegitimate child faced opprobrium, with her head shaved and the nape of her neck plastered with lime. In some cases, such women were tied to a raft and left to the mercy of water and wind. Their children, needless to say, became outcasts. Even between the August 1945 Revolution and the early 1980s, single mothers who had never married were objects of public scorn and the recipients of administrative sanctions.

Vietnamese Youth and Virginity

"What do Vietnamese youth think of virginity?"

I put this question to two women well placed to enlighten me. One, the former director of a research institute on Vietnamese women, noted that eight out of ten female respondents in a recent survey said they prized their virginity, while all the boys said they preferred to marry virgins. She also cited a survey by a women's magazine in Hồ Chí Minh City, which revealed that the majority of the girls interviewed objected to free sex. They were afraid that if the relationship failed, they and they alone would have to pay the price, not their partners.

My second interlocutor, director of a newspaper for women, presented a different view. "Virginity!" she said. "The girls of today do not give a damn." To prove her point, she gave me the latest figures for the young Hà Nội single women who had resorted to abortion. In fact, these figures do not convey the whole picture in Việt Nam, especially in the countryside, where Confucian prudishness and the family spirit still retain their grip.

Virginity remains a value respected by many in Vietnamese society regardless of the timid introduction of sex education in secondary schools and the wave of eroticism and sexuality on TV, in movies, in Western literature, and on the Internet since *Đổi Mới* (Renovation or Renewal, which began in late 1986). We are still far behind the West.

While virginity is not yet an outmoded Vietnamese value, different perspectives have emerged due to acculturation with the West. I doubt Vietnamese young people understand and approve of the concept of virginity as expressed by our national poet Nguyễn Du (1766–1820) in his masterpiece, *The Tale of Kiều* (Truyện Kiều), which has enchanted generations with its long, complex story in six-word, eight-word meter. During a spring outing, Kiều, a beautiful girl who is virtuous and talented, meets the man of her dreams in Kim Trọng, a student. They fall in love. Breaking the Confucian taboo, she dares visit him in secret to vow her eternal love. That evening, under the moonlight,

> Kim's passion swelled, a surging sea,
> He felt a certain license overtake his tenderness.
> She warned: "Don't play with love . . .
> Why hasten to pluck the flower?
> Some night my love will respond to yours."

Kiều resists Kim's advances because she wants to wait until marriage sanctifies their love. Yet she never realizes her wish. Obligated to sell herself for a bribe to save her father, she endures fifteen years of degradation and shame as a prostitute, then as the concubine of a merchant, and then as wife of a brigand. She attempts suicide. Alone in a house of ill repute, she recalls her first meeting with long-lost Kim Trọng, imagining him nearby:

> Pointless— a girl keeps her virtue for whom?
> I know I have stepped astray,
> Let those faithless in love block my bloom,
> Yet I held back from you.
> Wherever my heart goes, that pain follows it,
> Oh Kim, if we meet again—
> My body's used, it cannot give you purity.

Đổi Mới (Renovation or
Renewal) and Globalization

Vietnamese Culture Facing Globalization

Thanks to the "World Decade for Cultural Development" (1988–1997), the Vietnamese people (in particular, the intelligentsia) accepted the ideas of the UN (United Nations) and UNESCO (United Nations Economic, Scientific, and Cultural Organization) about the organic links between development, economics, and culture. Culture must hold a central position and play the coordinating and regulating role. Development should not only be measured by economic growth but must also consider individual and collective welfare as well as spiritual life and thought—in other words, advances in the quality of life.

Việt Nam, like any other nation, must work for sustainable development within globalization, an irreversible phenomenon, which, however, should not be accepted passively. We must all steer development in the right direction through concerted action on a world scale. Taking stock of a decade of globalization (1990–2000), *International Courier* (Courrier International, a publication of *Le Monde*, Issue No. 525, 2000) defined "globalization" as "the tendency of the capitalist economy to become world-wide. Indirectly, it describes the present state of capitalism." This definition depicts certain aspects of globalization as the source of the double crisis described by the Brazilian liberation theologian Leonardo Boff (1938–) in the monthly journal *Faith and Development* (Foi et Développement, February 2001):

"The social crisis opposes the rich to the poor as never before in history. The wealth produced is appropriated by a minority of elites belonging to a small number of countries and by some social classes in dependent and poor countries. The second crisis is ecological. The present world system encourages maximum consumption of all natural and cultural resources. The end result is the deterioration of the quality of life of humans and other beings in the biosphere."

Side by side with the other peoples in the world, the Vietnamese must shape a different globalization, an integration with a humane face, taking into account the interests of disenfranchised peoples and based on the principles adopted at the 2001 Porto Alegre World Social Forum's "Call for Mobilization," which advocated action to produce the following results: sound economy; sustainable society; multiform economy; collectivism; democratic, transparent, and responsible governments; care for the environment and society; co-operation based on equity and autonomy in international relations; respect for biological, cultural, and economic pluralism; respect for human rights; and respect for the interests of different generations.

Those goals can be achieved only in an atmosphere of world peace and reciprocal trust. After the fall of the Berlin Wall, which signaled an end to the Cold War, people asked: On which path should the world embark—dialogue or cultural conflict? I think that these two methods have been side by side on our planet for five thousand years. In globalization, we have both dialogue and conflict. It is up to all of us to bend the global character toward creative dialogue.

For formerly colonized and poor countries in general, the top priority is economic growth to ensure sustainable development. But Adrien Ntabona, professor of anthropology at Burundi University, thinks the top priority should be cultural development. He notes in *Faith and Development* (Foi et Développement, December 2001): "The fundamental global problem is first of all not a political or economic one, but an axiological one linked to the value system that makes a man a man."

In Việt Nam, the 1945 Revolution led by Hồ Chí Minh ended eighty-five years of colonial exploitation and under-development. The thirty years of war (1945–1975) spent to affirm and complete national independence cost us millions of lives (a half million from the First Indochina War Against France and more than three million from the Second Indochina War Against the United States). During the American War, ten per cent of our country was ravaged by seventy-two million liters of defoliants, with that destruction including twenty-five million cubic meters of commercial timber, a hundred and fifty thousand hectares of rubber plantations, and between nine and fifteen thousand villages. These figures do not address the human costs. Reconstruction of the re-unified country truly started only in late 1986 with the beginning of the policy of Đổi Mới (Renovation or Renewal), which can be characterized as adoption of the market economy and the opening of Việt Nam's doors to international relations with all countries.

French historian Pierre-Richard Feray notes that culture played a prominent role in Việt Nam's Resistance War Against the United States, when Russian SAM rockets were fueled by an ideal of poverty and by a culture that seems to have been key to the Vietnamese victory. To ensure nation-building in peacetime, he says, Việt Nam must again draw on its "advanced culture strongly marked by national identity," which associates tradition with modernity. But colonization and the long years of war, as well as cultural change coming from the West, have upset traditional values. As a result, cultural and spiritual clarity has blurred, especially among the young, many of whom seem to have lost their bearings.

Vietnamese values cover a very broad range as a result of the country's turbulent history and its position at the heart of Southeast Asia, since Việt Nam is a link between the Chinese and Indian worlds and a meeting place between East and West. The Vietnamese nation formed during three millennia by affirming the double historical process of mixing indigenous populations with the assimilation of people from multiple outside cultures, including Austroasiatic and Austronesian ethnicities as well as Chinese, Indian, French, Japanese, American, Russian, and Korean cultures. The result is the emergence of an original culture consisting of a Southeast Asian base on which foreign cultural grafts were later added and reshaped. A characteristic of Vietnamese culture is its ability to turn elements borrowed from foreign cultures into its own.

During the past several decades, scholars and artists have discussed the Vietnamese national character in dozens of seminars in an effort to discern positive and negative factors in our traditional values. It is regrettable that many of these studies lack objectivity, often stressing the positive qualities more than the defects. Such a bias could be justified during the resistance wars. However, now, as globalization increases competition, a more critical attitude would help our country's sustainable development.

We must preserve a strong cultural identity in order to add our voice to the voices from other nations and to enrich the global symphony. We must also avoid chauvinism if we want to participate in the international concert without playing wrong notes. To perform in this concert, we must learn from other cultures and practice a conscious acculturation in order to allow foreign elements to fertilize national culture by transforming it from within.

There arises the wider evaluation of Asian cultures. The 1997 monetary crisis devastated many small Asian dragons. In March 1999, an international seminar with a comparative perspective on Asian values and Việt Nam's development was held in Hà Nội. Thinking about that theme, I venture three remarks:

- First, there exist universal values, which neither the East nor the West can deny.

- Second, Asian values and Western values have differences and even contradictions. The two value systems will not eliminate each other but, instead, will become complements through passive and active acculturation.

- Third, before appropriating foreign cultural attributes into our culture, we must reserve a particular place for regionalization (assimilation of Southeast Asian cultures) and our participation in the Francophone Community.

In conclusion, the *Đổi Mới* policy has also had a negative effect. The adoption of the market economy and the opening to Western cultures has encouraged competition and, at the same time, has stimulated frantic individualism, fanning an unbridled search for material pleasure in contradiction to our traditions of community. Economic progress must not harm our cultural identity. In this new era, the balance between economic and cultural development remains our biggest challenge.

The Traditional Family under Fire

Traditional cultural values came into question in Việt Nam after the 1945 Revolution, which ended eighty years of French colonial subjugation. One of these values is the concept of the traditional family and its change over the years. Changes from the French colonial period throughout the American War to *Đổi Mới* (Renovation or Renewal in late 1986) have influenced family structure so that it is hard to find examples of traditional Vietnamese family life. The economic gains from *Đổi Mới* have not only upset old family values but have also affected traditional Vietnamese culture based on the three levels of community (family – village – nation). A Vietnamese proverb says:

> A drop of red blood is more precious than a pond of
> fresh water.
>
> *Giọt máu đào hơn ao nước lã.*

Such emphasis on consanguinity may sound anachronistic. But until about forty years ago, it was common, especially in the countryside, to find three or four generations living together under the same roof. Family members had a common denominator within the family's economic unit. They were mostly illiterate farmers, with the same joys and pains, cultivating the same plots of land and sharing the same ethical values based on Confucianism—the authority of elders, the superiority of men over women, and the patriarch's control over the entire family.

During the 1980s, many writers lamented the crisis of the traditional Vietnamese family. The novel *Season of Leaves Falling in the Garden* (Mùa Lá Rụng Trong Vườn, 1985) by Ma Văn Kháng (1936–) has a nostalgic tone. The short story "The General Retires" (Tướng Về Hưu, 1987) by Nguyễn Huy Thiệp (1950–) was a thunder-clap in the seemingly calm literary sky. This short story creates the disquieting image of a society in which a general from the 1945 Revolution finds himself completely estranged because current society is not what he thought he had fought for during thirty years of war. The general is lost in his own family, among his own children, and within his own village.

For more than a decade, scholars have conducted many research studies, seeking to understand the present state of the Vietnamese family. Some conclusions are optimistic. Professor Lê Thi (1926–), retired director of the Women's Studies Center, says:

> The positive, progressive side is the development of relations based on equality and democracy. The family is returning to its primary functions, which for a period were neglected or discarded. It is not facing a crisis but, rather, is finding itself in the midst of an impasse, a crumbling. If this were a crisis, it would be a crisis of maturity.

Lê Thi contemplates the family's future: What should the Vietnamese family preserve from tradition? What values should we adopt from modern culture? How should we combine the ancient and the modern? What about the role of the individual?

Other researchers, such as Nguyễn Tài Thư (1935–), are more pessimistic.

> The family is facing new problems for a variety of reasons. Quite a few people feel the family no longer offers the most stable place to raise and educate children. Fewer and fewer people among the rich and powerful as well as among the poor and the weak enjoy real family happiness. Family ties are less and less appropriate for preparing younger family members to deal with modern-day social relations.

Nguyễn Minh Hòa, a researcher in Hồ Chí Minh City, adds:

> The family is gradually losing its economic function. As a collective unit, the family functions as a consumer of social products and services. But now, society shoulders the traditional family function of educating children.

Increasingly, society also assumes more functions of protection and care both on the material and moral planes.

Since *Đổi Mới*, the media has regularly reported about the growth of social phenomena—fraternal conflicts over money, rampant adultery and divorce, ungrateful children, indignant parents, and an increase in juvenile offences. We can trace all these defects back to, among other things, the negative effect of the market economy, in particular, the feverish race after profit to satisfy material pleasures, resulting in an excessive emphasis on the individual and the decline of family morals.

Despite its primordial importance, the family is but one of many important traditional institutions. We must set any discussion within a general cultural framework. During globalization, we Vietnamese must amalgamate Eastern and Western culture. As an institution, the Vietnamese family should borrow from the Western family its democracy and individuality (but not individualism). The traditional Vietnamese family must divest itself of antiquated concepts (patriarchy, disdain for women, and the infallibility of male elders) and retain its positive elements (harmony between generations and justified pride in the family line). Many laudable, traditional practices prevail despite contemporary upheavals; we should perpetuate these while embracing new elements so that the Vietnamese family maintains a healthy existence.

The Market Economy and Matrimony

The August 1945 Revolution ended eight decades of foreign domination and introduced democratic principles and practices. One was the New Life model, which liberated our people from outmoded customs, including old wedding rituals, which had financially ruined many a family. Meanwhile, the newly urban rich had vied with one another in following Western ways, producing pitiful, unconvincing imitations.

Old-fashioned wedding rituals followed the etiquette pre-scribed by Chinese philosopher Zhu Xi (1130–1200). Although these rites were simpler in Việt Nam than in China, they nonetheless involved many steps, including a go-between's match-making negotiations, exchange of the prospective bride and groom's horoscopes, the formal marriage request, the formal betrothal, the wedding ceremony, the ceremony honoring the Goddess of the Red Thread (the elderly woman in the moon who uses her moonlight to bind a couple's hands with magic red thread), the ceremony for the Household Genie, the second-day visit to the bride's parents, and dues paid to the bridegroom's home village. The list goes on. For the engagement ceremony alone, the bride's family presented each member of the family and clan with a *bánh chưng* (a non-sweet, square cake about 15 x 15 x 4 centimeters and made from glutinous rice, green beans, and pork) or a *bánh giày* (a similar cylindrical cake), a roll of *nem* (pork pie), four areca nuts, and four betel leaves. Then, the family would wine and dine half the village on the wedding day to repay "debts of the month."

The August 1945 Revolution abandoned these old, onerous practices. During the two resistance wars (1945–1975), "New Life Weddings" consecrated marriages with a simple gathering of parents, friends, and colleagues. The parents and representatives from the office, factory, cooperative, or military unit where the bride and groom worked exhorted the couple "to remember their duties toward the Homeland during their newfound happiness." Music, singing, and poetry enlivened these meetings, which eventually became monotonous and unappealing. After peace returned, Vietnamese began to draw once again from the traditional and the foreign.

Adoption of the market economy in late 1986 brought a marked improvement in Việt Nam's standard of living, coupled with a deepening gap between rich and poor. Economic successes also revived some outdated and wasteful customs and practices. Research by *New Hà Nội* (Hà Nội Mới) newspaper highlighted effects of the market economy, modern living conditions, and recently revived customs. Of the four hundred families questioned in March 1995, 51.8 percent approved of evaluating zodiac signs governing the bride and groom's births, while 93.9 percent supported traditional betrothal rites, 11 percent approved of honoring the Goddess of the Red Thread, and 95 percent paid homage to the ancestors.

The revolutionary Wedding Tea with a few cookies and cigarettes served to a dozen people has evolved into a banquet attended in "suburban villages by people from all hamlets in the village. In cities, guests include the colleagues, relatives, friends, and acquaintances of the parents and the bride and groom." The number of guests may swell to eight or nine hundred. According to a survey conducted in ten urban and suburban districts of Hà Nội, 58 percent of families of ranking officials and 35 percent of traders had hosted banquets attended by at least six hundred guests. The average family (state employee, peasant) invites three hundred people. Impecunious pensioners and workers invite relatively few guests. A desire for pomp marks weddings of children of ranking officials and prosperous merchants. For the betrothal ceremony, a procession of pedicabs with golden roofs decorated with red fringes carries family members and friends bedecked with jewels and bearing many offerings, while a videographer records the procession. Marriages marked by ostentation accounted for 86.1 percent of weddings in Hà Nội's urban districts and 86 percent in the city's suburban districts.

Families assess wedding banquets in plush restaurants according to calculations similar to a business profit-and-loss statement. Parents carefully invite everyone from whom they have previously received an invitation. Guests must abide by a tacit rule: They should give their hosts a gift in cash, that is, an envelope containing between one-fourth and one-third of a state employee's monthly salary. This obligation is particularly devastating for retirees. Of those questioned, 88.2 percent noted it was a disaster to receive three or four invitations in one month.

When the wedding is over, the hosts draw up a balance sheet. Generally, the accounting shows a profit because the hosts invited as many prosperous guests as possible.

Divorce as Seen in a District of Hà Nội

Successive social upheavals have changed traditional family values, resulting in a steep increase in divorce. Hai Bà Trưng is a district in central Hà Nội. Its population between 1987 and 1995 was about three hundred thousand. During that period, the number of marriages ranged between twenty-two hundred and three thousand annually, while the number of judicial divorces was between four hundred and five hundred. That comes to nearly two divorces for every ten marriages. The figures in France for that same period were one divorce for every ten marriages, while in the United States the numbers were three divorces for every ten marriages.

Việt Nam's divorce rate is alarming for a country where matrimonial ties have been regarded as sacred. The People's Courts give these reasons for divorce in recent years:

- incompatibility of character: 39.6 percent
- adultery: 16.4 percent
- bad treatment of the wife: 16.2 percent
- family dissension: 11.3 percent
- one of the partners (usually the husband) has taken to drinking or gambling: 11.3 percent
- economic difficulties: 2.8 percent
- illness or infertility: 2.4 percent

What conclusions can be drawn from the above?

In Việt Nam, since the adoption of the free-market economy, the rampant pursuit of money has increased pressures within the family, yet the percentage of divorces arising from economic difficulties was only 2.8 percent. Most divorces (nearly 40 percent) arose from incompatibility. The cause of incompatibility, I believe, is rooted in the institution of marriage and the difficulty of marital relationships during all periods of history.

The other causes for divorce should be viewed in relation to the situation of the wife in the traditional Vietnamese family, which has been deeply influenced by Confucianism, in this case the rule of the father, the husband, and the family's other male members, who alone are traditionally responsible for ancestor worship.

Traditionally, wives could not initiate divorce, whereas husbands had the right to repudiate their wives for any of seven reasons— infertility, lechery, failure to perform duties attending her in-laws, malevolent gossip, theft, jealousy, and infirmity.

However, repudiation was not allowed in three cases:

- the wife had been in mourning for her father-in-law or mother-in-law during the required period of three years (i.e., she had helped her husband perform his filial duties)

- the husband had become rich since their marriage (i.e., she had contributed to his prosperity)

- the wife would be deprived of all means of support.

At present, the Law on Marriage and the Family gives the wife equal rights with her husband, especially the right to seek divorce.

Let us return to divorce cases in Hai Bà Trưng District.

The figure of 16.4 percent of divorces due to adultery would have been inconceivable in the old, traditional society, especially with regard to the wife. The husband had no need to engage in adultery, since he was entitled to polygamy. A folk saying noted that the husband could have "seven concubines and five wives." However, an adulterous wife suffered inhumane torture, both physical and mental. The back of her head was shaved and smeared with slaked lime. Then she was marched through the village, to be followed by hordes of jeering children. Young widows were required to observe strict chastity, for an adulterous-widow was similarly punished.

Things have changed during the last decades. Adultery is no longer rare, especially among young urban couples. With the end of polygamy and more open relationships, adultery has become a major reason for divorce. Other causes are vestiges of the feudal family. Bad treatment of the wife accounts for 16.2 percent of divorces. Wife beating is still fairly common. In some cases, the husband and mother-in-law bully a wife so fiercely that she takes her own life. Some wives (11.3 percent) have divorced their husbands because they were incorrigible drunkards or gamblers.

This picture of divorce in one Hà Nội district some years ago may nevertheless reflect the situation in the country at large. In any case, it is a sign of the times.

The Young and Our Traditions

The Resistance Wars Against France (1945–1954) and the United States (1954–1975) have receded in time. Fighters from those days are elderly, white-haired, and in ill health. In his article, "A Retrospective Look at Contemporary Poetry" (Nhìn Lại Tiến Trình Thơ Hiện Đại) published in *Literature and the Arts* (Văn Nghệ) magazine on November 25, 1995, poet and critic Vũ Quần Phương (1940–) noted that poems, which had once moved those veterans deeply, have lost their beauty in the eyes of today's young people. Similarly, Việt Nam's national epic, *The Tale of Kiều* (Truyện Kiều), no longer entrances the young as much as rock music.

I had thought that *Kiều*, the immortal masterpiece by Nguyễn Du (1766–1820), would survive all changes in taste and fashion because it is believed to portray the Vietnamese psyche. Someone has said not without reason: "So long as *Kiều* lasts, the Vietnamese language shall last. And so long as our language endures, our nation shall live on." It pains me that people think the younger generation is lukewarm toward *Kiều*. I shared my feelings with a friend, the poet Trần Lê Văn.

"Let us nurture no hope," Trần Lê Văn said, "that *Kiều* will enjoy the same fervor in the age of discotheques and computers as in our time and that of our fathers. But I do not think our young people are no longer moved by *Kiều's* lines singing the enchantment of love. Two years ago, I was invited to talk about *The Tale of*

Kiều to pupils at a country school in Chương Mỹ District [Hà Tây Province, now part of Hà Nội]. For more than an hour, excerpts from the poem enraptured those teenagers aged thirteen to fifteen. They asked me a hundred questions about *Kiều*. We members of the older generations must reveal to young people the beauty hidden in that treasure."

A few days after that conversation, I was asked to speak about Vietnamese culture to a class of about thirty students with an average age of twenty-five at the Franco-Vietnamese Center for Management Training. I improvised a test about *The Tale of Kiều* by asking two questions: "Do you like *Kiều*?" and "Even if you don't like *Kiều*, do you feel the beauty of some of the verses?"

Ten students said "Yes" to the first question; all thirty answered the second question affirmatively.

I was somewhat reassured, all the more so when, during a ten-minute break, I saw two pairs of students playing a traditional game of shuttlecock. Nothing could be simpler and cheaper than a game of Vietnamese shuttlecock, a true game for young people of the Third World. The only materials needed are a round piece of rubber, a piece of metal or wood, and a few feathers. No rackets are required. The shuttlecock is passed back and forth using the feet and, when necessary, other parts of the body, excluding the hands.

No one needs to despair about our youth.

The Cicada Generation

Many Vietnamese young people, especially children of well-off townsfolk, are dazzled by Honda motorcycles, Canon cameras, Sony DVDs, and Toyota cars. They think Japan is a land of milk and honey. They do not know how much sweat and tears as well as intelligence and energy the Japanese spent to reach their present living standard. Meanwhile, in the Country of the Rising Sun, some pleasure-seeking young people have forgotten the difficult past of their elders—their parents and grandparents.

Some sociologists compare the differences to those between ants and cicadas. The elders in Japan tasted war's bitterness—defeat and austerity. They do not ask for much. The next generation grew up in prosperity and abundance, craves enjoyment, and demands consumer goods. The elders feel a beer reflects great wealth, whatever the beer. Their children expect a list of beers.

Mme. Ogi Maoki, a teacher, notes that egotism and isolation are developing among young Japanese children: "Returning from school, the children rush to complementary classes or piano lessons. Pupils in my third form live only fifty to a hundred meters apart. But when I asked a student to take a lesson to a classmate, who had missed class, the student said he did not know his classmate's house."

Japanese children in the twentyfirst century grow up amidst computers and electronic games. Too soon, those children abandon childhood fairy tales, dreams, and poetic imagination. Obsessed by TV cartoons and computer games, they spend little time outside and have fewer human contacts than earlier generations. Traditional courtesy and politeness dim. Such is the generation of the Japanese cicadas.

In Việt Nam, the generation of the ant grandparents endured the American War (1954–1975) and usually had two children, since family planning has been obligatory for years. In contrast, the cicada generation born after the complete return of peace in 1990 comprises those under the age of twenty five. Đổi Mới (Renovation or Renewal, which began in late 1986) has brought relative prosperity, with foreign consumer goods, such as refrigerators, TVs, electronic tablets, smart phones, motorcycles, and Western foods, including milk products. This youngest generation knows neither the suffering of war nor the privations of rationing.

Vietnamese and Japanese cicadas have many points in common—thirst for enjoyment, lack of community, little respect for traditions, and an obsession with electronics. Japanese cicadas can justify themselves, for the consumer society is their society and the product of their country's post-industrial economy. However, the Vietnamese cicadas live in a Third World country, which cannot yet support itself as a consumer society. Our young people must temper themselves much more for the future, which will not be easy.

Allow me to raise only one point: the ants' education of the cicadas. The ants are anxious to spare their children the hardships they suffered during childhood. As a result, they spend without counting to give their children a comfortable life through modern conveniences and sophisticated products, such as ice cream, chocolate, cookies, and vitamin candies. Their children spend all day on lessons and educational tasks, including special courses. In many cases, these children have no Sunday off. Thus, they tend to be isolated, egoistical, unable to adapt, and without character.

A Story of Tomatoes and Watercress

One morning, as usual, the elderly itinerant vendor of vegetables stopped at our door and set down her two heavy baskets hanging from a bamboo shoulder pole. After buying food for the day, my daughter-in-law said, before going to the hospital where she is a doctor, "Dad, fresh tomatoes sell at ransom price, 7,000 *đồng* a kilo. Imagine that." She added cheerily: "As for the watercress, it's a give-away. A bundle costs 500 *đồng*, enough to serve our family of six."

My reaction was different. Our farmers face multiple hazards. In 1999, farmers comprised 80 percent of the population yet earned an average monthly income of 70,000 *đồng* ($5.04 US). I was happy to see tomatoes fetching a high price; I knew most farm prices would soon decline. The year before, farmers had sold their produce at low prices because they lacked the food-processing and transport needed to market surpluses. Farmers from a village in southern Việt Nam, which had been ravaged by floods, finally harvested a bumper rice crop. But a bountiful supply sent prices plummeting. Once again, the farmers lost much of their investment.

With temporary pauses during the American War (1954–1975), agriculture in the north of Việt Nam has been influenced by several factors:

Collectivization and Land Reform, which began before 1960, generated agricultural development surpassing the level of 1945, but then the extensive cooperatives organized between 1960 and 1980 brought about a decline in production. Between 1980 and 1988, we had partial de-collectivization involving targets for contracted assignments, which entrusted some production to individual peasants. Those farmers benefited from the profits, thereby creating agricultural development. After *Đổi Mới* (Renovation or Renewal, which began in late 1986), agricultural production surged, beginning in 1988 and continuing into the 1990s, as land in cooperatives was allocated on long-term leases to farmers, who held direct responsibility for their fields, as they do today.

Development of our irrigation network came with collectivization, when nearly all lowland rice fields were irrigated. The allocation of private plots in the late 1980s and the system of small pumping stations under local management ensured that irrigation was better adapted to individual farmers' needs.

Change in the selection of seeds (the green revolution) began for Việt Nam in 1965. Rice varieties with a shorter growing season replaced traditional varieties with higher stalks and longer seasons. Chemical fertilizers became more common.

De-collectivization brought positive results. Thanks to *Đổi Mới,* our living standard has improved. However, we are still far from the take-off point that would allow us to become another little dragon in Southeast Asia. Since 1996, economic growth has slowed. In 1998, we experienced unfavorable conditions: floods, droughts, fallout from the Asian monetary crisis, a drop in the number of foreign tourists, and a decline in foreign investment. The government and the National Assembly warned our people about numerous difficulties, which called for new efforts if we were to continue the policy of reform we had begun in late 1986.

Until recently, our economic development has been inspired more or less by the model of East Asia (Japan, South Korea) and Southeast Asia (Malaysia, Singapore, Taiwan, and Thailand), that is, the policy of export-oriented industrialization. Maybe we should revise this tendency. Let us note that these countries started their export-oriented industrialization at a much more favorable time in the international market. Japan took advantage of the circumstances of the Cold War, whereas Malaysia, South Korea, Taiwan, and Thailand took economic advantage of the American War in Việt Nam. Such advantages do not exist for Việt Nam and for the other countries that began industrializing later and are burdened by outdated technology and large populations in need of employment.

Consequently, to assure durable development while industrializing to increase exports, we must broaden our domestic market by boosting the purchasing power of our population (which is mostly farmers). To do this, we must develop our countryside and agriculture and increase internal savings. Let us not forget that the peasants made decisive contributions to our War of Resistance Against France (1945–1954) and our War of Resistance Against the United States (1954–1975) by their participation as soldiers and porters and by contributing food and supplies. Today, they contribute to our economic growth, with the result that Việt Nam has become the world's second largest rice exporter. If our peasants' products sell at low prices, the peasantry's purchasing power will remain low. The prosperity of both rural and urban citizens and the national economy will suffer.

A Traditional Village Facing the Market Economy

After my first visit in 1992 to Lệ Mật, a village famous for its snake hunters and snake breeders, I wrote about an annual ceremony commemorating the legendary exploit of Lệ Mật, a poor fisherman believed to have saved the life of a Lý Dynasty princess in the 1000s by killing an aquatic monster. A second visit several years later to Lệ Mật, which is seven kilometers north of Hà Nội, took me by surprise. Our motorbike was about half a kilometer from our destination when other motorbikes approached, advertising their restaurants with this message: "Savor Snake Meat at *Our* Restaurant!"

When we arrived at our destination, I found I could barely recognize the village I had described in 1992. That was six years after the beginning of *Đổi Mới* (Renovation or Renewal), which opened Việt Nam to a market economy and, in turn, created a boom in the snake business. Now, Lệ Mật has become a village with tough competition between dozens of snake eateries targeting foreign tourists and prosperous city residents out for a jaunt.

Mr. Quốc Triệu waited for us at the door of his restaurant. In his late fifties and sporting a healthy tan, he was brimming with magnanimity and self-confidence, for his business is among the earliest and most prosperous in the village. Quốc Triệu took us to his restaurant's place of honor in an oriental-style pavilion on the second floor, where he offered us an appetizer, a drink made from cobra bile. He said it would improve our eyesight and cure our lumbago. Then he left us to choose from a list of dishes, including civet, pangolin, black cat, monkey, porcupine, hedgehog, freshwater turtle, salamander, and, of course, snake. We had already seen these animals alive in cages at the restaurant's entrance.

We tasted a number of dishes—sautéed hedgehog flavored with citronella, roasted porcupine, cigarette-size spring rolls made from snake meat, snake meat rolled in flour and fried, snake meat and rice gruel, and snake meat cooked with sugar-cane juice. I confess that snake meat was not to my taste despite all its professed medicinal properties. Snakes marinated in rice whisky are said to help cure joint pains and are thought to be such an effective aphrodisiac that young people are advised against consuming the drink! While we sat at the table, a snake was killed in front of us and its blood dripped into a cup of rice whisky. I'm afraid I could not summon enough courage to taste the mixture.

Snakes have brought wealth to Lệ Mật Village, as Mr. Quốc Triệu's rags-to-riches story shows. He was born into an impoverished peasant family, which, from generation to generation, earned its supplementary income by catching snakes in tree hollows, paddy-dike holes, and from rhumbas of snakes in the bamboo forests. The family sold snakes to urban ethnic-Chinese Vietnamese, who prized snake meat and rice whisky marinated with snakes.

However, the trade brought little income. Life in the village was miserable. People starved during the great famine in the spring of 1945 before the August Revolution, and snake hunting was not without risks. Snake bites paralyzed or killed several people. Quốc Triệu benefited from his father's teaching, but nevertheless he was bitten by poisonous snakes. Although each family had its own recipe for herbal antidotes, Quốc Triệu had no medicine at the time. As a result, the fingers of his right hand are paralyzed, and he suffers from a less serious injury to his left arm.

At one time, Quốc Triệu sold venom from the snakes he bred to the state pharmaceutical service. His family lived a little better then, but he had to travel to the highlands to hunt snakes because few snakes remained in his neighborhood. True prosperity came to Quốc Triệu's family only with establishment of the market economy. People became more prosperous and more inclined to sample snake meat and snake whisky. Now, trucks from the highlands arrive in Lệ Mật every day to deliver bags of snakes. Competition among eateries and support services has depleted village solidarity, while our forest ecosystem suffers from no protections for snakes, which play their part in the wider eco-system by keeping rats and other rodents under control.

Indeed, the market economy has its own venom.

A Pedicab Driver

We were going out of town. A fine drizzle fell on the pedicab's nylon roof. I engaged in small talk with the driver pedaling from his seat perched behind my back. He was a thin man about fifty, with a rugged face tinged with bitterness. A certain stiffness in his carriage hinted at a military past. In fact, as he eventually told me, he was a retired army lieutenant.

The case of Mr. Hành, the cyclo driver, is fairly typical of the life of a North Vietnamese Army veteran of the American War (1954–1975). Of peasant stock, he was born in An Hưng Village, now part of the port city of Hải Phòng. While in primary school, he served as apprentice to his uncle, a tailor. In 1950, during the Resistance War Against France, French troops occupied Hải Phòng. Little Hành, twelve years old, earned his living by doing piecework for the French army's Supply Department.

In 1954, Hải Phòng City was liberated together with the whole of North Việt Nam. Hành secured jobs with privately run shops. At age twenty, he married a sixteen-year-old peasant girl. In 1961, he joined the army. After six months' training, he became a driver trucking munitions under massive US bombing on the famous Hồ Chí Minh Trail. In 1967, fighting raged on Highway 9 near the 17th parallel. B-52s carpet bombed night and day. Toxic chemicals sprayed by US aircraft laid waste the foliage in virgin forests, exposing the Trail.

As a political commissar during the American War, Hành supervised a 124-truck battalion. He directly commanded twelve trucks whose drivers had volunteered to carry new ĐKB rockets (similar to Soviet Kachiusa BM-21s) to Tân Cảnh Front in Kontum for coordination with the Spring 1972 Offensive in Quảng Trị, South Việt Nam. He narrowly escaped death several times while fulfilling his assignment and was awarded a Liberation Fighter Medal. American B-52 bombers struck Hành's battalion as it was regrouping. He was wounded by a bomb splinter in the back of his skull and by pellets in his armpit from a cluster bomb, also known as a baby bomb. Hành underwent six months of treatment, but the doctors could not remove all the pellets. One pellet is still inside his body, slowly shifting from place to place. Because of the shortage of experienced officers, Hành stayed with the truck convoys until he was demobilized in 1972. As a civilian, he worked in a shop, making artificial limbs for amputees. He shaped wooden feet, calves, thighs, arms, and hands before plastics were available. In 1976, as a wounded veteran, he enjoyed the right to early retirement.

Hành's family life has not been happy. Letters to and from home were rare for soldiers on the Vietnamese side during the war. Lucky families might receive three letters from a son or husband during ten years. After he was demobilized, Hành learned that his wife had deserted him.

These days, Hành's first child, a son of the former wife, supports himself with odd jobs in Germany. His second child, also a son, was implicated in a crime. His daughter has not been happily married. Hành married again, this time to a retired state employee. Their combined pensions cannot make ends meet. They have a baby boy, now a year old, and live in a dilapidated hut. Hành was pedaling a cyclo to supplement his meager pension.

At the time of this conversation, there were thousands of pedicab drivers in Hà Nội. Most were peasants from Nam Hà and Thanh Hóa Provinces, but some were state employees, students, and even intellectuals seeking extra income. This was a sign of the times, for no self-respecting man in traditional Vietnamese society would stoop to this occupation, especially in the days when the vehicle was a rickshaw. A rickshaw-puller, whom French colonizers and Vietnamese mandarins called a *coolie-pousse*, was at the bottom of the social ladder, together with prostitutes.

During the first days following the August 1945 Revolution, Hà Nội's new leaders banned pedicabs because they deemed cyclos contrary to human dignity. Yet this decision deprived thousands of men of a livelihood. Subsequently, the government took a more realistic policy, particularly in the face of the urban population explosion following the shift to a market economy. Now, Hà Nội's leadership has once again banned pedicabs from the city's streets, with the exception of tourist groups and processions for betrothal ceremonies.

Respect for Teachers Re-Emerges

Back in the days of Việt Nam's classical, Confucian-based educational system, a master did not teach for money but, instead, to fulfill a mission similar to that of a priest. The parents of his pupils provided for his material needs, including food, clothes, and lodging with a family. They supported the teacher's family members, who sometimes lived far from the master's classes. On the occasion of ritual feasts and holidays, parents offered the teachers gifts-in-kind and, more rarely, cash. The pupils' devotion to their masters extended to the afterlife. They would establish an association of disciples (*hội đồng môn*) to tend a teacher's grave and provide devotion to his memory after death.

For more than a decade, people tried to restore respect for the teacher, one of the moral values of ancient Việt Nam.

But why?

The socio-economic upheavals caused by thirty years of war (1945–1975), the opening of the free-market economy in late 1986, and the impact of the global informatics revolution have posed thorny problems for our educational system. A string of educational reforms has not been effective. School enrolments soared with the country's increasing postwar population and universalized primary education in former South Việt Nam after re-unification. During the 1997–1998 school year, Việt Nam had twenty-two million students. The teaching staff remained inadequate, even though it rose from 586,000 in 1993 to 820,000 by the end of 1997. Nevertheless, schools suffered from a growing talent drain. During the 1996–1997 school year, two thousand teachers left their jobs in Hồ Chí Minh City, 275 left in Long An Province, and 140 left the profession in Bình Dương Province.

The fact that teachers were abandoning their profession showed that the traditional ideal of the teacher had changed. Yet according to Confucian ethics, the teacher was superior to the father in the three fundamental social ties—king, teacher, and father. One adage says:

> You must regard anyone who teaches you an ideogram
> as your teacher;
> Even anyone who teaches you only half an ideogram is
> your teacher.

When education was limited to males, the traditional master taught his students the humanities and the duties of a man with good breeding. Thus, a teacher had to be exemplary. Westernized education under French colonization blurred this image of the master as a model of knowledge and wisdom, although the master remained an established authority extolled in textbooks. A child of six learned in his first reading lesson: "At school, I must listen to what the master says, and I must do whatever he says must be done. I owe him absolute obedience. I love and respect my master, just as I love and respect my parents."

Democratization brought about by the August 1945 Revolution shortened the distance between teachers and pupils. At one point, pupils called their teachers Older Brother (*Anh*) and Older Sister (*Chị*). However, after some decades, school administrators restored the old titles of Master (*Thầy*) and Mistress (*Cô*) to enforce tighter discipline. Today, the campaign to restore authority and respect for teachers is in full swing. On Teacher's Day (November 20), students offer their teachers so many flowers that prices increase tenfold in Hà Nội's markets. *New World* (Thế Giới Mới), a monthly magazine, organized a competition for the best student article about a teacher. More than five hundred students turned in submissions. The publication's effort was not aimed at reviving the obsolete model of the Confucian master but, rather, to encourage devoted teachers.

The Fight against Corruption

Corruption in all forms—nepotism, bribery, extortion, money under the table, kick-backs, abuse of trust, and embezzlement—has appeared at all times and under all regimes in all countries as a seemingly incurable vice. In Việt Nam, the fight against the envelopes epidemic, which has contaminated government offices and services, has become a major concern of the National Assembly. The evil has worsened since the adoption in late 1986 of Đổi Mới (Renovation or Renewal), which, while helping to improve the national economy and people's living standards, has created a race for money and material pleasure. Unbridled individualism, which was unknown during the years of wartime austerity (1945–1989), is due in part to the free-market practice of exalting competition in a negative sense of the word.

During the time of the kings in ancient Việt Nam, becoming a mandarin was not considered a lucrative occupation. Rather, holding a position in the mandarate was a privilege extended by the sovereign. A mandarin might accept modest donations to help make ends meet. However, the Confucian ethic could not stop the mandarins' corruption, which flourished under irresponsible kings.

Throughout Vietnamese history, many upright mandarins and intransigent scholars fought against corruption. In the 1300s, Chu Văn An (1292–1370), vice-rector of the Royal College and considered the model master-teacher in Việt Nam, submitted an unsuccessful request for execution of seven mandarins guilty of corruption. When his request failed, Chu Văn An tendered his resignation from his prestigeous position at the College and retired to the countryside. In the 1400s, humanist and national hero Nguyễn Trãi (1380–1442) took the same form of protest. In the 1500s, reclusive thinker Nguyễn Bỉnh Khiêm (1491–1585), also known as Bạch Vân (White Cloud), castigated corrupt mandarins (the rats) in his famous poem "Upping the Ante" (Tăng Thử, also called "Hating the Rats" – Ghét Chuột), written in five-word meter:

> Heaven gave human beings life,
> Shelter, warmth, food, and pleasure;
> Oh! And sages of antiquity
> Provided seeds for five cereals.
> Peasants could rear their children,
> Husbands cared for their families.
> But the rats were appalling
> With their truly wicked stealing,
> Shamelessly devouring fields of rice,
> Eating everything in the granaries.
> Poor peasants, men and women,
> Wept and wailed with hunger;

Human destiny couldn't bear this,
But the rats were merciless,
Recklessly occupying even the citadel!
Gods and people sought revenge,
Having completely lost their patience,
Announcing: "We'll kill you rats,
Expose your corpses in markets
To feed crows and vultures,
To protect those you devastated,
To restore peace and prosperity."

During the 1800s, Đặng Huy Trứ (1825–1875) demanded radical reforms. Confucian in the best sense of the word, Đặng Huy Trứ wrote *Handbook Governing Gifts* (Từ Thụ Yếu Quy) for the use of mandarins. In Đặng Huy Trứ's view, a mandarin was the people's servant, "the son of the lowly people" (*thứ dân chi tử*) or "the people's dog and horse" (*khuyển mã*).

During colonialism, Vietnamese controlled only a narrow strip of arable land along the coast because the French had occupied the fertile fields in the Southern Region (Cochin China, Nam Kỳ). Even a Royal Court with the best intentions could not pay its officials enough. A first-rank mandarin received only about three-tenths the pay of a district mandarin in China. Some mandarins received no pay because of deficits in the local budget. But a man serving the king must not clothe himself in rags. Further, he must host receptions on feast days. How could a mandarin maintain his integrity and meet these social obligations?

Đặng Huy Trứ's realistic position was based on moral purity. He held that a mandarin was duty-bound to refuse bribes, but he could accept gifts stemming from pure gratitude. He listed 104 cases where refusal was obligatory, drawing on examples from education, politics, economics, culture, and society. He analyzed each case, with comments and examples from history. Cases where refusal was obligatory included gifts from a candidate to an examiner, from a supplicant to an inspector, from foreign traders expecting favors, from a merchant hoping for a tax reduction, from someone hoping for gain in redistribution of communal rice fields, from a village hoping for exemption from labor to repair dikes, and from a defendant to a judge in hopes of leniency.

The author tolerated only five cases for accepting a gift: 1) annual ritual festivals (for example Tết [the Lunar New Year] or a harvest festival), 2) from someone for whom one had justly resolved a dispute, 3) from someone to whom one had lent support for legitimate promotion, 4) from north-south maritime traders (to thank local authorities for ensuring safe passage through their territories), and 5) from someone to celebrate a happy event (ambassadorial mission, promotion) or to commemorate a solemn occasion (funeral or death anniversary of someone's parents).

What do today's public servants think of those recommendations made by a mandarin more than a century ago?

Saying Hello to the Past

It has been three generations since my family settled in Hà Nội after leaving Tư Thế, our native village in Kinh Bắc, home of Việt Nam's ancient culture. Thanks to *Đổi Mới* (Renovation or Renewal, which began in late 1986), the people of Tư Thế have achieved a better life. Yet sadly, much has been lost. The look of my native village has changed dramatically. Brick and stucco houses have replaced the mud and straw huts, although perhaps with too much copying of Western architecture with its triangular pediments, flat roofs, and rococo ornaments. There remain no traces of the traditional village of my childhood memories. All of Tư Thế's ancestral temples were leveled or burned during the Resistance War Against France (1945–1954). The village bamboo hedge is gone. The communal house with its porch (an architectural marvel) and surrounding kapok and banyan trees near the market is also gone.

Many traditional villages have become unrecognizable because of the two recent wars (1945–1975) and Việt Nam's modernization—or Westernization. Few have remained immune to cultural pollution.

However, Đường Lâm, which is four kilometers west of Son Tây Province Capital, remains an exception. The tall, urban-like roofs that indicate rampant industrialization elsewhere have not disturbed the horizon at Đường Lâm. Painter Phan Kế An, a close friend and native of Đường Lâm, explained: "In the old days, a rule kept us from building houses higher than the communal house. That rule no longer holds. Yet even now we have only a few multi-storied houses." Phan Kế An added, "The main reason may be the villagers' poverty, for they support themselves largely by cultivating rice. Trade is negligible, and the village has few sideline professions beyond raising cane sugar, making soy sauce, and weaving a little homespun cloth."

Poverty has saved Đường Lâm's cultural heritage, although this is a materialistic poverty measured by the presence of imported luxury articles. Living standards have improved, including new houses made of local laterite brick. Census results show that 60 percent of households enjoy an "easy life," 33 percent are "well-off," and only 4 percent are rated as "poor," with the remaining labeled as "other." Around six hundred villagers have attended university, and all villagers have completed elementary school.

Visitors to Đường Lâm can easily lose their way in the labyrinth of paved alleys and footpaths bordered by the reddish-brown laterite walls that surround the laterite houses, which are characteristic of Việt Nam's Midlands. They can see the architecture of a traditional Vietnamese village with its communal house, pagodas, Taoist temples, clan houses of worship, and even a Neolithic excavation site.

The region surrounding Đường Lâm is bathed in an atmosphere of spirituality honoring the memory of illustrious Vietnamese. Phùng Hưng (life: 761–802; reign: 795–802), also called Great Father-and-Mother King of the People (Bố Cái Đại Vương), is worshipped as a liberator of our country from the Chinese T'ang Dynasty (618–907). Ngô Quyền (life: 897–944; reign: 939–944), another national hero, routed the Chinese fleet on Bạch Đằng River, ending a thousand years of Chinese rule. Visitors can savor the quiet setting of these leaders' tombs and temples.

The Mông Phụ Communal House is a wonder with its impressive framework of ironwood timbers. There, visitors will find the altar to Giang Văn Minh (1573–1638), a laureate doctor, who salvaged our country's honor while serving as Việt Nam's ambassador to China. The Chinese emperor ordered Giang Văn Minh killed for daring to one-up the emperor in verbal jousts. Nearby is the temple honoring Lady Mía (Lady Sugar Cane), who introduced that crop to the village in ancient times. Another famous Đường Lâm villager is patriotic scholar, Kiều Oánh Mậu (1854–1912), who wrote a remarkable commentary on our national epic, *The Tale of Kiều* (Truyện Kiều).

In September 1940, the Indochina Fine Arts College evacuated to this haven of peace in order to avoid the Japanese occupation; the College remained in Đường Lâm until the August 1945 Revolution. In contemporary history, the bravery and self-abnegation of the Đường Lâm people during the thirty years of our two recent wars for national liberation have earned Đường Lâm the title of Heroic Village of the People's Armed Forces.

Appendices

About the Vietnamese Language

Vietnamese is a mono-syllabic, tonal language. Its Romanized alphabet is similar to the English alphabet but with no *f, j, w,* or *z.* The alphabet has two *d*'s. The *đ* with a bar through its stem has a hard sound like the English *d,* while the *d* without the bar is similar to the English *z* (northern accent) or *y* (southern accent). For clarity in English, Vietnamese sometimes distinguish between the two *d*'s by writing "*dd*" for the hard đ with the bar and "*dz*" for the soft *d* without the bar, as in Ngô DDình DZiệm.

The Vietnamese alphabet has additional letters: â, ă, ê, ô, ơ, and ư. Vietnamese nickname them:

- Â is *a* with a hat.
- Ă is *a* with a saucer.
- Ê is *e* with a hat.
- Ô is *o* with a hat.
- Ơ is *o* with a whisker.
- Ư is *u* with a whisker.

To make matters more complicated, Vietnamese has six tones. These vary with pitch (that is, where the tone starts), melody (how the sound wavers), and duration (how long the sound is maintained). The tones are crucial to a word's meaning and to the accuracy of a person's name.

Below are the six Vietnamese tones, with examples of varied meanings:

- LA   no tone   a mule
- LÀ   falling tone   the verb "to be"
- LẢ   falling rising tone   exhausted, weak
- LÃ   waving tone   with "*nước*" (water) = fresh water
- LÁ   rising tone   a leaf
- LẠ   low, short tone   strange, foreign

Both hearing the difference between tones and duplicating the sound are easier for the foreigners who sing or play musical instruments.

Vietnamese will play with tones, much as English speakers will play with words in puns. Hữu Ngọc recounts how soldiers greeted Hồ Chí Minh after President Hồ's long trek through the jungle by shouting, "*Hồ Chí Minh muôn năm!*" (Long live Hồ Chí Minh!). President Hồ teased his troops by answering with the same words but with different tones, saying, "*Hồ Chí Minh muốn nằm!*" (Hồ Chí Minh wants to lie down!).

A foreigner saying the wrong tone may be speaking nonsense or even using an obscenity. Luckily, the Vietnamese are remarkably gracious and delighted with foreigners who try to learn their language, no matter the level. Of course, the Vietnamese delight in stories of foreigners' mistakes as much as native English speakers may enjoy the humorous variations caused by those who mix up homophones.

The hardest consonant sound for foreigners learning Vietnamese is *ng*, as in the family names Ngô and Nguyễn. The sound is like the *ng* in "sing." It feels like you swallow the sound. Foreigners also find pronunciation of *gi* baffling. However, this sound is easy. *Gi* is equivalent to a *z* for a northern accent or to a *y* for a southern accent. Thus, "*gia đình*" (family) sounds like "za ddinh" with a northern accent or "ya ddinh" with a southern accent.

There are other pronunciation subtleties, which those learning the language will quickly master.

For Westerners, Vietnamese has the advantage of a Romanized script, which makes the language far easier to learn than Chinese, Japanese, or Korean. Because the Romanized script was developed rather late in the evolution of the language, there is also the great advantage of consistency. Thus, the same sequence of letters is always pronounced the same way within a given regional accent. In contrast, a Vietnamese person learning English must hear words pronounced or consult a dictionary because of the many variations. For example, the English sequence "ough" can be pronounced many different ways, including "bough," "cough," "dough," "drought," "fought," "rough," "thorough," and "through."

Pronouns present a challenge for foreigners and for Vietnamese, since the language uses dozens of personal pronouns for "you" and "I." Most pronouns are based on family words, such as "older sister" – "younger brother"; "grandfather" – "grandchild"; "uncle" – "niece" (with four words for "uncle" based on paternal or maternal and older or younger than the parent). Speakers raise the status of addressees for "you" and lower their own status for "I."

Years of peace and *Đổi Mới* (Renovation or Renewal) have brought a rapid opening in individual freedoms, but older Vietnamese all remember the days before 1990, when they could not have individual conversations with a foreigner, regardless of nationality.

Visitors to modern-day Việt Nam quickly discover that Vietnamese at all levels of society delight in the chance to meet casually on the street or in tea stalls and cafés, where they will share stories by using informal sign language and bits and pieces from any spoken languages that work.

A Chronology of Vietnamese History

10th–3rd century BCE   Era of the legendary Hùng kings (Lạc Việt tribes); Bronze Age, Iron Age; era of the Việt bronze drums; kingdom of Văn Lang (2879 BCE – 258 BCE)

3rd century BCE   Kingdom of Âu Lạc tribe unites with Văn Lang Kingdom; Chinese defeat King An Dương, establish Cổ Loa Citadel

179 BCE– 938 CE   Feudal China dominates; patriotic insurrections; Trưng Trắc's victory over the Chinese (40 CE), reigns as Việt Nam's first historical ruler (40–43); Queen Bà Triệu (248), Lý Bí (542), Mai Hắc Đế (722), Ngô Quyền (938); development of *Nôm* ideographic Vietnamese script not accessible to the occupying Chinese and to those who can read Chinese script; rich heritage of oral poetry (*ca dao*)

1009–1225   Lý Dynasty establishes capital in Thăng Long (Hà Nội, 1010 CE); builds One-Pole Pagoda (1049) and other pagodas; takes name Đại Việt (Great Việt, 1054); establishes Việt Nam's first university (Hà Nội, 1070), begins triennial mandarin competitions (1075); develops dikes, agriculture, handicrafts, pottery, printing, silk, and brocade; Taoism and Confucianism expand; *chèo* theater develops (11th century); earliest extant written poetry by Buddhist bonzes (11th century)

1225–1400 Trần Dynasty defeats Mongols (1258, 1285, 1288); growth of Confucianism; development of Vietnamese medicine, ceramics, statuary art, *tuồng* theater (13th century); establishment of Trúc Lâm (Bamboo Forest) Buddhist sect (late 13th century); rich literature in *Nôm* (Vietnamese ideographic script) and *Hán* (classical Chinese ideographic script); extensive histories compiled

15th–17th centuries First period of Later Lê Dynasty; struggle against Ming Chinese domination (1407–1427); Emperor Lê Thái Tổ (Lê Lợi) defeats Ming, establishes the Later Lê Dynasty (1428–1789) and a highly developed administrative system, redistributes communal land, economic development; Hồng Đức Legal Code (1483); first commerce with Dutch and Portuguese traders; struggle between Lê and Mạc usurpers (1527–1592); dominance of Confucianism with influence of Buddhism, Taoism, and indigenous beliefs (including mother goddesses); introduction of Christianity (16th century); invention of Romanized *Quốc Ngữ* script (17th century); Christian priests publish first Portuguese – Romanized Vietnamese dictionary (1651); struggle between the Trịnh Lords (North) and Nguyễn Lords (South) (1570–1786); important literary works, histories, geographies, political treatises in *Nôm* and *Hán*

Early 18th century–1802	Second period, Later Lê Dynasty; crisis between Trịnh and Nguyễn lords (1570–1786); corruption and depravity at court; intense poverty for the population, economic crisis; crisis in Confucianism, renaissance of Buddhism; growth of popular arts, poetry, communal houses; final crisis of the feudal regime; Tây Sơn Peasants' Uprising, national re-unification of North and South; short period of national renaissance under Quang Trung (1788–1792), *Nôm* becomes official script, unprecedented development of popular literature in *Nôm* and *Hán*; Nguyễn Du writes national epic, *The Tale of Kiều*; outstanding women poets, Lê Ngọc Hân and Hồ Xuân Hương
1802–1858	Nguyễn Dynasty (1802–1945), restoration of reactionary feudal regime (*Gia Long Code*, 1815), incompetence and corruption, economic conservatism hinders development of commerce; exploitation of peasantry through taxes and corvées, foreign policy of submission to Chinese Court; Huế Royal Palace, Huế tombs, and Huế's Vauban-style citadel built
1858–1900	French attack Đà Nẵng (1858), occupy Gia Định (1859); Huế imperial court transfers three eastern provinces of Cochin China to France (1860–1864), patriotic insurrections, French occupy three Western provinces of Cochin China (1867), French first occupy Hà Nội and other localities in northern Việt Nam (1873), French full occupation of Hà Nội (1882), Harmand Treaty (1883) makes Việt Nam a French protectorate, Treaty of Huế (Patenôtre Treaty, 1884) finalizes French colonial rule with three different regions; failure of the Save-the-King

Movement (1885); École française d'Extrême-Orient (French School of Asian Studies) established (1898); numerous insurrections (1858–1910); patriotic literature in *Nôm* and *Hán* emerges

1900–1939   French pacification ends, first period of colonial exploitation (1900–1914); use of *Quốc Ngữ* Romanized script spreads; patriotic movements, strikes, insurrections; Phan Bội Châu's Đông Du (Go East) Movement sends young nationalists to China, Japan to study; French begin educational system using French and Romanized Vietnamese script; University of Indochina established, Hà Nội (1907); Lycée du Protectorate established in Hà Nội (1908); Indochina College of Fine Arts established, Hà Nội (1925); French close national-level triennial mandarin examinations (1913); World War I (1914–1918); early influence of October Revolution (1917); French ban competitive mandarin exams in Chinese script (1919); Nguyễn Ái Quốc (Hồ Chí Minh) is founding member of French Communist Party (1920); second colonial exploitation (1918–1940); independent press appears and plays greater role (after 1920), widespread demonstrations at funerals for patriot Phan Châu Trinh (1926), founding of Vietnamese Communist Party (1930), Depression (1929–1933), Soviet–Nghệ Tĩnh Uprising (1930–1931), political ferment; *Quốc Ngữ* becomes dominant script, New Poetry Movement introduces new forms, personal material; Popular Front in France (1936–1939), Indochinese Communist Party functions more openly; World War II begins

1940–1945	Half of France falls to Germany (June 1940); Japan invades Việt Nam (September 1940), administers Việt Nam through the French Vichy regime, creating a dual yoke of occupation; Hồ Chí Minh returns to far north of Việt Nam (January 28, 1941) after thirty years overseas; Vietnamese Communist Party forms the League for the Independence of Việt Nam (**Việt** Nam Độc Lập Đồng **Minh** Hội or Việt Minh), widening the nationalist movement to include non-communist patriots (May 1941); two million die in famine in northern Việt Nam (spring 1945); Japanese Emperor Hirohito broadcasts surrender speech (August 15, 1945); Việt Nam's largely peaceful August Revolution seizes political power across the country (August 16-30, 1945); Provisional French President Charles de Gaulle meets with US President Harry Truman in Washington (August 22, 1945), with regaining post-war Indochina as a French colony first on de Gaulle's list of priorities for discussion; Vietnamese Emperor Bảo Đại formally abdicates to the Việt Minh (August 30, 1945), ending a thousand years of Vietnamese monarchy; Hồ Chí Minh reads Declaration of Independence for the Democratic Republic of Việt Nam (DRVN, September 2, 1945), with Hà Nội as capital
1945–1954	DRVN begins campaign against 95-percent illiteracy (September 3, 1945); France, supported by USA and Great Britain, lands troops in Sài Gòn, French War begins in southern Việt Nam (September 23, 1945); intensive negotiations between President Hồ Chí Minh and French representative Jean Sainteny in Hà Nội (1945–1946), formal talks in Fontainebleau, France break down (spring-summer 1946); French

attack Hải Phòng and Lạng Sơn (fall 1946),
DRVN government withdraws to the northern
mountains (fall 1946), French push toward Hà
Nội, the DRVN capital; President Hồ Chí Minh
promulgates his "Call for National Resistance,"
nationwide Resistance War Against France
begins (December 19, 1946) with France using
US materiel and funding, while DRVN (despite
overtures to France and the United States) has
no outside recognition or assistance

1950–1954 Mao Zedong announces formation of People's
Republic of China (PRC, "Communist" China,
October 1, 1949), PRC recognizes DRVN (January 18, 1950), Soviet Union recognizes DRVN
(January 30, 1950), Hồ Chí Minh meets Chairman Mao Zedong and Party Secretary Joseph
Stalin in Moscow and secures military assistance
(February 1950); Vietnamese army overruns
string of French forts on the Vietnamese-
Chinese border, opens access to China and Soviet bloc (September 1950); Vietnamese army
(with Chinese advisers and Chinese materiel)
defeats the French army (with American advisers and American material) at Điện Biên Phủ
(May 7, 1954), signaling the "death knell for
colonialism;" US President Eisenhower sends
Ngô Đình Diệm from USA to serve as prime
minister of South Việt Nam (June 25, 1954);
Geneva Conference (May 8 – July 21, 1954)
provisionally divides Việt Nam into North
Việt Nam and South Việt Nam through Agreement on the Cessation of Hostilities in Viet-
Nam (Geneva Accords) signed between the
DRVN and France (July 20, 1954); Vietnamese
revolutionaries in South regroup to North,
as stipulated in Geneva Accords, USA begins

intensive CIA disruption of Geneva Accords in the North, heavy build-up of US materiel in the South, Catholic refugees from the North arrive in the South (mid-late 1954), DRVN government returns to Hà Nội (October 10, 1954)

1955–1975   Ngô Đình Diệm deposes Bảo Đại, establishes Republic of Việt Nam (ROV, South Việt Nam) with himself as president (October 23, 1955), refuses to allow elections in July 1956 to unify Việt Nam as stipulated in Geneva Accords, institutionalizes repression (10/59 Law, October 1959) against southerners with family members regrouped to the North in compliance with the Geneva Accords; founding of the National Front for the Liberation of the South (NLF) with wealthy Sài Gòn lawyer Nguyễn Hữu Thọ as chairman (December 20, 1960); first use of US combat troops in South Việt Nam (1962), US-backed coup against President Ngô Đình Diệm of South Việt Nam (November 3, 1963); US President Johnson fabricates the Gulf of Tonkin Incident and quickly retaliates with first US bombing of the North (August 4-5, 1964), US Congress passes Gulf of Tonkin Resolution, allowing presidential discretion in managing the war (August 7, 1964); two battalions of US Marines land at Đà Nẵng, South Việt Nam (March 1965); USA uses first B-52s against North Việt Nam; North Vietnamese begin making plans for resistance against B-52 attacks (April 12, 1966); beginning of Tết General Offensive in South Việt Nam (January 31, 1968); beginning of diplomatic talks between the DRVN and USA in Paris (May 13, 1968); formation of the Provisional Revolutionary Government of South

Việt Nam (PRG, June 8, 1969), PRG becomes
one of the four parties at the Paris Conference,
along with DRVN, ROV, and USA; death of
President Hồ Chí Minh (September 2, 1969);
private bi-lateral talks between DRVN and
USA at Paris result in an agreement, which
US President Nixon refuses to accept (October 1972); Christmas Bombing of Hà Nội and
Hải Phòng with B-52s, known in Việt Nam as
Điện Biên Phủ in the Air (December 18-29,
1972); Agreement on Ending the War and Restoring Peace in Viet-Nam signed in Paris between four parties (DRVN, PRG, ROV, USA,
January 27, 1973), prisoner exchanges follow;
North Vietnamese military design team works
on 305TG1 Plan to end the war (April 1973);
North Vietnamese Campaign to Liberate the
South begins (March 1975) with expectation
the campaign will take two years, senior leaders of ROV flee the country (March-April
1975); end of the Vietnam War, known in Việt
Nam as the American War (April 30, 1975)

1975–1986   US rice imports and financial assistance end
for South Việt Nam, creating hunger and eco-
nomic distress in addition to residual wartime
destruction; officers of former ROV placed in
re-education camps to prevent a counter revolution; many private businesses in former ROV
taken over by the DRVN government; borders
close, contact with the West closes; Khmer
Rouge persist with incursions into southern
Việt Nam; newly formed National Assembly
formally re-unites North Việt Nam and South
Việt Nam into the Socialist Republic of Việt
Nam (SRVN), the current name of Việt Nam,

with Hà Nội as capital (July 2, 1976); further
collectivization under Party Secretary Lê Duẩn,
strict rationing across the country, difficult
economic conditions, typhoons, and other natural disasters; increasing incursions by Khmer
Rouge into southern Việt Nam, which began in
early 1970s; SRVN becomes a member of the
United Nations (September 20, 1977); Khmer
Rouge genocide in Kampuchea (Cambodia)
kills between 10 and 30 percent of population
(UN figures); Việt Nam sends troops to Kampuchea (Cambodia, December 28, 1978); the
then US government politically backs Khmer
Rouge; China, politically backed by the then
US government, invades six Vietnamese border provinces to punish Việt Nam (February
17, 1979); USA and Western countries, except
Sweden, institute an even more stringent embargo against Việt Nam (1979); "hard times"
for population, everyone is gaunt; a few villages
quietly experiment with privatizing their fields
(early-mid 1980s)

1986–present   Party Secretary Lê Duẩn dies; VIth Congress
of Vietnamese Communist Party establishes
policy of *Đổi Mới* (Renovation or Renewal)
to open Việt Nam to a market economy and
friendship with all nations (December 1986);
first small-scale (very small-scale) enterprises
begin in cities; villages privatize land, leading
to greater incentive and far greater production;
all Vietnamese troops return from Cambodia
by September 1989; Việt Nam begins to export
rice, becomes a major world rice exporter and
also exports oil (1989); Việt Nam begins to
enjoy first peace in modern memory (1990);
exports bring foreign exchange and foreign

goods; travel restrictions ease; greater openness and greater individual freedoms, literary
experimentation begins (late 1980s), tourism
begins to flourish (early1990s); bilateral talks
with ASEAN, the European Union, and the
United States, formal normalization with all
three (1995); Internet download access available (1995), first Vietnamese material up on
the Web (1997); Việt Nam hosts Francophone
Conference (1997), emphasis on development
and international commerce, growth of cities,
only pockets of hunger but greater disparity
between rich and poor; entry into WTO (January 11, 2007); Việt Nam holds rotating seat on
UN Security Council (2008–2009); Việt Nam
hosts international academic conferences, regional games, ASEAN meetings; large numbers
of young Vietnamese study in Western countries, international student groups study for a
semester in Việt Nam; widespread use of cell
phones, smart phones, Internet, tablets, Google
search, Facebook, Skype; orientation toward
personal greed replaces traditional emphasis
on community; growth of inter-locked corruption and bureaucracy, corruption becomes
institutionalized, including in the educational
and health systems, decline in education and
health services; influx of world cultures along
with greater interest in traditional Vietnamese
culture, growth of village festivals; temples,
pagodas, and churches refurbished; larger,
more ornate ancestral altars in individual
houses

Henri Oger's *Mechanics and Crafts of the Vietnamese People* (1909):

Sketches of Hanoians' Vibrant Life

Mechanics and Crafts of the Vietnamese People is the result of the study that Henri Oger (1885 – c. 1936) conducted from 1908 to 1909 during his military service with the French army in Hà Nội.

Accompanied by Vietnamese sketch artists, Henri Oger traveled the streets of Hà Nội and the city's outskirts to create an inventory of the residents' impressive diversity of crafts and trades. He did not overlook a single segment the private and public life of the period as he was gathering his collection of more than four thousand drawings and sketches. These documents provide us with images of gestures, crafts, tools, and artisanal products, along with corresponding descriptions.

École française d'Éxtrême-Orient (EFEO) in Hà Nội, in collaboration with the General Sciences Library of Hồ Chí Minh City, published a re-edition of Oger's entire work in 2009. Other than the esthetic quality of the drawings, which in themselves constitute an art book, *Mechanics and Crafts of the Vietnamese People* (where "mechanics" refers to the less common meaning of the word as "mechanical details") is a unique witness to the local small industries and activities that prevailed in northern Việt Nam at the beginning of the twentieth century.

First Edition (1909)

After assembling thousands of unique graphic works, Henri Oger faced the task of publishing his collection, which proved both a technical and financial challenge. A team of thirty Vietnamese artists worked for more than two months in Vũ Thạch Pagoda to engrave onto wooden blocks the more than four thousand drawings with their descriptions in Chinese and Vietnamese ideographs. However, local printers could not run the wooden blocks beneath their rollers.

Thus, it became necessary to stamp the woodblocks onto traditional, handmade paper (*giấy dó*) for publication of *Documentary Art Archives of the Ethnography and Sociology of China and Indochina*, which included Oger's "General Introduction to the Study of Crafts of the Vietnamese People." *Documentary Art Archives* consists of two volumes. The first is an introductory text by the author (160 pages and 33 plates); the second is the album of seven hundred plates in-folio (65 cm x 42 cm), including more than four thousand drawings, plans, and engravings. The work was probably completed in 1909 but without copyright, since it was published in Việt Nam.

Henri Oger's book is a rare publication, for he printed only sixty copies. Scholars have found only two copies in Việt Nam. The first, which is incomplete, is in the National Library (Hà Nội); the other, which is complete, is in the General Science Library (Hồ Chí Minh City). The latter is the copy EFEO chose to use because of its good state of conservation and the good relations EFEO has established and maintained with the General Science Library. Some copies may be in private hands, but we do know that other copies of the 1909 edition are available in a few libraries outside Việt Nam. These include Johns Hopkins University, Baltimore,

Maryland, USA; Southern Illinois University, Carbondale, Illinois, USA; University of California, Berkley, California, USA; Cornell University (microfilm), Ithaca, New York, USA; and The Library of Art and Archeology, Sorbonne, Paris IV, France.

A Unique Perspective on Vietnamese Culture at the Beginning of the Twentieth Century

Young Oger did not hide his ambition to acquire a deep understanding of colonized Vietnamese society, thereby allowing him to denounce the contempt with which scholars at the time viewed local people and their practices. Oger's approach as defined in his introduction stems from the principle that "the current state of Indochinese and Sino Studies requires the development of large reference systems and inventories." Based on this conviction, he set out to establish a large collection showing multiple aspects of Vietnamese daily life, art, and small industry. This quest for an exhaustive approach to a vast area of knowledge is one of the remarkable aspects of Henri Oger's work, making him a pioneer. His ambition was to paint in broad strokes a picture of material Vietnamese civilization, that is, the culture's physical and viewable attributes as opposed to spiritual characteristics.

Oger completed his enormous task without support from professional institutions staffed by trained experts. His work stems from a new area of cultural anthropology, which at best had barely been introduced. At the time, sociological and ethnographic field studies were rare. Scholars enhanced their academic work mostly with first-hand accounts and information from reports and travel diaries by amateurs (e.g., missionaries, military personnel, and explorers).

Henri Oger's immersion into the everyday life of ordinary people helped him to question ideas commonly held during the French colonial period, especially the opinion that Vietnamese small industry was absent or insignificant. Oger asserted that this view neglected the important artisanal and commercial activities developed by farmers, workers, and city-dwellers—activities that provided indispensable financial and practical resources not available from the production of rice.

The Premises of Technical Anthropology in Việt Nam

Henri Oger's method of collecting and investigating indicates a social analysis of technical systems, particularly regarding the central place afforded to the study of gestures. He insisted on demonstrating the different phases of a worker or artisan's actions to depict the full use of a tool or basic machinery. This method of sequencing a particular process allowed the author—in his own words—to "group the series together," identify, and then study chains of operation.

Furthermore, Oger held that the study of a particular people's civilization is the study of its material civilization. Thus, he developed his interest in the gestures where the human body itself is the instrument. Ultimately, Oger highlighted four elements in technical processes: 1) the material which the artisan used (e.g., tools and other means of work); 2) gestures; 3) sources of energy that resulted in the movement of objects (e.g., running water and traction); and 4) the specific representation in technical gestures.

Each of Oger's comprehensive surveys ranked collected data according to existing classification modalities and applied typological principles of hierarchical sets. The author distinguished four technical categories: 1) industries based on primary materials (e.g., agricultural trades, fishing, hunting, transportation, and harvesting); 2) industries transforming natural products (e.g., paper, precious metals, and pottery); 3) industries adding value to the products already prepared (e.g., commerce, stonework, and lacquer painting); and Vietnamese private and public life (e.g., musical instruments, magic, games, and toys).

Little information exists on Henri Oger's collaborators—the thirty artists and engravers who created the work. We have some of the artists' names: Nguyễn Văn Đăng, Nguyễn Văn Giai, and

Phạm Văn Tiêu from Thanh Liễu Village, Gia Lộc District, Hải Dương Province, and Phạm (Trọng) Hải from Nhân Dục Village, Kim Động District, Hưng Yên Province. It seems the most talented and prolific among the artists was Nguyễn Văn Đăng (1874–1956).

An Amalgamated Collection

While Henri Oger's introduction follows the above-mentioned four categories and uses a chronological order, the collection seems free of ordering.[1] Readers might discover on a single plate the images of a child flying a kite, the punishment for guilty adulterers, a traveling fruit seller, a boatman navigating his sampan, the tools for wood sculpture, and ceremonies for burial of the dead. These contrasts within and throughout the plates remain a mystery, since Henri Oger's introduction includes nothing about the drawings' arrangement. The most likely hypothesis is that the printers assembled the drawings without consulting Henri Oger.

The artists' simplicity of line and care to show the best content even when sacrificing the rules of perspective, body posture, and facial expression renders each drawing a unique and powerful work and also makes this collection a unique national heritage by demonstrating a century of rich Vietnamese techniques and knowledge.

While Henri Oger's empathy was undoubtedly sincere, he was trapped in the evolutionary perspective that dominated social sciences during his time. He states, "The Vietnamese people are

---

1. With this in mind, we endeavored to reorganize Henri Oger's work to make it more accessible to the public, while simultaneously respecting the author's intentions. See: Tessier, Olivier, 2011. "Du geste au dessin: La vie à Hanoi au début du XXe siècle saisie par Henri Oger" (From Gesture Drawings: Life in Hà Nội in the Early Twentieth Century as Captured by Henri Oger), *Asian Arts*, Special Issue: Imaging People in East Asia, ed. Alain Arrault et al., Volume 66, p. 99-116.

the class of semi-civilized people engaged in appreciable but slow progress." He punctuates his text with judgments, which contrast with positive appreciation, for example: "The tailor has no taste. He doesn't know how to draw" and "The local vender, like many primitives, looks for a good price rather than for quality." Today, readers would assess those remarks as disregard for the other or racist. Indeed, Henri Oger was a man of his time; he was convinced by the intrinsic superiority of his bourgeois Western civilization over all foreign societies, an ideology which legitimized colonialism and France's mission to civilize.

Reproduction by EFEO, Hà Nội (2009)

Given the unique nature of documents collected by Henri Oger and the drawings' scientific and esthetic value, EFEO in Hà Nội decided to re-edit the work in its entirety in two volumes. The first volume is Henri Oger's original text, *General Introduction to the Study of the Mechanics and Crafts of the Vietnamese People*, in three languages (French, Vietnamese, and English). EFEO enriched the work by adding a biography of Henri Oger written by Pierre Huard, a well-known scholar. A preface by Philippe Le Failler and Oliver Tessier from EFEO explains the scope of Oger's work, its historical context, and Oger's pioneering spirit in anthological inquiry based on his case study about artistic production and the use of *dó* paper.

The second volume is a reproduction of the seven hundred woodblock prints (most of them with many drawings), which were numbered and reworked based on a standard pattern. As an added value of this reprinting over the original publication, Vietnamese readers have translations into Vietnamese Romanized script (*Quốc Ngữ*) of the legends and annotations written in Chinese (*Hán*) and Vietnamese (*Nôm*) ideographs. To respect the original, EFEO inserted the translations in a gray band at the bottom of each page.

Finally, in parallel to a print run with two thousand copies, a DVD version with one thousand copies has a recognition system integrated into the images, thereby enabling readers to click on a drawing and see a dialogue bubble containing Henri Oger's notes in three languages. A similar system exists for the translation of *Nôm* and *Hán* footnotes into Vietnamese Romanized script.

The new, complete edition (2009) of Henri Oger's work is available in fourteen libraries in the United States, seven in France, and one each in Germany, Great Britain, and Singapore. Interested readers can find the locations of these libraries by entering "Henri Oger" in the search line at www.worldcat.org. After the book's display page appears, enter a US postal zip code to bring up the list of libraries. DVDs of the 2009 edition are available through EFEO's Hà Nội office, www.efeo.fr/base.php?code=221.

Conclusion

Now, it remains to exploit the historical information—social and cultural—highlighted by these seven hundred plates of drawings and sketches. While the re-publication of this inventory contributes to a better understanding of Vietnamese material civilization, that step is not an end *per se*. This collection should feed into not-yet-published research in multi-disciplinary areas.

The following presentation, which is specifically organized to accompany the vision Hữu Ngọc has presented in *Việt Nam: Tradition and Change*, contains a sample with 219 images from the more than four thousand sketches and drawings Henri Oger collected for *Mechanics and Crafts of the Vietnamese People* (1909).

Without pretending to present an exhaustive list of possible avenues for further exploration, we at EFEO would like to introduce the brief thirty-two pages of drawings that follow to highlight the relevance and usefulness of Henri Oger's pioneering work for historic and contemporary Vietnamese Studies.

Let the work begin.

Olivier Tessier
École française d'Étreme-Orient (EFEO)
Hồ Chí Minh City, Việt Nam

Oger Drawings

Ancestor Worship

Altar at the foot of a banyan tree

Religious ceremony at home

Mother Goddesses and Shaman Practices

Mother goddess

Shaman collects amulet blood from a cock's crown

Shaman ceremony

Wet-Rice Culture

Collecting fertilizer

Building a dike

Harrowing

Sowing gold
paper ingots

Transplanting

Scarecrow

Wet-Rice Culture

Irrigating   Harvesting   Threshing

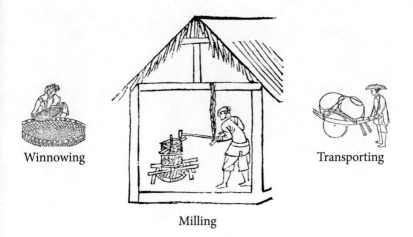

Winnowing   Milling   Transporting

Other Kinds of Farming

Herding ducks

Tending vegetables

A pig goes to market

Bamboo shoots

Building a haystack

Harvesting fruit

Fishing

Emptying a pond to
nab the fish

Trapping a fish to grab
through the top hole

Fishing baskets

Hunting

Swooping up a frog

Hunting snakes

Snaring a porcupine

Building a Peasant's Hut

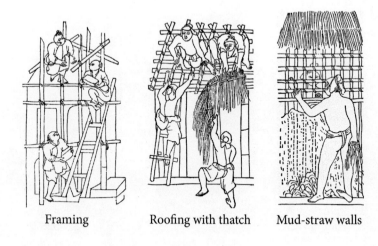

Framing Roofing with thatch Mud-straw walls

Building a Town House

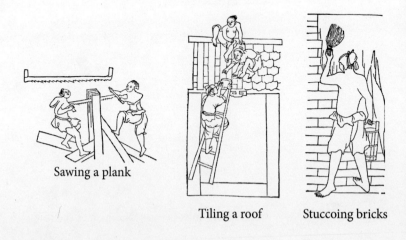

Sawing a plank

Tiling a roof Stuccoing bricks

Hospitality

A peasants' meal

A feast after a ritual

The Kitchen

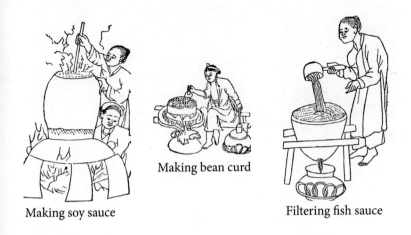

Making soy sauce

Making bean curd

Filtering fish sauce

Household Chores and Crafts

Laundry   Night-soil pick-up   Washing the dog

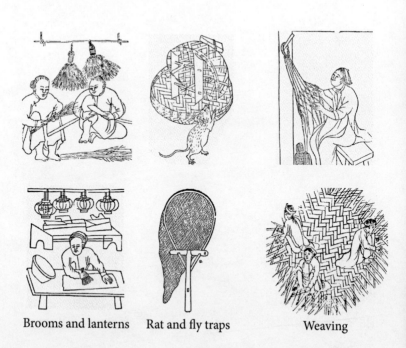

Brooms and lanterns   Rat and fly traps   Weaving

Women at Home

Lacquering teeth

Searching for lice

Hammock

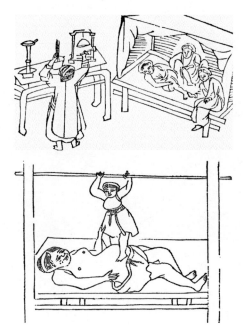

Birthing a child

Lullabies and stories

Village Life

Village watchmen

Stone watchdog

Prosperity symbol
with yin-yang

Sharing a betal quid
starts a conversation

Village market

Porter

Porters waiting

Village Festivals

Moving deities to the village temple

Moving a deity

Temple entrance

Cooking Race

Knife dancers

Boat Race

Comings and Goings

Leading a cart   Pulling a mandarin   A "monkey" bridge

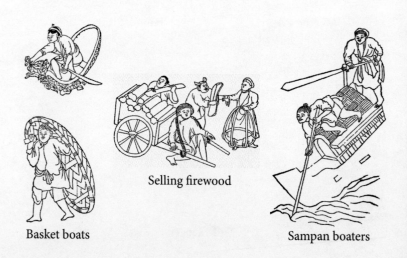

Selling firewood

Basket boats   Sampan boaters

Town and City Life

Entrance to a Vietnamese hotel

French café

Town life in the Vietnamese Quarter

Shops and Merchants

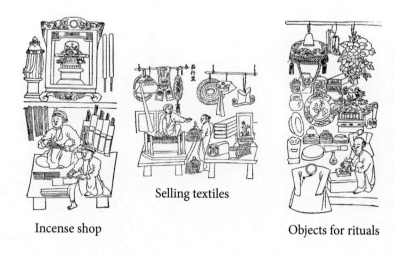

Incense shop

Selling textiles

Objects for rituals

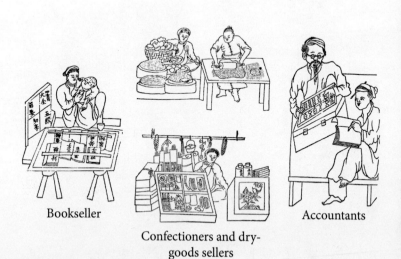

Bookseller

Confectioners and dry-
goods sellers

Accountants

Health and Medicinal Practices

Left: Rites for the ill

Above: Deity against demons

Below: Pharmacy

Acupuncture

Ear cleaning

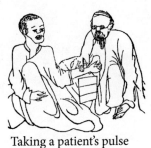

Taking a patient's pulse

Buddhist Practices

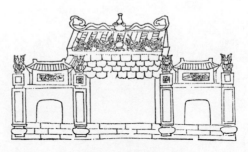

Pagoda entrance

Statue of Buddha

Frontpiece   Bodhisattva Avalokitesvara   Preface

Buddhist Life

Preparing an altar

Burning incense

Chanting a prayer

Villagers in a Buddhist procession

A Confucian Education

Students learning ideographs by practicing with a wooden frame

Reading the mandarin exam questions and writing answers

Laureates' names on a stele atop a tortoise, a symbol of longevity, and
a Confucian laureat returning home from the examinations

Confucian Scholars and Their Implements

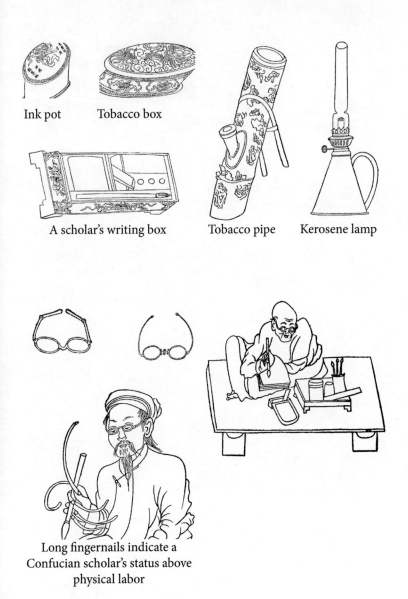

Ink pot

Tobacco box

A scholar's writing box

Tobacco pipe

Kerosene lamp

Long fingernails indicate a
Confucian scholar's status above
physical labor

Making Paper and Ink and Then Printing

Mulberry prep   Framing and drying   Grinding ink, printing

Making Silk

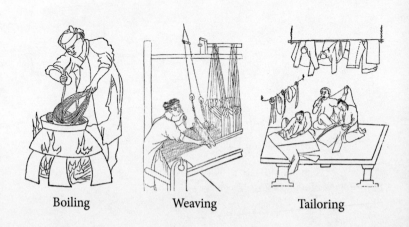

Boiling   Weaving   Tailoring

A Mandarin's Life

Writing an edict, a procession on an ordinary day, and at rest

Left: Military mandarin

Right: Statue of the king

A mandarin's ceremonial procession

Lacquer

Harvesting and stirring sap   Pounding lime for lacquer

Churning, decanting, and filtering lacquer

Painting objects, a ceremonial fan, and lacquering a Buddhist statue

Other Arts

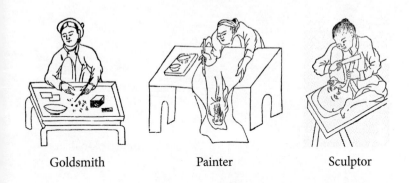

Goldsmith   Painter   Sculptor

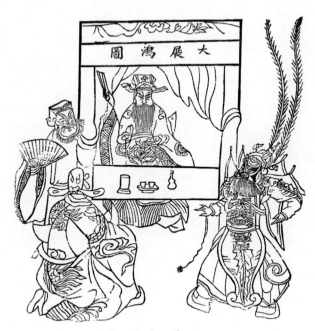

A theatrical performance

Musicians and Their Instruments

Sixteen-string zither

Monochord

Buffalo-skin drum

Bamboo flute

Phách for *ca trù*

Nhị two-string violin

Long-necked lute

Đáy for *ca trù*

"Singing rope"

Engagements and Weddings

Preliminary bethrothal, wedding gifts, wedding ceremony

Groom and bride's processions taking the bride home to the groom's family, elder preparing the wedding bed

Funerals

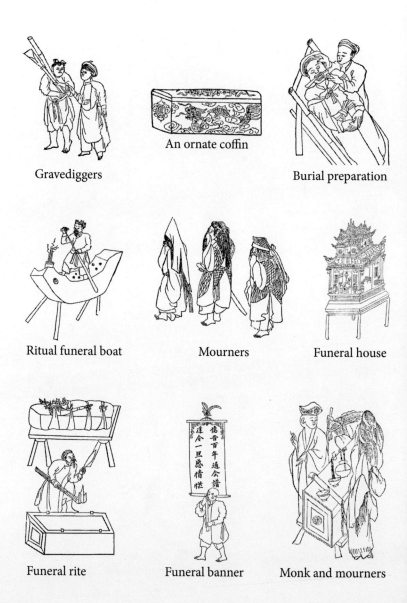

Gravediggers

An ornate coffin

Burial preparation

Ritual funeral boat

Mourners

Funeral house

Funeral rite

Funeral banner

Monk and mourners

Re-Interment After Three Years

Left: Tending the spirit of the deceased for three years

Right: Ceremony to begin the exhumation

Carving a headstone

Reburial in a terra cotta box

Exhumation

A rich man's tomb

Hats and Headdresses

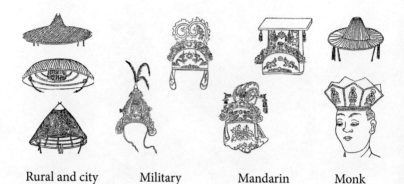

Rural and city   Military   Mandarin   Monk

Shoes and Sandals

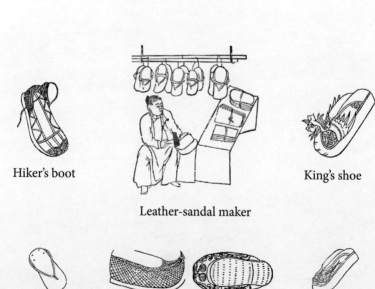

Hiker's boot

Leather-sandal maker

King's shoe

Peasant's shoe   Funeral and rich man's shoes   Mandarin's shoe

Jackets

A monk's jacket for ceremonies   A peasant's shirt   A rich man's shirt   An official's jacket for court

Full Outfits

A scholar in street garb   A peasant in his raincoat of leaves   Townspeople in festive dress

Games for All

Playing with dice

Tug of war

Toy raft

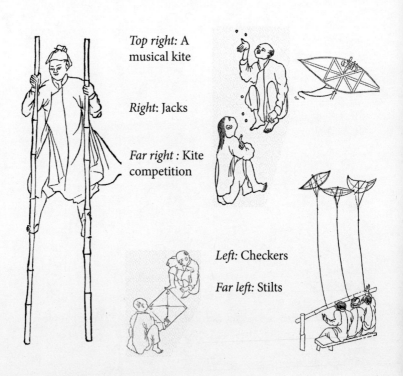

Top right: A musical kite

Right: Jacks

Far right : Kite competition

Left: Checkers

Far left: Stilts

Adults (Usually Men) at Leisure

A singer and client

Opium addict

Card game

Boules

Teaching a magpie

Tết — Lunar New Year

Top left: Driving away evil spirits. *Top center:* Cleaning the family altar. *Bottom left:* A Tết pole, offerings, and firecrackers. *Bottom center:* Writing Tết maxims. *Bottom right:* Lighting a huge firecracker.

Tết dragon dance

Index

Pages with quotations appear in italics.

Am=American;
Ch=Chinese;
Fr=French;
VN=Vietnamese;
EFEO=École française d'Éxtrême-Orient

343

Molière (French playwright, 1622–
1673), 46, 189–91
Mongol invasions (mid 1200s CE),
xiv, 14, 39, 88–89, 99–102,
218–19, 222, 225, 292
Montesquieu, Charles–Louis (French
writer, 1689–1755), 55, 75,
129, 155
mother goddesses. *See under* religion,
spirituality & beliefs
Mus, Paul (EFEO scholar, 1902–
1969), 127
music
"New Music" (1936–1945), 191–94
ca trù (VN traditional songs), xvi,
147, 180–82
drums, xiii, 24, 30, 37–38, 47, 176,
181, 185, 196, 222–23, 291, 334
other instruments, 181, 185, 334
Musset, Alfred de (French writer,
1810–1857), 56, 190

Nam Sơn (VN painter, 1890–1973),
xvi, 194–97
Nam Xương (VN playwright, 1905–
1958), 46, 191
National Assembly, VN, 122, 124–25,
272, 279–80, 298–99
Nationalist Party (Việt Nam Quốc
Dân Đảng), *120–21,* 156
Neolithic Age, 37, 173, 283
Nghệ Tĩnh Uprising (1930–1931),
229–30, 294
nghĩa, xii, 3–4
Ngô Đình Diệm (VN premier,
president South Việt Nam,
1954–1963), 16, 236, 296–97
Ngô Quyền (VN king, reign: 939–
944), 101, 208, 221, 283, 291
Ngô Thì Nhậm (VN scholar, 1746–
1803), 102, *110–12*
Ngô Văn Chiêu (VN provincial
governor, 1878–1932), 238
Nguyễn Ánh. *See* Gia Long
Nguyễn Bỉnh Khiêm (VN poet,
1491–1585), 102, 188, 219,
233, *280–81*
Nguyễn Công Trứ (VN poet, 1778–
1859), xv, 139, *145–48,* 179,
181, *215,* 230

Nguyễn Đình Chiểu (VN writer,
1822–1888), xv, 151–53
Nguyễn Đình Nghị (VN playwright,
1883–1954), 191
Nguyễn Đỗ Cung (VN painter, 1912–
1977), 123
Nguyễn Dữ (VN writer, 1500s), 219
Nguyễn Du, (VN author, 1766–1820),
3, 8, *13,* 21, 102, *135–37,*
139, 146, 151, *167–68,* 179,
233–34, 268, 293
Nguyễn Đức Chính (VN crafts artist),
178–80
Nguyễn Đức Nùng (VN painter,
1914–1983), 123
Nguyễn Gia Thiều (VN poet, 1741–
1798), *144–45,* 204
Nguyễn Gia Trí (VN painter, 1908–
1993), 196
Nguyễn Huệ. *See* Quang Trung
Nguyễn Hữu Cảnh (VN scholar,
1650–1700), 228
Nguyễn Hữu Cầu (VN general,
?–1751), 219
Nguyễn Hữu Kim (VN theatrical
director, 1920s), 190
Nguyễn Hữu Tiến (VN *chèo*
scriptwriter, 1875–1941), 185
Nguyễn Khắc Viện (VN scholar,
1913–1997), xxiii, xxiv, 43, 73
Nguyễn Khuyến (VN poet, 1835–
1909), xv, *153–54,* 222
Nguyễn Lân (VN scholar, 1906–2003),
122
Nguyễn Lữ (Tây Sơn rebel, 1754–
1787), 107–108
Nguyễn Mạnh Bổng (VN writer, c.
1897–1951), 190
Nguyễn Minh Hòa (VN researcher),
262
Nguyễn Ngọc Tư (VN writer, 1976–),
168–69
Nguyễn Nhạc (Tây Sơn rebel, 1753–
1793), 107–108
Nguyễn Phúc Cảnh (VN prince,
1780–1801), 239
Nguyễn Quyền (VN activist, 1870–
1941), 79
Nguyễn Sáng (VN painter, 1923–
1988), 196–98

Quan Công (Chinese legend, Guan Yu, c. 160–c. 219), 41, 102, 230, 234

Quang Dũng (VN poet, 1921–1988), *161–64, 221*

Quang Trung (Nguyễn Huệ, VN king, reign: 1788–1792), xiv, 9, 38, *107–12*, 229, 293

Quốc Ngữ (Vietnamese Romanized script). *See under* Vietnamese language

Quốc Tử Giám (VN's first university, 1076). *See under* Confucianism

Rageau, Christiane Pasquel (French author, 1935–), *126*

Red River Delta. *See under* Việt Nam: regions, Northern Region

religions, spirituality & beliefs. *See also* Buddhism, Confucianism & Taoism

ancestor veneration, xii–xii, 11, *18–22, 22–24,* 25, 41, *42–44,* 58, 63, 120, *164,* 165, 173, 195, *215–18,* 247, 265–67, 282, 300

Cao Đài, 11, 233–37

genies, *18–20,* 36, 48, 63, 83, 197, 264

geomancy, 106, *208,* 213, 220

Hòa Hảo, 11

mediums, 41–42, 101–102, 225–26, 236, 311

mother goddesses (Thánh Mẫu), xii–xiii, 19, 25, 38–42, 84, 165, 210, 236, 292, 311

World of Mortals (This World), 13, 41, *162,* 181–82

World of Shades (Other World), 12, 42–43, 73, *135*

yin and yang, *19–20, 233,* 320

Renewal (late 1986). *See Đổi Mới*

Renovation (late 1986). *See Đổi Mới*

resistance against invaders

Ba Đình (1886), 14

Resistance War Against France (1945–1954). *See* French War

Resistance War Against United States (1945–1975). *See* American War

Resistance Wars Against China. *See under* China: invasions & Việt resistance

Rhodes, Alexandre de (French Jesuit, 1591–1660), 56

rice farming

ancient times, xiii, 5, 10–11, 29–30, 34, 47, 52, 108

customs, 11, 16–19, 34, 39, 44–47, 72, *147, 150,* 175–76, 184, 208–209

localities, 201, 202, 204, 218, 221–22, 226, 229, 233–36, 271, 282–84

modern times, 16–17, 33–35, 59, 272–73, 298–99

Rimbaud, Arthur (French poet, 1854–1891), 158

Rivière, Henri (French naval officer, 1827–1883), *112–14*

Rossi, Tino (French singer, 1907–1983), 192

Rousseau, Jean Jacques (French writer, 1712–1778), 15, 55, 75, 129, 155

Royal Court. *See also* Confucianism

Chinese, *93–98,* 293

French, 239

Hà Nội (until 1802), 38, 53, *67–69, 98–112, 137–44,* 178, 181–84, 196, *206–209, 210–13,* 293

Huế (1802–1945), 73–79, *112–20,* 121, *145–56,* 164, 178, 293, 331, 329

Rudravarman III (Chăm king, reign: 1061–1074), 227

Sadoul, Georges (French filmmaker, 1904–1967), 55

Sài Gòn

before 1945, xvii, 77, 79, 151, 164, 189, 228, 247

after 1945, *228, 237–38, 296, 297*

name & as location, 29, 79, 151, 228

Saint-Saëns, Camille (French composer, 1835–1921), 238

Sainteny, Jean (French diplomat, 1907–1978), *128,* 295

Save-the-King Movement (Cần Vương, 1885–1889), 74, 78, 118, 166, 228–229